Grit
&
Gratification

*What games do we play
with fate—with life?*

The Whistling Girls & Crowing Hens Series
Book 5

Jan Anthony

This is a work of historical fiction. Names, characters, places and incidents are products of the author's imagination, and media articles are used fictitiously and are not to be construed as real. Any resemblances to actual events, locales, organizations or persons, living or dead, are entirely coincidental.

Copyright © *Jan Anthony*, 2024 All Rights Reserved
This book is subject to the condition that no part of this book is to be reproduced, transmitted in any form or means; electronic or mechanical, stored in a retrieval system, photocopied, recorded, scanned, or otherwise. Any of these actions require the proper written permission of the author.

ISBN 979-8-3483-9123-2

Library of Congress Preassigned Control Number 2024925264

**Published by
Mother Courage Press**
Editor/Publisher Jeanne Arnold

Grit
&
Gratification

What games do we play
with fate—with life?

The Whistling Girls & Crowing Hens Series
Book 5

Jan Anthony

*Creative stories based on personal letters,
prose, poetry, journals, diaries and imagination*

Dedication

Dedicated to the women in my life
and all those who love them,
but especially Bea for her love
and her poems and journals.

Prologue

Waves and waves
crashing on the shore
of my being.
Thundering, foaming surf,
emotionally exciting,
building to a thrashing crest,
shooting up
into the air!
Against rocks, stumbling rocks,
washing away sand,
wearing corners round,
splashing spray again,
roaring,
consuming,
engulfing
waves and waves
crashing on the shore
of my being.
I hear my voice, talking,
trying to pretend,
trying to hide existence
of this sea of violence,
in this ocean of love.
by Bea Lindberg

Chapter 1

Jan on January 25, 1981

Both of my kids seem to be doing well without having me hover over them after their father and I divorced when they were in their teens. I moved into an apartment one block away from their house after I was outed as a lesbian to family and friends, at church and at work.

In the homemaking chapters of my life, I knew nothing of Adrienne Rich and other authors and scholars who later helped me understand the effects of women living under patriarchy. I knew of no one like Mary Daly. There *is* no one like Mary Daly who inspires me to share her wisdom about male-oriented religions subordinating and isolating women, making women sinful objects while assuming and adapting sacraments from women's natural, sacred gifts within women's once revered bodies and souls.

Role models like Rich and Daly inspire frustrated women struggling to identify and redefine the same turmoil that was going on inside of me. As if guided by a higher power or intuition, I first found *The Second Sex* by Simone de Beauvoir.

Ms. Magazine was newly published. My personal patriarch, my husband, hated my reading those issues. I would not do so in front of him because he would punish me with his silent sullenness, perhaps based on his innate fear of my discovering what society did not want me to know—that I was not alone.

Strange that I should want more. In comparison to most women, I had everything anyone could want: a monogamous and successful husband, awesome children, a devoted dog, good neighbors, many friends and a home overlooking Lake Michigan. What a view, especially on the night of the full moon!

I labeled all that "the velvet chains of acceptable middle class values."

Why did I want to resume having a career, even a part-time one? Alone in my house all day, I had not expected to find myself as the married women's version of "Eleanor Rigby… She's leaving home. Bye, Bye." Yet I did identify with this woman in, of all places, a Beatles' song.

When Nick Dixon invited me to work part time at Lakeshore Medical Center to edit its little newsletter, he knew I could do the work because of my part-time job as a feature writer at our local daily newspaper. I was his friend, another Unitarian, a neighbor, someone he considered as a good mother and a faithful wife to my husband.

No one knew what hid under my surface, under my skin, in my heart; and no one, even I, imagined that sometime soon I could be described as "being on the cutting edge." But not on the cutting edge of technology or style; more like risking to fall off a cliff.

The cast of characters in this continuing scenario includes the following:

Bea Lindberg is my lover and soulmate. And she gives in return that love completely as we create our unique life together by trial and error and some success with our children, extended family and friends. She is also my friend, my sister, my business partner, my primary person, my woman.

Bea launched me into a tailspin of emotion that began in December 1973. She is the only person—a woman—to love me unconditionally, and I have found in loving her how much I love myself as a woman, as a mother, as a daughter, as a whole person filled with goodness and charged with energy—some negative but mostly positive. My children had her as their Unitarian teen coordinator in our church and they enjoyed her music and laughter. She is creative, intelligent, talented, exciting and unpredictable.

Alex Carnigian, my ex-husband for twenty-five years, my high school sweetheart, an excellent father, a patriarch, is a victim of societal expectation for males that is intensified by his ethnic heritage. He is moralistic for himself and his wife, yet liberal for others, a quiet introvert, intelligent but boring—perhaps only tired.

He's been jealous and seething with internal rage since I stopped obeying him. He hates Bea. He continues to hold power over me because he controls our children's security and our property. I left my children and my home rather than have a custody fight that I would lose and be officially and publicly outed, harming my financial and career options and who knows what else.

Marge Manley is the first in our Unitarian women-friend's circle to be a happy divorcee. Still, it took her years to recover from her ex-husband's rejection. My best friend for over a decade, she was the first adult women I truly loved with intense emotion. When I told her that I loved her, she politely declined any serious relationship and used my secret affection and longing for her to her advantage. Alex hated her for being my friend and for setting a bad example for me to follow, as if I didn't have a mind of my own.

After our divorce and his having many women practically standing in line to be his chosen one, he became involved with Marge who now seems to be the hostess in my former home.

Marge was also my Bea's closest crony when I wasn't around to complete our threesome. Marge also works at Lakeshore Medical Center and panders to our two administrative bosses—and to Alex. She avoids me now, and when we do gather in the same room, she looks away as if we are merely two co-workers among many. I wonder if Alex knows anything about her colorful past. Marge is envious of Bea's talents and dreads Bea's emotional flair-ups. And she envies the extraordinary love that Bea and I share.

Randall (Randy) King is now Lakeshore Medical Center's VP of Human Relations, my immediate boss, former office mate and confidant when he joined the hospital's administrative staff. He's a solitary, young, intelligent and extremely handsome Machiavellian bachelor who abuses his new power like "the radiant youth" in Oscar Wilde's *The Picture of Dorian Gray*. Randy King was intrigued by an older and intoxicated Bea to perform the sexual act that could, in my opinion, set new sexual harassment legal action standards in the workplace.

Nick Dixon replaced the benevolent Clark Young as CEO of Lakeshore Medical Center and is a superficial hustler and a colossal male chauvinist, to use a currently popular expression. Nick once described Bea as "abrasive" when she was hired by Randy to work with me at Lakeshore Med, but Nick is one of the most abrasive persons I know.

Bea was let go from her job. Now I am anxious about our security. I'm the only one to support the both of us. I can't afford to lose my income, which is what we fear if we were to tell what happened or take him to court. So, we remain silent.

Carolyn Schafer became my communications assistant to fill Bea's position. Her warmth, cheerfulness and creativity make our department whole again after Bea's leaving. The Goddess sent Carolyn to me.

Then there's me, Jan Anthony, with our teenage children: two of mine, Matt and Jenny, and four of hers: Josh, Jim, Jill and Joel; our ex-husbands; and my father, Carl (Barney) Anthony, our only remaining parent. In addition to these close relatives, we deal with varieties of accepting new and old friends; our homophobic ex-friends and many relatives who act as guardians of morality and heterosexual privilege; our lesbian support group women and assorted liberal personalities, our Mother Courage feminist bookstore regular customers, my co-workers, and Society.

Society must deal with the results of conservative Republican President Ronald Reagan, the second-rate actor turned governor of California. He became president after defeating Jimmy Carter, a Democrat and an honest man running for another term after struggling to free over fifty hostages held in captivity in Iran for 444 days. Go figure! The hostages were released on the day of Reagan's inauguration.

Now, during and after all these hectic times and relationships, I continue relating with comedienne Phyllis Diller with her raucous gallows laughter. Our mutually domestic topics have shifted, however, from our being common housewives with moldy ironing stored in plastic bags in the refrigerator to my being a small town religious liberal who has been transformed into minor-league feminist lesbian activist, an underpaid professional working woman and, I presume to my immediate administrators and a few others, an embarrassing social outcast. Yet Diller still speaks for me saying, "My 'consciousness' is fine; it's my pay that needs raising."

Bea on February 16, 1979

Jan Anthony and I used our first Mother Courage logo for our bookstore for a year or more, and I considered it quite symbolic with a strong woman with a determined look emerging from an oval nautical rope shaped like an egg "breasting" out of bondage (more like "chesting") to break the waves wherever the ship goes. She's the figurehead on the prow of her ship. And it's time real women are allowed to skipper that ship.

A woman called to complain about the image of the "nude woman surrounded by a rope." It didn't give her the same feeling I intended, so I designed a new one of a nautical life-saving ring with our Mother Courage name on it, but I added thick crossed bars at the bottom that made the circular ring into science's female symbol. We've used that ever since as a life-saving buoy for women.

The tensions of our partnerships in the bookstore plus the stress that Jan brings home from work—the crap from Jan's boss Randy King and his right-hand man Chuck McCarthy—cause us to get testy and fight for our equal say in what goes on around us.

<<<◇>>>

All that was all forgotten when Jan took off from work and we closed the store for our Valentine luncheon at an ornately endowed Victorian-style restaurant. Some entrepreneur renovated a timeworn corner saloon and fabled whorehouse into a fine dining establishment.

The hostess greeted and guided us past a cozy bar built under the stairway leading to private dining rooms on the second floor. Our table on the first floor was next to stained-glass windows that shielded us from pedestrians' views. Dining couples, most likely straight, clustered about at white, linen-covered tables among lush red window treatments set in the wood-paneled Victorian décor with walls covered with gilded portraits—and we didn't give a damn if we were singled out or not. We settled in with the menu and, for a definite change, we ordered pomegranate martinis. Though I kidded Jan about missing her olives, we toasted and tasted the ruby-red cocktail, a Valentine treat. It takes her a long time to make up her mind when it comes to what to order, but she quickly spotted a sensuous meal—a deep-dish pan of Spanish paella with chicken thighs, shrimp with their feelers, bits of vegetables topped with freshly opened mussels in their shells floating in saffron seasoned rice soaking in garlic.

The wine and elegant food made us hungry for more, so rather than go back to work, we decided to go home to make love in the afternoon. "Who cares if I'm not at work now," Jan whispered across bits of cuisine left on our fragile chinaware and fragrant flowers in crystal vases on the table. Her eyebrow rose like Lauren Bacall's, Jan's crush in early teens. "If you want me, just whistle. You know how to whistle, don't you? You just put your lips together and blow."

I paid the check and whistled and laughed our way past more straight couples waiting their turn for their intimate luncheon.

It was good that February's blustery weather forced us to keep the bedroom windows closed. No one could hear us during climaxes exploding with our forbidden afternoon of our naked, noisy, playful power. Its intensity flourished in remembering our savory lovers' feast, and our tongues delighted in having each other for dessert.

When Jan slid into her chair behind her desk late that afternoon, she looked across her desk at Carolyn with both eyebrows raised and gave her a satisfied smile. Carolyn was happy that Jan took time off to be with me and thanked Jan again for arranging time for her to meet her long-distance lover when her Roger came to her.

Jan on February 24, 1979

I read a book review in *Time Magazine* and had Bea order Dorothy Tennov's book on romance, *Love and Limerence*. This new word for me, "limerence" is the ultimate, near obsessive form of romantic love, and I've got it, had it, and hope to never lose it. Regrettably, the book also codifies the agony of romantic love and makes me feel that if my limerence continues as long as I want it to, it may, perhaps, be the death of me.

The reviewer explains limerence as "Pressure in the chest (literally 'heart-ache'), acute longing for reciprocation, fear of rejection, drastic mood swings, the growth of passion through adversity, and intrusive thinking about the LO, or 'limerent object.'"

I've experienced all of this for so long with feelings swooping between ecstasy and pain. Tennov explains my condition. "It's because my beloved seems to reawaken an unresolved problem and then seems to be a solution to it. But I have to accept now that my beloved brings her own set of unresolved problems with her."

Bea experienced it too when we found out that we were brave enough to return each other's passion, but now that we're settled together, I think hers is lessening. We don't write poems or long, loving letters anymore. We live and work together now. Tennov describes a lesbian home "… an island of peace in a homophobic society, our only refuge. Then our lover is often the only other person who provides our social reflection." The last is not the way we live with people around us all the time. But still it applies that *"Under siege by the dominant culture, we feel we cannot afford anything but security, mutual validation and predictability within the private world of our relationship."*

The italics are mine, and I understand that being limerent is filled with negative hazards like walking down The Yellow Brick Road.

According to Tennov's take on gay limerence, "Adversity in the form of social resistance to our sexual preference may account for the high voltage which often charges our relationships initially. The tension generated by our forbidden preference, combined with the special 'gender empathy' unique to same sex relationships, makes this initial limerence period memorable for many lesbians. Unfortunately, it doesn't last."

And, "...if a relationship does persist after limerence has ended, it is because some other bonding has taken place or because circumstances make it difficult to disengage."

And, "...the bonding necessary to keep our relationships together in a hostile culture is precisely the sort of relentless us-against-the world stance, which makes sex infrequent in our long term relationships."

I hope not! Yet I know I primarily think of her first in our relationship and then me, and I feel that she thinks of herself first and then me.

One more quote today: "The relationship between limerence and sex remains extremely complicated. Despite virtually unanimous agreement among interviewees that sex with LO under the best circumstances provides the 'greatest pleasure' knowable in human existence, it appears that the very nature of limerence and the very nature of sex conspire to undermine the happiness except under the luckiest and most extraordinary of circumstance."

May that be so for us!

Chapter 2

Bea on May 15, 1979

I bought a classic sailboat, a 17-foot National One Design with a bronze centerboard and rudder, from a guy who kept it in his garage for years. I have to have a boat! Now with Barney out of the float business, I can squeeze my boat into the basement of our bookstore.

We named it *Courage* which I painted on its transom. Eventually we'll sail it from the River Woods Marina, but we have to test it out on Braun's Lake first. It has a twenty-five-foot wooden mast that's stepped into a mast step on the boat's center deck. In order to transport it, we have to take the mast down when we tow it on land and put it up again when we dock where we're going to sail.

One day we were practicing this maneuver in our driveway. Of course, we have electric wires to avoid and our house and our immediate neighbor's garage to miss if I drop the mast while lifting it. It actually weighs only about twenty-five pounds when you hold it in its middle span, but it turns into a great unwieldy timber when you boost it on your shoulder and try to aim it into the little square step on the deck. Meanwhile Jan runs around on the ground circling the trailer and boat, attempting to manage all the cables and connections, praying that it all doesn't topple over.

The mast has a set of spreaders across the top part, making it look like a tall, skinny cross. While struggling with this once, Jan said I look like Jesus Christ on his woeful steps toward Golgotha.

Our neighbor Joe ran over to help us. We said, "Please no, Joe. If we can't do this by ourselves, we can't sail the boat."

We did it in the driveway and were confident as we pulled it to Braun's Lake for our first outing. No one was there. It was early in the spring so the boat launch was ours. I was proud to hoist the mast and get the *Courage* launched. My crew, Jan, had never sailed before, had hardly even been on a private boat other than for fishing, but she paddled us away from the dock while I prepared the sails to capture the wind. For some reason I couldn't control the boat and we headed across the small bay toward a resident's pier. The spreaders nicked the corner of the pier's corrugated sunroof while I tried to figure out what was wrong.

Ha! I had neglected to drop the centerboard. And when we did, we got stuck in the mud. Without a motor, Jan quietly pushed off from the pier and we back-paddled into deeper water. Well, once that was fixed and no one hollered at us, we headed across Braun's Lake in the breeze. On the way back I had to teach Jan to duck every time we had to tack the boat so she wouldn't get knocked overboard by the boom. I also had to teach her how to handle the jenny (sail on the right) at the bow of the boat.

The billowing clouds and the springtime winds added to the chill, but our life-jackets kept us warm for the afternoon, as did our brandy. We headed for the dock and it was easy folding the sails and loading the boat on the trailer, but when the car pulled the boat away from the dock to unstep (lower) the mast, I braced myself to pull it out but found my strength weakening. We were both exhausted. Jan was quietly supporting me from the ground, prepared to use the lines and wires to stabilize the mast we'd planned to unstep and secure it on the boat.

I had to think this problem through carefully, and I rested by drinking a beer. We couldn't drive home with the mast up and I was too tired to get it out, especially when it had been pressed firmly into place with the swelling from the dampness and power of the wind on the sail. Finally, I whipped up my determination and almost burst a blood vessel or two mustering up the strength of a sumo wrestler, wrenching and pulling the damn thing out and down on the deck. I did it. And we toasted our posting with a shot of brandy before lashing the mast to the boat for the hour's ride to our store's basement, where we had to maneuver around traffic to back the boat into the narrow doors.

But we did it! And we both celebrated with a couple shots of brandy with beer chasers when we made it home safe and practically sound. Then I collapsed in my chair.

Jan's invitation for May 31, 1979

"Come and launch Bea sailing through life on her birthday. 7:30 p.m., Saturday, May 31, 1979. Dress nautically if you like. A gift suggestion: Autograph a bottle of wine to be used on future boating outings. RSVP Jan at 363-2393."

To create the flyer invitation, I found some clip art in my files showing a small, slightly listing sailboat with the backs of two people looking forward into the wind. I drew more hair on the back of the head of the man at the tiller so it would look more like Bea's head and I would seem to be leaning over the side of the boat. I added "*Courage*" in Letraset letters to the back of the boat, or as Bea and real sailors call it, "the transom."

We filled our house with her family and our friends, including those in our lesbian rap group who wanted to mix with the others to celebrate Bea's birthday. My gift to her was a brandy cane from the medical supply store. It held five vials, enough to fill the cane when the handle was screwed off. I had her name monogrammed on the metallic band.

We also paid our year-round season sailing fees so we could keep the *Courage* on its trailer at River Woods Marina's outdoor storage and we won't have to kill ourselves by taking down the mast. It would be all ready for next year's adventures on Lake Michigan.

Jan on August 10, 1979

My dad and I had a long talk at the shop late this afternoon. He always sits with his chair leaning back against the old radiator, his hands in the same position as when he held his deceased Chihuahua Chico in his lap. He "upholstered" cushions to the oak frame chair using foam rubber covered with red plastic sheeting stapled to the slats on the back and under the wooden seat. The chair's top rung is wearing away after years of his leaning back to nap and to warm himself against that cast iron relic radiator filled with hot water and some hot air. To cut down the drafts blowing in from his windows, he salvaged leftover 4th of July parade float lumber to construct indoor storm windows that he covered with heavy grade, vaguely transparent plastic sheeting. The plastic changed his clear, summertime view of the end of the boxcar railroad tracks at the turn of the river into cataract vision.

Fortunately, we'd cleaned up, paneled and painted his offices in the back rooms of Mother Courage Bookstore, but we dared not throw anything away. After he approved of our using his storefront for our bookstore, we had to haul his mounds of artificial flower boxes and display papers from the front rooms down to the deep and narrow basement. It took several trips. We used his Rambler wagon, filled it with boxes and even piled some on its roof, then drove around the busy streets to get to the building's basement with its huge back door. We must have looked like the sled full of stolen toys from Dr. Seuss's *The Grinch Who Stole Christmas*. Now the lowest level is filled with the debris of his dreams as an artificial florist next to the faded, larger-than-life-sized replicas of fish, flags, fictional and authentic human figures used on Lakeshore Bay's best parade floats since the early 1930s.

Three generations of my family worked together until he stopped building floats after Lakeshore Bay's patriotic binge of the nation's bicentennial year in 1976 when they honored Carl Barney

Anthony as Mr. Goodwill. He and Chico rode on their own little float with an Uncle Sam's hat that we built for his glorification to ride in the largest Fourth of July parade since World War II.

<<<>>>

It's good that I see my dad almost every day when I come to the store. I get a big hello from him when I come in and hang up my coat in the back closet. Sometimes he leans against the back doorway between the bookstore and his workroom and the three of us chat. Dad and Bea talk together during the day. But usually my dad keeps his space and Bea keeps hers. One time Bea and I started arguing when he and I could tell that she had been drinking at the store. He backed away quickly and stayed out of our way. Another time he invited her to take over his sign business when she made posters at his drawing bench with his show-card paints. She was happy that he respected her potential but she politely declined his offer.

He loves that I've traveled and enjoyed my experiences living in Germany in the mid-1950s. He would take my letters and follow my husband and my travel routes on his National Geographic maps. He never complained that I had left him for three years as a U.S. Army wife and a high school English teacher for Army and State Department teens. The only time he said he may have needed me was to decorate the floats for Fourth of July parades. He told me he had money set aside to fly me home. Luckily he found out that Don Nobel, his black bachelor neighbor who lived next to him in the basement apartment beneath the pool hall, had artistic skills. He hired Don to be his assistant and Don worked with my dad whenever help was needed, even after I returned from Europe, started raising a family and continued decorating floats.

Barney's personal life is almost as complicated as mine. He's never said anything about our relationship. I know he likes Bea. Nor about my getting a divorce, though I am sure it gives him grief; he loves Alex like a son.

He finally found Helen Anderson who moved into Dad's attic apartment that my mom built during World War II when Dad enlisted and served as a Navy Seabee for twenty-nine months with many months in the South Pacific. Helen was not a pleasant person. She drank a lot and almost set herself on fire when she fell asleep and dropped a cigarette in her chair. She continued to live there, even when my father was the only relative left to care for his angry, judgmental invalid mother who lived in my old bedroom. Helen died in 1963, when Jenny was about two.

He's certainly treating me better than I treated him when he had his long relationship with Helen when my mother was at the County's mental institution. Over the years, I have learned from him to be sympathetic with others and not pass judgment on their decisions. I have true compassion for him now that I didn't have then.

He's lonely. He doesn't have much business that I can see but he comes to work every day walking or driving his worn fake-woody brown Rambler station wagon. Fortunately, Social Security gives him a steady income that he never had in all his sign painting years so he has some money now. In fact, one of the first splurges of his newfound financial security was to buy my nine-year-old son a life subscription to *National Geographic Magazine*, an act that may have influenced Matt with his many travel adventures and with his college major—geography.

Several times before Dad qualified for Social Security, he had to borrow money from my husband to pay his taxes. That was hard for him to do; yet he would not rent the empty upper flat in his home nor the barely utilized storefront full of artificial flowers that stood like a dusty artifact of another of his unfilled dreams until we made that space into Mother Courage Bookstore.

He told me that he misses being touched. What could I do about that? Years of his life have been without intimacy. My schizophrenic mother had been in and out of mental institutions since 1941, and he isn't into trying any unsolicited touch—that I know of. And why should I know?

I felt strange having him tell me that he needed touch, especially when I'm consuming the touch I want with delightful gratification and joy. He looked at me directly, humbly. He's so frail. I shook my head sympathetically, merely said, "Oh, Dad," and walked around the desk to give him a gentle hug around his boney shoulders as he sat in his chair with his hands still in his lap as if he's holding Chico.

In the early 1950s when I was a newly married senior student at UW-Madison, I discovered that that my dad brought Helen home to sleep with him. I was flamingly self-righteous. She had taken my mother's place while my mother was institutionalized. She had insinuated her way into his and my life and finally into the little upstairs apartment. My mother knew the woman was in her home because she'd mention "that woman" when I'd visit her at Lakeshore Bay's County Hospital, and my mother knew who and what Helen was when my mother would have a chance to come home on rare occasions and be with my dad. That other woman also brought Chico into his home and when she died, my dad was left with that damn dog. He and the dog were touching all the time. He took better care of Chico than he did of me. Now Chico's gone; the dog died a year ago last January.

I'm humbled having judged him when I was in my idealistic stage of life. During our confrontation about this other woman in 1953, he said that I would understand when I grew older. Now, here I am in a complete and loving relationship with Bea for several years. I suppose others considered it worse than adulterous while I was married, but I didn't consider my behavior as adulterous then. I knew I was finally getting what I had wanted in my life; it wasn't wrong for my beloved and me. I earned the right to love my woman lover—in the past, the present and the future.

And now that I'm divorced and openly promoting our feminist bookstore, we're highly visible and conspicuous partners in a relationship considered by many to be unnatural and perverse. My dad has never said one negative word about my new life though he loves Alex like his own son; nor has he indicated any hostility about my loving Bea—not one disapproving word! But he and I never talk about it. I know that he knows what it's like to love a beautiful and creative woman. He loved my mother when she was married to her first husband and had a young son. She fought for custody of her son during her divorce proceedings, married my father and was five months pregnant with me when her son was killed when a car hit him in sight of my mother. Perhaps my dad's love for an intelligent and artistic woman like my mother is why he understands why I love my Bea so much.

Never in my entire life do I remember hearing one racial or anti-Semitic word from either my mother or my father in an era rife with unchecked prejudice against anyone who was not a white Christian. That was also true for sexual orientation, although most people didn't even talk about men or women being in those situations, except in whispered tones or vague innuendoes. I wonder if his friends and the few relatives he may see ask about me. What does he feel or say to them?

What a gift I've been given—even though I was fiercely angry with him for living with another woman while my mother was confined in mental institutions. He has given me the gift of acceptance and support and unconditional love. And now after all these years, he needs what I can't give him: a special person to be with, someone to touch him.

Bea on September 2, 1979

We've been figuring out what would happen if Barney needed to come to live with us. We'd work it out by rearranging the dining area into a bedroom for him that would be close to us in the evenings, and near the television and the second bathroom. We agreed on that, but we hoped in our hearts that it wouldn't be necessary. We tried not to think of the somber options. My dad, Ducky, widowed, retired from his supervisor's job and living independently, shifted in and out of nursing homes and apartments, had a lady friend who had her own place, and he dropped dead on his neighbor's floor—the Sunnyside Liquor Store.

Bea on September 16, 1979

Good morning! I'm moving in a warm glow all day. What I worried about being hazardous turned out to be wonderful. Jan was even concerned for me. But we pulled it off. My youngest son Joel married Karen, and I had to be the mother of the groom with my ex- and relatives and all those straight people surrounding us. It was awful shopping for a dress! What do merchants think mothers are, stupid? All those frills and patterns. Yuck.

But first, we had to get through Karen's bridal shower. Jan sat next to me and tried to be invisible. Karen went around the table and held each person's shoulders to introduce each to the group. I was easy. She described me as Joel's mother, but what would she say about Jan? She put her hands on Jan's shoulders and said that Jan is Bea's friend, and paused and added, "and my friend too."

The wedding rehearsal in a Lakeshore Bay Lutheran church was relatively painless and the rehearsal pizza party at the restaurant where the two had worked was great with lots of good jokes.

Her parents are pleasant but quiet, and the wedding and reception were a full-blown do with all that a bride could want.

I had my hair done and did last minute shopping on Saturday. I finally found a simple white satin long dress that hung gracefully on me. No frills. Just a necklace around my neck and a narrow satin cord around my waist. I left for church at 2:30. Jan came later and sat in the back pews. She would mill about and I could always find her when I looked for her. All my kids and more were in the wedding.

What a terrific reception. My ex-husband's relatives were hanging about in one corner. I had prepared Jan for my former in-laws, but when Jan saw Jake's sister, she told me she looked like a red brick wall. All the cousins were there. Marge came too, and all my kids' friends from the old days when they hung around at my house. We laughed so much and told family shaggy dog stories that probably will turn into legends. We all danced to a great band. My son Josh danced with Jan. Marge hadn't been asked to dance so she grabbed Josh and made him dance with her too.

My youngest is a married man and his wife is wonderful.

Bea on November 14, 1979

Jan loved the ring I made for her and I loved making it. When we came home from the bookstore, I made supper and Old Pal Marge came over to wish Jan a happy birthday.

Another gift for her was Jenny's asking Jan to be the parent involved in her Thoreau High School's "Rites of Passage" committee, which challenges the students to analyze their lives, set goals and make decisions. They meet on a regular basis with other students, selected teachers and a parent to check that the student is on the right track for the future. Jan would have been so distressed if Jenny had chosen her dad.

Matt called and said he'd be home soon from his cowboy college in South Dakota to run cross country at UW-Oshkosh's national race, and he told her he will transfer to Madison for the next semester to be "in a more cultural environment." Having Matt closer to home is another present for her.

We decided to save our dessert of apple pie and ice cream for later and eventually we ate it in bed—and then I had her.

I wrote my first poem in a long time.

> I am rich beyond measure.
> Your soft body is my pillow—
> Lush cushion of delight—
> Luxury that cannot be bought.
> It's my bonus that comes with love
> For the time when the tide of our passion ebbs
> And you draw a circle around us

With our love enclosed—
Our softness mutually comforting.

Mother Courage is doing OK, but that's about it. Customers come by to chat and sometimes they even buy something. Often friends and family stop in and since we joined the Milwaukee Feminist Writers group, some Milwaukee lesbians even visit our store.

Chapter 3

Jan on February 1, 1980

Last night, Mary Daly stood on the auditorium stage above us sitting in the front row with other women at UW-Whitewater auditorium. She stunned us with her inspiring views on feminist theology, ethics and women's history. Betty Hannamen, Bea and I drove fifty miles to hear her speak, and Daly didn't let us down. She repeatedly overwhelms patriarchy with her knowledge, attitude and personal power. And she did so again last night. Determined not to waste time on the male powers structure, she refused to take any questions or comments from men in the audience. She does that in her classes too, now that the school must admit women to the formerly all-male school. She's wasted too much time and energy on male privilege, she said, and she will not do it again. Several men walked out.

From my research, I learned that she's a Ph.D. three times over and she challenged the Jesuit-run Boston University male administrators into giving her tenure. The Catholic college never realized what a swarming hornet's nest she'd create, and she continues to buzz and sting their male-dominated religion and patriarchy's legacy of abusive power.

She was threatened with dismissal from the school when she published *The Church and the Second Sex* in 1968. She said she wrote it with a great sense of pride, anger and hope. In those years of protesting, she became a cause and the Boston area men and women went all out to protest her termination and the loss of her teaching career. She was finally granted tenure, but her book became out of print after three years. Unable to affect the "publishing house patriarchs," she moved on to become "a postchristian feminist"

(Capitalization is from her book at our store.) with her second feminist book, *Beyond God the Father: Toward a Philosophy of Women's Liberation*, which was published by our own Unitarian Universalist Beacon Press in 1973.

A rush flowed through me when she spoke of Simone de Beauvoir and her book, *The Second Sex,* as one of her early inspirations. It was also that for me, and cheers would come from the crowd and us when she'd challenge us to overcome our cultural and religious suppression, to refuse to suppress or limit our perspectives, questioning any of the preconceived patterns of male-dominated culture.

With vigor she declared that men have had control over research. Now women scholars are uncovering hidden history, herstory, which we never really heard about in our education. This new scholarship is piecing together the fragmented dreams we were brought up to ignore, the sexuality we were taught to deny, the language with words that ignore our existence, the pride and esteem we give to others but seldom to ourselves.

Christians revere the 1,980 years since the birth of Jesus; the Hebrew tradition signifies their year as 5741. Feminist scholars now count women's heritage starting from 9980 years ago at the dawn of civilization when women were leaders.

While referring to centuries of male scholarship, her hands created a square with her fingers sifting through the contents as if it were a box of kitty litter and its contents indicated centuries of male-dominated research re-search and re-searched the same old history from their point of view. In promoting her latest book, *Gyn/Ecology*, which I brought from our shop, she used new language and words, saying that women's access to humanity is blocked not from the state, church and culture, but by language itself. That truly spoke to me with my abandoned novel I tried to write using gender-free pronouns and our church women trying to de-genderize our UU hymnbooks by our penciling in feminine pronouns.

She urged us to self-define "spinster," "hag" and "crone" by choice, neither in relation to children nor to men. "Be a Spinster whirling and spinning in a new time and space," she challenged us.

She asked questions about women's histories that are so painful to hear when she answers them: What about Indian women burning on their husbands' pyre? What about the millions of women burned as witches? What about the brutality of clitorectomies in Africa? And the Chinese custom that the bound foot is the most erotic and desired portion of the entire female body.

Her speaking on the ultimate threat of female bonding helped me to understand my boss and others of his ilk. She said that when women break through to self-knowledge, we find our inherent strength that has been denied. When the male attains insight about himself, he realizes that his role-defined strength is because he hides his weakness. He knows he must fear the combination of even two or three Sparking Female Selves, for Sparking Spinsters confirm each other, and our converging power is the reason why strong female-identified women frequently find ourselves isolated in patriarchal institutions surrounded by token women.

I will cherish this night and Mary Daly's autograph that she signed in one of our already owned books. It's dated "Jan. 31, 1980" and she wrote "To Mother Courage—Courage! Mary Daly."

I will forever remember following the crisp, bright whiteness of the full moon guiding my driving home along the two-lane road with sharp, black shadows against glistening white drifts piled along our asphalt path and the glowing crystal reflections from the snow-covered countryside.

The Milwaukee Journal woman reporter had been sitting near us in the front row and when we read her article today, she stressed Daly's refusal to speak to men and that she was sitting among a row full of lesbians. I don't think that the two of us wore any defining marks on ourselves and we didn't wear any self-identifying t-shirts labeling our sexual orientation and Betty is certainly straight

Bea on February 2, 1980

I didn't write daily little pocket diary notes this year. I broke that habit for the first time for many reasons, mostly negative; but my recent research into past diaries made me realize their value and I've chosen a ring-binder format so I can write more. But I still go beyond the daily margins.

We sailed our *Courage* a few times but not as much as we wanted because I had to stay at the bookstore and Jan had to work a lot on hospital PR projects. Art wise, I painted three new canvasses and mounted my own show at our Mother Courage Bookstore and Art Gallery. I also repaired two friends' instruments, a mandolin and a lute, and I built a dulcimer for Betty Willing.

I arranged to have my daughter staff our bookstore on Saturdays. We stopped our Sunday hours and this gave Jan and me full weekends together, which is much better. But still we are adjusting. Jan vacillates between wanting input from the store customers against what's practical, so she complains about not being there on Saturday; yet she enjoys the freedom. Together we are able to accomplish more.

My Jill is not steadily employed elsewhere and now Mother Courage is helping to send her through college. We don't owe any money except our usual current monthly bills. Yes, we have cash flow problems; especially with the new mall opening with two big-chain bookstores in it, but damn it, the store is giving Jill a regular income and paying for my insurance and a few incidentals. We will hang in with the store for a while longer and roll with the punches.

Another challenge among many women-owned bookstores is finding feminist books to sell. We had been ordering our small press publications from Women in Distribution (WIND). Sadly, they went bankrupt a year ago after five years of feminist bookstores being able to order small press books from a single source. Of course, some of those small bookstores didn't or couldn't pay their bills because of inexperienced and undercapitalized business practices. All of women-owned presses and small bookstores have suffered. WIND stocked every title of every press and its failure is disastrous for the women distributers, the presses and us.

Fortunately, Carol Seajay, an enterprising businesswoman and bookseller, publishes the *Feminist Bookstore Newsletter* for us subscribers so we know about new and reprinted titles by Marge Piercy, Toni Morrison, Alice Walker and other less known independent women authors. Seajay and her women's bookstore network explained the differing terms and transactions that each bookstore staff would now have to know so the women could order from dozens of publishers rather than a single source. So, by our fingernails, we are keeping our radical feminist revolutionary storefront mission in business—just.

Bea on June 20, 1980

Emotional trauma erupted when Jan tried to claim her divorce settlement visitation rights to the forty acres of Door County property. She had signed over the acres to Alex so he wouldn't have to sell them in their divorce settlement, but she negotiated visiting the land. When she arranged for the first visit, he informed her that I would not be allowed on the property. When Alex wouldn't give Jan the keys to the trailer, barn and outhouse, we simply searched all the area hardware stores and bought locksets with keys to match the numbers on those he had installed.

Jan's Lakeshore Med colleagues Sue Manning, Jennifer Kindly and Jan's office mate, Carolyn Schafer came on the first weekend of our summer week's stay with Joanne Zekas and Betty Willing coming up on the second weekend.
Our five guests are straight, well maybe four straight and one bi but it doesn't make a difference because we respect and enjoy each other and we had a grand time, even if I did carry my pistol.
Woodridge has an outhouse but no bathing facilities, so we drive to swim in Buckaroo Lake and wade far enough out to take off our bathing suits. We float a plastic raft to hold suits, soap and shampoo—and we'd plop our dog Luv in the raft when she gets too tired to swim. Luv loves watching us skinny-dippers in the warm water playfully mooning the sun.
Jan made sure she maintained the land while she was enjoying her "visitation rights" and mowed the tall grass and weeds around

the barn and trees nearby. During one after-brunch conversation, we heard a dreadful screaming outside the barn and I ran out to discover that Jan had uncovered a rabbit warren with a screaming litter of bunnies. She'd run the mower over the hole and frantic furry bunny babies escaped from under the whirling blades. Jan could have fainted from empathy for all Beatrix Potter creatures but none, it seemed, were chopped into bits and pieces.

But a snake lurked in the deep grass and glommed on to one bunny running about above ground. More shrill screaming. Jan ran inside with Joanne, Betty and Luv watching through the fly-specked window until Jan gagged at the chain of violence she touched off.

In the spirit of my pioneer foremothers, I grabbed a shovel and smashed the snake near its head until the blows forced out the screeching bunny, and then I whomped the snake on its skull several times until it stopped writhing. Now what were we to do with a screaming, snake-smelling, traumatized frantic ball of fur? I eased the bit of bunny-puff on the shovel, carried her into long grass, gently slid her off in a shady spot and left the rest up to Mother Nature to do must be done. Returning to the disaster scene, I scooped up the dead snake drooping from both sides of the shovel and threw it in the opposite direction over a stony ridge that borders the rock edges of this land. Wiping my hands together to rub off any remains, like a conquering hero I swaggered inside to the liquor shelf and poured myself a stiff victory drink that I lifted to acknowledge the applause and cheers from my admiring visitors.

Jan had turned away from the current disaster scene knowing that a greater disaster was bound to happen if and when Alex sells the land.

Jan on July 3, 1980

Dear Matt,

Tomorrow's the 4th of July and the weather should be perfect here. Grandpa enjoyed an exciting and successful float paper sales year, and Bea and I will be decorating a car and a truck tonight at the shop. Jenny will be missed because she sprained her ankle sliding into second base in a Rock League game. (When your team, the Stones, is in the Rock League and the Diamonds team is the top, you shouldn't even consider sliding into second base.)

I don't see Jenny enough. We both have such busy schedules and I miss her. I haven't heard about her trip to California yet or what kind of situation you're in. Jenny said that you found a place to live in Madison, but she said it with some reservation in her voice. When I asked her about it, she said that you didn't mind living in places like that. What does that mean?

We're having several friends and families over to Grandpa's for the parade and for a picnic and we'll be watching the fireworks from the marina docks in the evening.

I've decided to try to extract myself from working under Nick, Randy and Chuck and have been sending out query letters and résumés. It's very comforting looking for another job when you still have one of your own. So far my dedication and open house plans for Lakeshore Med in September are moving forward. I'm going along with workable and creative ideas and if I should leave before then, someone else can carry on to a successful program. If I'm still here, it will all work out smoothly and I'll be able to finish the celebration of the new hospital addition with pomp and flair.

I came back to work from Door County: first to the American Booksellers' convention at McCormick Place in Chicago where, on the second day of frustration about long lines at the food and drinks courts, we created a gourmet luncheon at home and put it in our cart with a bottle of champagne and glasses. We popped the cork and everyone in our small press corner cheered.

Another day we managed to have a grand Italian supper at Ricardo's on Rush Street with the three portraits over the back bar by Ivan Albrecht, the artist who painted the portrait in *The Portrait of Dorian Gray* movie. (The only problem with that movie is that the Dorian Gray actor reminds me of Randy King.) Do you remember Ricardo's restaurant from one of our family trips there? Well, anyway. Albrecht is one of Bea's favorite painters too.

We enjoyed a peaceful weekend in Door County. I found some much-needed resolution and peace of mind, which is adding to warm, deep feelings of playfulness and happiness and greater emotional security. Though setbacks happen occasionally, by the reality of living and working, I regain my resolve and get back on course again.

Speaking of courses makes me think of the passages we've channeled by being sailors on Bea's boat. Often it's humbling. I had to paddle on the bow of the *Courage* from the pier to get out of the harbor on one calm sailing day. Wouldn't you think some of those big power launches would give us a tow out to catch the wind?

We'll be thinking about you a lot tomorrow on the 4th! Let us know how you are.

Love

Bea on July 8, 1980

On the 4th we enjoyed a memorable evening with Marian, Sharon and their New York women visitors watching Lakeshore Bay's good old fireworks. Marian's closest friend of the two, Linda, was once her lover.

Like Dorothy with her ruby slippers, Marian is from Kansas and after teaching high school art for a year or two, she worked for Hallmark in Kansas City. When she moved to New York City, she and Linda met at Midwestern's offices and became free-lance artists. Marian had actually worked on *Sesame Street* projects, visited the set and met many of the cast and production crew, including Muppets creator Jim Henson. Midwestern's Creative Department hired Marian and brought her to Lakeshore Bay.

We made front row seats at our marina by sitting on blankets at the edge of the river pilings. We dangled our legs over the water and watched a flotilla of private boats flowing past us out into the lake. We drank wine and sang songs until the spectacular pyrotechnics began. Several times we sang loud and clear out over the river, "The Bells Are Ringing for Me and My Gal," and we put our arms over each other's shoulders to sway back and forth together. I don't think anyone caught on to our exhilaration and to the double meaning that those words had for the six of us women celebrating out loud our freedom to be ourselves that 4th of July night.

Each morning, I listen on my multi-band, hand-held radio to hear the scratchy weather report and determine if the day is good for sailing. Most often the winds and waves are too strong for our *Courage*—or there's no wind at all. Marian and Sharon went out with us once when all the elements seemed perfect, but the wind stopped, we stalled and were eaten alive by flies before the wind picked up again. We would have jumped into the water but Lake Michigan was too cold.

One Monday, Jan and I sailed off our marina dock into the river. It's not easy maneuvering under sail without a motor, but we did it and sailed out with the wind onto the lake, staying close to the shoreline. When we sailed back to our dock, I never estimated the height of the high row of pilings and iron posts that supported the corrugated sheeting keeping river water from eroding the harbor walls. When a brisk wind pushed us against the river current, I smartly aimed the boat to the dock, gauged the wind and let go the sheet to put us perfectly beside the dock. I yelled at Jan to let loose the jenny, and as usual, she couldn't hear me with the sail flapping and the wind blowing.

I hollered to Jan, "Get your foot off the sheet!"

"What's the sheet?" she shouted back.

"The rope, damn it!"

"Oh!" as she finally responded to my command.

Sorry to say it, but the wind blew the loose mainsail and the wooden mast boomed out towards the corrugated sheeting and its tall posts. *The Courage's* boom hit every post: Boom! Boom! Boom! Boom! Boom! as we slid in the water to a stop at the dock. Jan had actually tried to stop the boat by grabbing one of the posts but quickly realized she had no footing. Fortunately, she let go or she'd be hanging off the sheeting with the river below ready to receive her.

What a landing! I was relieved that just a few spectators saw what we call, "Our Chinese fire alarm." It's enough to have them watching two women sailing a boat without a man at the helm, let alone watching us make a mistake.

The incident broke some fittings up on the mast that had to be fixed. Our buddies Marian and Sharon helped us get the trailer and boat parked as close to the marina's old brick tool shed as possible. Jan then hiked up on the sloping garage roof, leaned out over the edge, almost hanging by her toes to reach the tips of the split spreaders, and followed my directions to repair the damage.

Of course, other marina members again watched us from their cushioned seats with their cool drinks and wondered what would happen next to these women whose antics, I assumed, were quickly becoming boaters' cocktail time chatter.

Matt had given us his old two-horse engine that had to be started by coiling a rope around the top flywheel. The entire boat was covered with a shiny, lemon yellow deck that had a wooden coaming and an oval cockpit in the center. Because of its shape, I had to install the motor mount at the stern and, to start the engine, I had to leave the tiller, crawl over the stern deck and yank the rope. Then when it detached from the motor, if you're lucky it ends up back in your hand.

When it won't start, which is often, I have to do the whole procedure again. Also, once started, it would often conk out. Imagine what fun that whole business is.

One time the motor conked out just as we were in the center of Lake Michigan's waves meeting the on-coming Wood River currents. I sent Jan to the bow of the *Courage* with an oar where she bounced and leaned over the edge to try to paddle us forward. She told me later that she could almost hear the slave ship drummer pounding the beat to get the slaves to row harder.

Yells came down to us from women friends who had managed to get themselves a ride on a huge cigarette boat that powered past us toward the open water. Jan waved her paddle at them, but she said it wasn't done as a friendly gesture.

Finally, a kind soul offered us a line and towed us to our marina.

Another embarrassment.

When we did manage to sail to the dock in a calm and capable manner, I had to look around to drive one of their damn rust-bucket cars, hitch the trailer to it and back into the water at the dock, haul the boat on to the trailer and find a place to park it all. The driver's seat was almost dragging on the ground so I couldn't see much out the rear and the exhaust practically asphyxiated me before we could put the *Courage* back on the lot to wait for the next chaotic escapade.

What tension! What fun!! What adventure!!!

Chapter 4

Bea on February 18, 1981

My firstborn son Josh was married in September. My ex-husband also was married one week before Josh's wedding—to my old-time, dear friend Angie Murak. That was a shock and quite an emotional strain, I'll tell you. It still is, but I'm improving. Our old friend Marge went off to Mexico with Alex last winter and to Spain and Portugal in August. Best of old friends—and now enemies? Honestly, don't these men have any creative imagination than to choose our best friends for their wives and travel companions?

My son Jim is getting serious about marrying his girlfriend now that his two brothers are married, and I had to go over to meet her parents. Jake and Angie were there too. OK but—!

Jan is increasingly dissatisfied with how three Lakeshore Med's executives treat her and she's trying to get a long-deserved salary increase. Since we bought our house together and became legal partners in Mother Courage Enterprises, we have blended our money. (I have a little bit tucked away just in case.) Jan hands me all her paychecks and we've invested some in mutual funds. But I take care of everything financial, all the bills, the taxes and the mortgage. She's granted me complete financial responsibility and her salary supports us. Some couples like us keep separate savings and checking accounts. We have both our names printed on our checks. In the meanwhile, she is searching for another position and is sending out résumés, but no genuine offer has come through

Stress is getting to her. She finally took her sad, rusty brown Toyota Celica to Penney's auto shop to get the tires fixed. When I drove her there to pick up her car, we heard that the job was hopeless. The rims were rusted onto the tires. The mechanic broke a stud trying to get the first one off and stopped the job. Now she must drive the damn second- or third-hand junker she bought to the expensive dealership to solve that problem before the air leaks out of the tire again. The mechanic installed the white wall half of the tire to face the inside. Jan insisted he switch the tire back. "Why should I have white wall tires when no one can see them!" Big deal!

We had a noisy row in front of the maintenance manager. His mechanics fooled around all day with that car and then they screwed up remounting one tire? Besides, what difference do whitewalls enhance the little Celica's image when duct tape's holding the damn car together. As if disguising the grungy gray tape by spraying brown paint over the patches makes the car sporty again.

It's not the car. It's the image, the metaphor of how Jan's being paid less than her peers, emotionally harassed and pressured by Randy to leave.

Jan was furious that I didn't support her with all this tire business and forcing her to argue with me in front of this guy. Why should two women have a fight over tires—in public?! Rather than duke it out with the mechanics, she finally gave in to me, which makes her angrier because she promised herself she wouldn't give in all the time like she did in the past with her husband. And I was pissed—just because. Gurr! Yes! Pissed at each other, we made another mistake and drove to our lesbian rap group.

On that Night of the Tires, we met at the house of a newer couple. Each of us drove in our separate cars, her beat-up car as proof of not earning enough to buy a better one.

In the midst of discussing how to cope with other lesbian issues, the smug hostess made a crack about alcohol, and Jan stood up and marched out to her beleaguered Toyota. I ran out the door to followed her in my 1978 burgundy Olds Cutlass ragtop sedan that I inherited from my father's estate. Both of us hollered at each other on the way to our cars parked in front of their house—and pulled away with gears and whatever is left of her tires screeching. Our closeted hosts must have been positive that their neighbors heard us. What we did was stupid, yet it's so hard to understand how complicated it is for us to deal with even the most mundane issues.

Inviting newcomers didn't make our lesbian support group grow stronger. Their individual quirks caused us to break up. I know we've helped each other by meeting and sharing the politics of being lesbians. It's important for all of us to have that support. Mother Courage Bookstore, which I always emphasize as "a full-service bookstore" to diminish its feminist/lesbian stigma, is the only outlet for finding books and music that affirm our women's lives. We needed each other more, but individual idiosyncrasies create issues too. Merely being lesbian is no guarantee for liking each other, even when it's crucial for us to have others to turn to, to be treated as worthy human beings rather than viewed as perverts who practice "deviant sexual acts."

Fortunately, the two of us have our Unitarian church and many straight friends who love, accept and try to understand us. At least many in our church do, but it helps for us because our minister Tony Logan came out of the closet and those who are uncomfortable with him have moved elsewhere. Understanding us is tough because often Jan and I don't understand each other either.

Before we fell in love late in 1973, I read where some "expert" defined the term "homophobia" as an irrational fear, hatred and intolerance of homosexual men and women. Hell. I didn't need to have a "term." My father disowned my brother when he came out to him, then my mother had a nervous breakdown. My brother jumped in Lake Michigan in Chicago in March. Somehow a TV reporter found my name and called me at my home with four sick kids to tell me they were airing the video of my brother's body being dragged out of the lake on the 6 p.m. news. He asked me how I felt about it! I know about irrational fear, hatred and intolerance first hand. It's lucky for me that my parents are dead or I'd be blamed for killing them now by being with the woman I love.

It's weird. Most of the others in our rap group are ten or more years younger, some college students, and some divorced moms with little kids. And they are worried about their husbands, parents and siblings finding out about their being lesbians, how they separate during the holidays, where can they go together as a couple or meet someone without going to a bar. Meanwhile, though Jan hasn't come officially out to her father, Barney seems comfortable with us and he's happy to see Jan almost every day at the store. But we're concerned about how our teenage and young adult offspring are dealing with their mothers being lovers. And as far as holidays go, we let our six children go with their spouses or other relatives on those days while we invite our lesbian friends who are left out of their own families to come to our home for a big meal and comfortable companionship.

But actually, I'm not a lesbian. I've spent more than half my life being a straight woman and a mother of four. Why now that I've chosen to be with the person I love—who happens to be a woman—should I be labeled "LESBIAN"?

Jan on February 20, 1981

Debbie's party in their rented lower flat brought together several lesbian rap group friends, some new couples who had left their husbands and blended their lives together, and other women friends of our hosts. It was a dreadfully frigid night with the cold penetrating the tired old house on the edge of Downtown. After our potluck buffet, the wine and beer flowed freely. The antique double sliding doors separating the kitchen from the living room's diminishing fireplace heat were closed with the merry-makers clustered in the kitchen with several of the younger crowd now fueled by smoking pot.

Our young friends' choice of intoxicants didn't concern us. We prefer the liquid kind. So we shared a few drags off the hand-rolled "cigarettes" circling the kitchen. It's not the first time we've been with generous company sharing their offerings.

I stood close to my beautiful, bodacious Bea in a black shirt, trim black pants, boots and cowboy hat as we talked and laughed with the crowd in the midst of the once trendy kitchen appliances sitting on worn linoleum surrounded by shady faded floral wallpaper illuminated by a single ceiling globe on a sandy-colored ceiling.

A strikingly handsome young woman friend with raven-colored hair began regaling the two us with stories in her uniquely husky voice about being an apprentice plumber. She chose plumbing she said, "Because of all the trades, if you make a mistake in plumbing, all that happens is—you get wet."

Then right in front of my face, Bea put one hand on the back of her neck, the other around her waist, pressed her body close and gave her a full-blown kiss smack on the mouth for what seemed to be long enough for me to be visibly shocked, physically queasy with out-of-focus eyes glazed over in amazement.

Was it impulse? The heady pot, beer, the wine? An impulse to test me, to show me she can do anything she wants in front of me? I don't know. I felt as if an anvil had been pressed onto my chest. I quietly slipped out of the kitchen through the double doors and sat dumbfounded and wounded on the floor and fed the fireplace coals for what seemed like hours while women came and went past me.

When Bea told me it was time to go home, I uncoiled myself from my meditative pose, said thanks and goodbye to our hosts, drove home and went to bed without touching. Not one word was spoken from either of us about what happened to have crushed me so hard—nor why.

Jan on February 22, 1981

My Jenny's not happy as a college freshman. It's probably because she never learned to play the game of answering tests and writing themes. Not much of that was done at her alternative high school to prepare her to "play" those games, yet she has the intelligence to succeed if motivated. I think growing up following a super-high achieving brother and having hard-working and high-achieving parents didn't encourage her to excel.

I couldn't understand Jenny's asking her father to help her with homework to analyze the groundbreaking feminist story of *The Yellow Wallpaper* by Charlotte Perkins Gilman. We sold the Feminist Press edition of it in our store and I often recommended it as symbolic of what happens when an intelligent and independent wife is "isolated for her own good" and forced by her oppressive doctor husband "to rest" in a room until she goes mad, a powerful metaphor for rage and anger. She starts to strip off the wallpaper as if to peel away her skin to find her true self. In the process she also erodes away domestic boundaries by eating away hateful yellow wallpaper.

Why did Jenny ask her father rather than me? What does he know about being patronized, repressed and imprisoned? When I had a rare occasion to see Alex, I commented on his helping Jenny with this assignment and told him my positive insights in the book, hoping he would see parallels my life. Perhaps he could see the writer's striving to make others understand about women trying to live beyond being domesticated inferior beings. He looked at me, almost in distain, and asked, "When did you start eating wallpaper?"

Carolyn Schaffer on February 25, 1981

Of the twenty-five projects for Randy's weekly report list, fourteen are "A" priorities, including today's event, an international endoscopic demonstration with over seventy-five experts viewing the live demonstrations on TV sets from three close-circuit color cameras transmitting every word and move of our own famous gastroenterology specialist and others from Wilhelmshaven, Germany; Liverpool, England; New York City and Milwaukee's Midwest Medical College.

We're responding to the media and helping with details to make this day run smoothly. Live TV teaching demonstrations of this magnitude have been performed outside England only once in Egypt and another in Germany.

In contrast we also have a new chaplain, Episcopalian Father Jay McConnell who seemed pleasant enough when I interviewed him for our employee newsletter. He's replacing our dear Father Arthur Boulton who retired after many years of service to Lakeshore Med and the Episcopalian Church. The new chaplain's assistant is a Catholic nun, Sister Eugene. Father Jay explained in the newsletter, "We are to share duties ministering to the spiritual needs of our patients, their families and employees." I suppose employees could make an appointment to see one of them for spiritual counseling. I don't think I would, though. I'd rather get by with a little help from my friends.

I remember when our friend Joanne Zekas was a patient. When she was interviewed in the admitting process, the nurse asked her about her religion. Unitarian Universalism was considered as "Other." When the nurse asked Joanne if she would like to see a chaplain, Joanne told her she would call Jan Anthony.

The original hospital founders and trustees have been associated with the Episcopalian denomination for over one hundred years, making Lakeshore Medical Center the Protestant hospital in deference to St. Agnes, which is Catholic and operates under its religious restrictions. That's why the two hospitals consolidated psychiatry, obstetrics/nursery and gynecological services solely at Lakeshore Medical Center balancing St. Agnes solely at pediatrics.

In reality and in comparison to St. Agnes, Lakeshore Med is non-denominational. Jan quoted Administrator Clark Young who stated the principle: "We care for people and their needs; how the patient came to this need is not the problem. Whatever brings people to us, if we have the means, we shall serve them; and we will do our best to have whatever means we shall need." Jan created an award-winning, five-fold photo brochure based on those noble words.

Other than the original, tiny, unassuming brick chapel with stained-glass windows on the site of the first hospital buildings, there are no religious symbols in hospital corridors and rooms nor statuary on the hospital's limited landscape and gardens. Our new logo may look somewhat like the sign of a cross, but it's a yellow and blue mix between what I think of as a Celtic cross, but more likely four flower-shaped petals.

We miss Father Boulton. I'll always remember his excited plans for his bishop's visit and how he told us he would arrange for everything so as not to bother us with another project. He ordered a full-sized sheet cake for the reception and had the baker decorate the entire top with frosting of our blue and gold logo. It was a surprise that after the cake was eaten, the bishop and almost everyone else showed blue teeth when they smiled at each other.

It seems as if he'd been our chaplain almost as long as his administrator friend Clark Young, who devoted his life to the hospital for thirty years before retiring and passing the torch on to Nick Dixon. I wonder what Nick will think or say about handsome young chaplain who told me he wears a gold earring in one ear as part of a ship crew's rite of crossing the Equator twice, or something like that—and many believe him. He doesn't have the gay gene gestures and walk like Father Boulton.

Father Boulton could sometimes cut a vindictive edge in his voice about those who have hurt his feelings, but he was always so gracious to those who showed respect for his work. He would accompany Madeline, our jovial School of Nursing administrator, to hospital functions, or should I say they would accompany each other, and they made a good-humored and charming couple, probably because Madeline left Virginia, her long time housemate, at home.

Unlike most ministers, Father Boulton's prayers at hospital events were ecumenical and sensitive to others' religious principles.

He was also house parent of the male nursing students who lived in a home next to the women's student nurses Victorian mansion. Randy lived in the men's dorm for a while, but he discovered that the old house was too drafty and cold for his liking. Soon after, Randy moved into the historic Marquette Apartments on Main Street two blocks from Lakeshore Med. It's the same apartment complex where Jan rented a tiny "room of one's own," where she lived from February to April some time before she was divorced, supposedly to write her androgynous novel. After she moved back to her family and her big home, she kept renting the room, a convenient meeting place for her and her friends.

What infuriates Jan is that Chuck, Randy's subordinate, has moved in with Randy—and Bea was supposedly "let go" from working with Jan at Lakeshore Med because of an unfounded "rule" forbidding a supervisor and a subordinate from living together, even though there's a fair amount of nepotism and living and sleeping together among the hospital staff. After that, I replaced—or am striving my best to replace Bea at the job.

Father Arthur Boulton on March 10, 1981

Hi Jan and Bea,

Life goes on here in Door County. It is not easy financially but I feel The Good Magnet brought me here and that things are falling into place.

It's taking me forever and a day to settle in because, in essence, we are trying to incorporate the effects of two households into one, but I let Bobby drag his stuff along in the event he should want to split. Utilities and food are atrociously high here and we're making the most of our trips out of town.

I did want to share this fact with you; namely, that I am still happy that I came here. I realize in retrospect too that outing from Lakeshore Med was long overdue for me. With lousy knees and sore feet, trudging those corridors in pain was no picnic. My attempts to find other work met with naught and going the social work route was fine until things became impossible for me when I was required to complete two semesters of 12 credit hours. I am too weary.

I'm thinking of you and loving you—forbid I should preach—but I share the thought that one must recognize wounding and do one's utmost to avoid the source of that wounding whatever the price! I don't know what lies ahead of me. I have some money in a sock so my trust is being tested. I am surviving. I came here for tranquility and peace. I have them. I came to the country for clean water, wholesome environment, hopefully too, some good interpersonal relationships that I think are possible. So if I'm poor? I was poorer without knowing it by pushing myself beyond my endurance at The Med.

The recent respite in the extreme weather gives us harbingers of liveliness to come. Here the snow remains pristine and lovely, despite the temperatures. I have seen beauty here and have had time to enjoy it.

Love, peace and caring,
Arthur

PS Tell Carolyn Hi and thank her for her friendly article about my retiring.

Jan on March 14, 1981

Marge Manley issued a memo to hospital managers and supervisors from the Human Resources Manager listing ten successful employee incentives:

- Interesting work
- Appreciation of work done
- Feeling "in on things"
- Good pay at marketplace values
- Promotion and growth
- Good working conditions
- Loyalty to employees
- Help with personal problems
- Tactful discipline
- Job security with uniform standards

What a crock!

Jan on March 18, 1981

My letter to Sister Mary, president of St. Veronica's Hospital nearby in Grange, illustrated how public relations positions are churning about in our area. I sent a personal letter and résumé to her.

Dear Sister Mary

"I can imagine your personnel office is flooded with public relations résumés like so many drops of water rushing in to fill the whirlpool's vortex.

"I was as surprised to hear about Karen's leaving your hospital to work at St. Agnes as I was when I heard about Ken's leaving St. Agnes for a position at the Hospital Council.

"Perhaps this may add to the current turbulence around our hospitals, but, confidentially, I too would like to find a new environment where I could meet new challenges and use my administrative skills and creative efforts to better advantage..."

I got the interview with Sister Mary whose PR person was hired to join our competitor's team at St. Agnes for a salary from $7,000 to $9,000 more than I make! Depressing and disgusting! And Grange may not be so bad for me to work—even with all the crucifixes and statues around. I could still be a strong feminist in Lakeshore Bay with my bookstore, and my private life could be more private—maybe.

"Oh, God!" I shuddered when I walked by all the saintly statues and Jesus dying on the cross, but I was determined to overlook that which seemed more immaculate than the chauvinistic crap that I was suffering at the Med. I could work for a religion-based college or a hospital because they're up front with their traditions and dogma. What was now getting to me at my own hospital was a phony and insidious infiltration of religious practices. And it's good practice for me to be interviewed in a positive rather than the hostile manner I'm getting now at my hospital that I would love to stay at for the rest of my career. As in my acrimonious divorce, it would be so much easier if the negative male influence would go away rather than my having to leave.

I wrote the customary "thank you for the interview" note but was politely notified by letter that I didn't get the position.

Jan on March 22, 1981

The out-of-town rejection letters stressed how many applicants applied and who was chosen. Many of the local contacts said they'd put my letter on file for future reference. The blind ad queries went unanswered. I couldn't help but wonder what, if any, were their real reactions: an angry feminist who speaks out against male domination at seminars and writes inflammatory commentaries to the newspapers; a well-qualified professional, true, but she owns that rabble-rousing women's bookstore; that divorced woman who left her wonderful husband and children and became—a lesbian.

On a recent Monday morning, a bong, bong, bong of chimes came over Lakeshore Med's speaker system and the gentle voice of Sister Eugene introduced herself and read selected and noted Bible verses to comfort the ill and injured.

I couldn't believe my ears. I'm supposed to be the Communications director and I never directed any Bible nor religious sentiments of any creed to accost our patients and employees of all faiths, nor did anyone inform me about this new practice for Carolyn to notify employees in the hospital newsletter.

I did find out, through my network, that Nick's wife who founded our Women's Health Clinic went home that night angry as a wounded wolf and demanded to know, "Who the hell approved reading the damn Bible verses over the loud-speaker system. I almost vomited when I heard them."

"I did," he told her and she shut up.

It's a part of the hospital's innovative new marketing plan to improve its image. St. Agnes, the Catholic hospital, is thought to be the spiritual hospital and Lakeshore Med is the sectarian one. So, my hospital's marketing committee uses Sister Eugene to try to alter that image by insidiously implanting Christian Bible verses that we are forced to hear every morning. Of course, she uses Bible verses; that's what she knows.

Our bookstore alone has healing spirituality sources, many using gender-free language where all could find comfort through meditation: Barbara Walker, Maya Angelou, Judy Chicago, Jean Houston, Shakti Gawain, even Medieval Catholic feminist poetry written by Hildegard of Bingen and Julian of Norwich.

I felt chills when I read this new book, *Mother Wit: A Feminist Guide to Psychic Development* by Diane Mariechild. In a quiet time at the store, I read one of her healing meditations that, for the first time in my experience, lead me down a path in the forest to a cabin where an old woman emerged as The Wise One. A woman of great wisdom! The wisdom of the ages. The wise old woman who lives deep within me, someone I could find within myself and absorb into my own experience. What a breakthrough!

After recovering from shock of being assaulted with literal Bible verses read on our PA system, I borrowed our Unitarian Universalist denomination's new gender-free hymnbook and typed several of the Bible-based readings that would fit Sister Eugene's and, I'm sure, the Marketing Committee's goals. I gently made an appointment and went to her office, sat with her to make only a few suggestions about considering the use of gender-free language but also to incorporate other bias-free religious principles in her readings that would not exclude patients of non-Christian faiths. Always gracious, my offerings may provide her some alternatives to consider.

She was polite.

Jan on March 25 1981

I answered a blind ad for a community relations director at a large hospital that sounded perfect for me. Then I discovered the ad was for a position at St. Agnes. I can imagine the smug grin on St. Agnes hospital administrator's face when he told Nick Dixon that I'd applied for a job with his competition. St. Agnes never responded to my letter.

After that I sent cover letters and résumés to many in the area, but I had to chance it that many manufacturing executives and other men in business may be or have hospital trustee or board member connections or be in the Rotary, Kiwanis, etc., which does not include women as members.

I started by writing an old UU friend, head of prestigious executive retreat and conference center located near Lakeshore Bay.

"Dear Henry,

I write this letter with feelings of nostalgia mixed with excitement because somewhere in the mid-sixties your predecessor offered to restart my career position at your foundation, but I was unable to accept the position because of family responsibilities.

(My husband refused to allow me to accept it.)

"It was the spark that ignited my growing professional life to the point where I am now ready to take on new responsibilities with multifaceted challenges in a new professional environment…"

To the Wisconsin Natural Gas Company's PR guy I knew from a IABC meeting: "When it is time for you and your associates to evaluate your current staff needs, I hope that you will consider my energy, experience and abilities to fill your future public relations and communications requirements. My present position at Lakeshore Medical Center is rewarding in every way except financially and I am unhappy to have to look for another professional position…"

Mid-week after my initial letter, I called him on the phone as I had indicated that I would in my letter, and then I responded with a thank you letter.

"When you said you thought I was a fixture at Lakeshore Medical Center, hit the mark because that's probably the problem here. Thanks so much for your sincere, insightful, empathetic and affirmative response to my letter and phone call."

Later, I found out that my friend and founder of our Lakeshore Bay Women's Network was suing the Gas Company for job discrimination, and I'm sure they were not looking for another woman who could be a trouble-maker. Plus, I heard he was quite a womanizer.)

From a large classified display ad for Assistant Manager, Publications at the Jos. Schlitz Brewing Company challenging job seekers "to GO FOR IT," I responded:

"I'm ready to *GO FOR IT!* as the criteria listed in the ad describes my qualifications exactly.

"In addition, I've always known that I could only work with integrity for an institution or a product that I could believe in, like my hospital. Well, I believe in people, in joy and celebration, and, unlike many women, beer is my favorite beverage; therefore, I would be happy and proud to be among those to promote it and the people who make it."

Bullshit! My favorite adult beverage is a martini or two.

Bea on March 30, 1981

Last night we had a Spring Fling Full Moon ceremony and party at our house. Jan encouraged Carolyn to bring her daughter Jane and her friend to join in with our straight and lesbian women friends—and Carolyn was so pleased to have them join her and find out what we and her mother do together on every full moon. They were home on spring break from law school at the University of Indiana in Bloomington. We didn't invite our own daughters because they had enough to deal with our feminist-lesbian orientation without finding out that we were leaning toward a witchy pagan experiment, searching and learning about those aspects of this religion that Jan and I are learning to accept for ourselves.

(When Carolyn started working with Jan after I was "let go" from being Jan's co-PR person, Carolyn fit in so well that Jan often said that the Goddess sent Carolyn to her. It was months before Jan put some clues together to indicate that Carolyn oldest daughter is a lesbian and that Carolyn's lover Roger also has a lesbian daughter. Ironically, Jan said that Carolyn never used the "L-word," yet she was comfortable being with us and didn't need to talk as much about her daughter's orientation as she did about Roger's daughter's accomplishments. Both daughters are feminist activists fighting for the advancement of women's rights. Carolyn once described Roger's daughter, a nurse of small stature who lives in San Francisco, as a real fighter, someone who can defend herself as a martial arts expert who wields a mean broom stick to defend herself if needed, especially when she leaves her hospital after her night shift ends.)

We started our party with a ritual for the Spring Equinox from Z Budapest's *The Holy Book of Women's Mysteries*. Our theme was the ancient annual springtime story of the return of Persephone from the underworld to unite again with Demeter, her mother whose happiness changes the seasons from barren winter to green and fertile lands again. I modified some of Z's rituals. We weren't ready to do all the woman kissing and blessings that Z suggests at her Susan B. Anthony Coven #1 and at women's festivals where they find places to run naked—sky-clad, they call it—and dance around bonfires in valleys and on hilltops. Our women hold hands to create a circle.

Because I had time to do the research, I assumed the leader's role as High Priestess. I spoke my version of Z's words: "We invoke you, oh Persephone, the ever young maiden, and Flora, the new life that is all around us. We invoke you by root, by stem and by bud, by leaf and by blossom. We invoke you by seed, by life to transfuse our lives and souls with your fresh energy. As you have risen from the ground, so shall your sisters. As you have united with your joyous mother Demeter, so shall we unite with our mothers while in life, and close the gaps of socializations that separate us. Bless your sisters who call upon your guidance. Make our heart fill with love for one another, for our sisters and mothers and offspring. So mote it be!"

Then I poured wine into a large goblet, drank from it and passed it around the circle once. The first round is to toast the rejuvenated Goddess. Then again, we went around the circle to bless new projects or relationships in each woman's life.

We moved over to the table full of food that everyone brought, blessed all that and closed the ritual saying "Blessed Be!" Then the women followed my gesture, one that I've never read about, seen or heard. While still holding hands in our circle, we lowered them while bending our knees, raised them high to the sky, together in celebration while we cheered with rising volume, "AAALLLLLL RIGHT!!!!!"

And we laughed and hugged each other, poured wine or opened sodas and scooped up the food. We had shared a simple ritual but the party went on for hours.

I'd made a date with Betty Willing to come to the store with her fiddle and I had my guitars and we played good music, practicing together for the party or for who knows what? So we played at our house and everybody sang and talked over all the party noise.

Jan told me she overheard Beth Johnson's exclamation when she recognized Carolyn's Jane who sat close to her friend in a small space. Beth asked Jane, "Aren't you the one who spoke so eloquently at my graduation ceremony? Yes! You were our valedictorian! You told the truth about our lives. You challenged everyone to do away with injustice and prejudice and face up and create a new future, especially when it comes to women's issues. I was so proud to be a woman who could identify with you and your words and be among those who make your speech a reality." Jane smiled in appreciation and Beth enthusiastically moved closer to continue talking with laughter and determination about their common battles for equity and justice.

I finally dosed off in my chair around midnight but the party went on with Jan hugging the women and walking them to their cars until the last one left, and she put some of the house back together again. She wondered today why most of the cannibal sandwich fixings with top grade beef, deli rye, chopped onions and various sauces that we had prepared were not eaten. Too many vegetarians at this party, I guessed. And we probably made a political food faux pas.

We're recuperating this morning. Jan slept late and I coasted until the spring sun came out in the afternoon to warm us and send us on our way to the Milwaukee Repertory Theatre to experience *A Streetcar Named Desire*, and then we treated ourselves to a terrific seafood dinner.

Chapter 5

Bea on April 4, 1981

Jesus! We had another Friday night blowout when Jan came home with her ego shattered by a bad job evaluation but her salary is raised $3,000. I wish someone would raise my non-existent salary by any amount. She went a little crazy and I got plastered listening to her. I couldn't cope with her so she called Betty Willing, who loves joining us at the bar, to come over.

Jan poured Betty a vodka on the rocks and us some Gallo jug wine. We had had our vodka martinis before some supper. We clicked our glasses together and Jan let loose. "He's got me by the balls, Betty, and I'm powerless in his grip that's clenched and ready to break me." She raised her glass like a wounded but courageous warrior. "I resent having to surrender!"

"We don't want you to lose any of your vital parts, Honey." And Betty declared her favorite response, "He's like all those assholes."

"I'm so tired and worn and weary, Betty. I've failed! I trusted those guys, especially Randy. Why did I trust them, especially after I trusted my husband and he's still trying to get even with me?"

"My husband is an asshole too, and I sure don't trust him. And you know, I never trusted that Marge either, from the start, years ago!"

"She doesn't bother me, except at work. She can have Alex if she wants him. But I had joyful dreams of working with wonderful people, doing great projects, making the best of everything. Like Bea says, 'I make shit into sunshine.'"

"Don't stop your dreaming, Jan. You and Bea have accomplished a lot already."

"But we have so much to deal with and I don't think we can make it. My dreams of joy are erupting into nightmares."

"Is it that bad, Honey?" as Betty put her hand on my cheek.

"Good night, you two," I said. "I've had enough. I'm going to bed." And I left Jan to ease Betty out the door and in her car to drive home to deal with her own problems. I wonder if she made it. She always does—eventually.

We're trying to recuperate today. I drove to the sports shop to buy two sets of snorkeling fins and masks with the $75 that I earned from an art job.

Bea on April 19, 1981

The first space shuttle, Columbia, and its crew, John Young and Robert Crippen, landed safely this week in California after orbiting the earth thirty-six times in two days. What an accomplishment for our country and the world. Ironically my accomplishment is that I bought a compact five-sleeper camping trailer, a 1973 canvas pop-up model in great shape, and we'll have our adventures heading to the East Coast for our next vacation in May.

Jan brought flowers for me Wednesday and packed for her two-day HPRW meeting at Green Lake. I shut the bookstore a bit early that afternoon and went to see Jill. The next day I said "Fuck It" to the store and shut the door again to run errands. Just sitting there is driving me bananas.

Jan keeps telling me to paint or draw or create something to sell so I have something to do with my time. I've read practically every book. She doesn't understand that you can't instantly turn on creative work. It has to happen.

I've given in. I'm taking the first steps to publishing Rachael Sandler's abuse book for children by attending a publishing course at UW-Milwaukee one night a week. Maybe I'll gain some ideas to convince Jan and Rachael that we are not the ones to do her book for her. Both Rachael and Jan won't give in. Rachael invited us to brunch at a crowded little Jewish deli in Milwaukee before we had a meeting to take her hand-written "manuscript" of two legal-size yellow pages to be illustrated with my drawings to make a book. I don't know what to draw on the subject of sexual abuse. Rachael said she needs a book to help the children she counsels to talk about their sexual abuse. She wants to show her students in therapy that they can tell her about abuse without shame and guilt. And I'm supposed to illustrate—what? Besides, we're supposed so split the profits—Ha!—Three ways. That means we have to put out cash that we don't have to pay for two-thirds of a major gamble.

At least Jan and I broke some of the tension when we went to Milwaukee's Downer cinema to laugh at the French film, *La Cage Aux Folles*. It's great to sit in a crowd and join in the laughter with others who are accepting and understanding the gay antics that aren't so different from other people—with a dash more flamboyance.

Bea on April 21, 1981

During the long hours of waiting for customers and reading at our bookstore, I deliberated over Mary Daly's 1978 book, *Gyn Ecology, The Metaethics of Radical Feminism*. When I finished the final chapter, "Spinning: Cosmic Tapestries," I talked with Jan for hours, sharing Daly's enlightened perceptions and scholarship, her riveting wisdom that gives us new insights into male power, dismembering, laying waste, even killing women and wasting their contributions to the well-being of our earth, our spirituality, our culture and women's selves. Astounded from what I was learning about women's conditions around the world for centuries, I helped Jan adapt one of Mary Daly's purest, less inflammatory messages for Jan's submission to the HPRW's newsletter to be mailed this month.

"Some Terrific, but Humble PR with Radiant New Action Is Needed to Increase Departments' Value"

When the results of the 1978 Wisconsin Hospital Association Membership Survey circulated through this office, one segment of the nine-page report seemed especially significant to hospital public relations people.

Administrators were asked to respond to this statement: "Please give a priority rating (1.2.3.) in order of importance to those members of your hospital family listed below whom you feel can assist your hospital the most in dealing with elected public officials."

Of the categories listed, public relations personnel ranked sixth—out of seven. Top priority went to 1) administrators; trustees; 2. medical staff; 3. auxiliaries; 4. other administrative staff; 5. hospital financial management; 6. PR personnel; and 7. nursing service administration.

Something is mixed-up when the awareness of the value of public relations is so low. It is vital to circulate enough pertinent information via many media so that trustees, medical staff, auxiliary, employees and others in the community can "assist your hospital the most in dealing with elected public officials." Either the public relations departments are not being used to help do this or administrators are not aware of the PR work that is being done.

A fable for this time is about one of the most miraculous public relations experts in modern creative fiction, the spider named Charlotte in E.B. White's story *Charlotte's Web*.

In it, a young pig named Wilbur is saved from being butchered through the creative, aggressive work of Charlotte, a spider who inhabits the same barn. Charlotte saves him by weaving into her web, which hangs over Wilbur's bed in the barn, the words "SOME PIG" in block letters.

The farmer and people from miles around who come to see the web concluded that Wilbur is "no ordinary pig." Only the farmer's wife has the wits to remark to her husband, "Well, it seems to me you're a little off. It seems to me we have no ordinary *spider*."

Charlotte weaves other slogans for this miraculous pig that she read from old papers left in the barn. He is "TERRIFIC" and "WITH RADIANT ACTION."

The hero pig lives out the PR prophecy created by the spider because he believes it too.

Like all truly creative geniuses, Charlotte is extremely versatile, being able to use whatever material is at hand in order to carry out her promotional plans. The barn's rat, Templeton, is sent to bring Charlotte ads from the newspapers in the dump, which she uses as a thesaurus of sorts. The ads also help her with her spelling problems.

The very last slogan she weaves—"HUMBLE"—boosts Wilbur to a big win over a larger pig in the competition at the fair by eliciting empathy from the judges. Wilbur's miraculous nature is confirmed and he knows now that the farmer will never butcher him but will keep him as long as he lives.

Charlotte has saved the day by creating and weaving magic words. Yet at the end of the story, "Nobody, of the hundreds of people that had visited the fair, knew that a gray spider had played the most important part of all."

Jan was cautious about acknowledging Mary Daly's unique language and her crediting women as spinsters who weave their webs to change the world, nor did she mention Daly's other chapters on how women have been sacrificed throughout history as Daly writes of powerful and anguishing details on Indian suttee, Chinese foot binding, African female genital mutilation, European witch burning, American gynecology and Nazi medical experiments. We're saving Daly's blasting "ammunition" should we need it in future confrontations.

I'll always remember these atrocities perpetrated on women and legitimized by male-dominated customs. Their unjust powers that we have inherited still exist.

Jan on May 1, 1981

We have all of our plans set for us to invade St. Agnes Hospital again during National Hospital Week near the end of May with our four-by-eight foot foam core panels featuring electroencephalography, obstetrics, radiation therapy, hemodialysis, the world famous Digestive Disease Center, and our education programs in nursing, radiology and medical technology. All have accompanying photos, our in-house produced brochures and publications, and of course, the coup de grace—Carolyn's beautiful banners that she's making for most departments on her own time at home so she can leave work on comp time to see Roger.

Bea on May 3, 1981

Barney's 78th birthday is today and after church we stopped at his house to give him his gift—a tape recorder so he can tell his stories on tape for posterity. We gave him a quick lesson on the machine, ate some cake that we brought.

What a week! Getting our camping trip out east routed by AAA, I bought a fire extinguisher, a propane gas tank, utensils and other camping gear. We even hosted a Saturday night UU Supper Club serving my Monterey Jack casserole. What a blast!

Most of the gay guys we know are open and friendly, not bitchy and hateful as portrayed in some movies. I don't remember details about movies that Jan's experienced, like *Midnight Cowboy* where the two losers love each other but overtly hide it by spewing out "faggot" and "queer," and how the cowboy, who hates himself for being gay, bashes in the face of an old cruiser. (Lesbians are usually sadistic prison matrons or schoolteachers who commit suicide.) I know our gay friends seem happier because they found our church where we can be together among straight people and feel safer than most other places where we're a minority.

I don't exactly know when it began, but our minister Tony Logan has been "out-of-the-closet" with the congregation and the community, and he can be more relaxed about being himself. He doesn't pretend to have a girlfriend anymore, as I advised him. Tony and I came out to each other when he became our new minister in 1975. Most of our congregation love, respect and accept him, whatever his sexual orientation. Not everyone did, however. Some people don't come to our church anymore, including the Dixons and Jan's ex-. Who knows how our relationship and those of us who are feminist rabble-rousers may have caused some to leave our church? Oh well, we'll more than make up for those dropouts. Our UU community welcomes newcomers and our sympathetic straight allies to join a new spiritual home and fill the spaces left by homophobic ex-parishioners. All species of people are more alike than they are different.

Our single friends like Tony may be ready to settle down. The others like Bob and Louie, Dick and Pat seem happier in a monogamous relationship rather than the indiscriminate cruising that others consider typically gay behavior.

Speaking of cruising, Jan and I avoided the Al Pacino movie *Cruising*, which never made it to Lakeshore Bay (I don't like Al Pacino anyway). But I know I couldn't stomach this movie. There's enough violence in this world and more than too much toward homosexuals. This movie, compared to the other gay bashing American films, intensifies the negative aspects of the gay men's lives and somehow justifies violence against them—and maybe even us.

"The old glory days of promiscuous gay sex may be coming to an end," said one of our gay friends—promiscuity not only in gay sex but the one-night stands as in what happened to Diane Keaton's straight woman character in *Looking for Mr. Goodbar*! I have strong opinions based on I what I read, see in the movies and hear from others who speculate that the promiscuity of the Sexual Revolution will end for everyone. Concepts of open marriage and sexual experimentation, coupling or tripling, swapping or swinging may soon begin to slow down for those in that scene. I agree that it's time. And I'm happy being monogamous again as I was when I was married and straight for twenty-one years.

I shudder when I think about our vulnerable gay male friends. Not only are there blatant films with openly gay sex scenes that may incite more hate crimes, but now stories are circulating in gay publications and in a few medical journals about a "gay cancer." Infected gay men are spreading the disease before they even know they have it—and it's killing its victims. Rumors are that there's no medication to save them; and no one with clout or financial resources, including President Reagan, is motivated to stop the growing epidemic in gay population centers in the U.S.—and other parts of the world.

I wonder what may happen to our gay guys.

So far, the rumors indicate that this disease does not affect lesbians or exclusively straight heterosexuals. But another aspect of the disease is emotional: that it may inflame even greater homophobia itself and that exaggerated homophobia could cause emotional damage to a person who has homosexual feelings and infect humanity with more fear.

What a cruel mess.

Bea on May 8, 1981

Yesterday was another busy day with odd jobs and having our neighbor dig over the lawn with his Rototiller to prepare our vegetable garden. I picked up travelers checks and our AAA's trip ticket. Our route gave AAA quite a challenge.

Jan on May 9, 1981

I don't know where to start as I try to settle myself down this evening. It may as well be from the beginning.

Bea was installing the fire extinguisher in our little canvas-top, pop-up trailer when Marian and Sharon stopped by and we sat inside the tent at our small table and chatted about our trip until the phone rang in the house. Bea jumped out to answer it.

"It's probably Jill calling from the store with some problem. I'll get it."

With an urgent look on her face, Bea stuck her head through the zipper opening in the canvas.

"It's Jill at the store all right. When she opened the store, a man came up the steps from the basement. He had a key to the downstairs door that he showed Jill so she wouldn't be more startled at finding a strange man in the building. He said he was Hugh Humphrey, one of Barney's friends who had an appointment to help with some sign work—and Barney hasn't come. Hugh had been waiting, phoned him several times but the line was always busy. He walked up the stairs when he heard Jill come into the bookstore and told her that Barney's always been on time in the past—and why is the phone line still giving a busy signal?"

Bea took a breath and held out her hand to stop me from jumping past her. "Wait until I finish the story, Jan. Jill then called Barney's home phone, and the line was busy each time she called. Then she called us."

"Please come with us, Sharon." I asked. "You're a nurse in case something's wrong."

So the four of us jumped into our cars and pulled into the back yard next to my dad's car.

Oh, God!" I shuttered. "What's wrong now? His car is here. There's something definitely wrong!"

The first to rush in the back door and through the hall, we made a line with Bea, Sharon and Marian following behind. I called for him, opened the kitchen door and I noticed his flickering TV on the credenza with its images rolling over and over. I followed that into the dining room and stunned to see my father on the floor to my right; the cord from his 1940s heavy black desk phone had somehow been wound around him.

"He's alive," I breathed. Bea came right to my side. "Dad! Dad! Can you hear me? We're here. We'll get help for you. We're here now."

But we couldn't use the phone to call for an ambulance because the headset, its base and the cord were all around him as if he had tried to call for help but passed out. Bea and I stepped over him to begin to unwind the cord while our two friends watched in shock. We didn't even give Sharon a chance to evaluate his condition. As if Bea and I had practiced rescuing skills, the two of us gently lifted him enough to unwind the tangle of phone and wire. He must have struggled to be so wound up. I wonder how long he lay there. God. If Hugh and Jill had not missed him, he could have been there for the whole weekend until we missed him on Monday.

We stayed at his side, talking to him even if we weren't sure he could hear us. Our friends opened the front door when the ambulance pulled up and in seconds, the neighbors starting gathering and asking questions. I followed the medics carrying my dad on a stretcher into the ambulance and directed them to take him to Lakeshore Med as I pulled myself in next to him, "Bea, call Jenny and take care of everything before you come to the emergency room."

The siren parted the traffic as we raced south down Main Street, the route of each Fourth of July parade. We turned at 21st Street and then down into the covered entrance of my hospital's new emergency department with my doctors and my nurses ready to take care of him.

Dr. Lindon took over immediately and RN Dana Martin brought a chair into the trauma room for me as I watch as much as I could. I saw no blood, no broken bones or head wounds. He did not respond to any of the techniques Dr. Lindon applied.

He was a trauma and emergency specialist trained at the hospital where the Midwest Medical College of Wisconsin teaches these specialties. He is my friend and we all worked together to have a grand open house and promote the ER's services. I had advertised it as "Emergency Medicine: More than a room." Then he approached me. "Jan, if efforts are used to try to save his life, your dad would probably not return to his former self. He would be comatose and on a life-support system at the County home—perhaps for years."

I knew what I had to do. "My dad would not want to be kept alive if he could not function as an able human being." And I thought, *"He's had his fill of hospitals and institutions with my mother being there for almost half of their lives as husband and wife."*

"I called for a neurologist for his opinion," Dr. Lindon said. And he left me in the room with the glass door open but with the curtain drawn. I could hear quiet voices from the nurses' station.

Jenny appeared soon after and that's when I began crying, but I pulled myself together quickly so she wouldn't cry. Dana brought in another chair and Jenny and I held hands while I told her what had happened and what the doctor and I decided, at least until the specialist came, perhaps to give us more hopeful signs. Jenny could barely look at her grandfather like that. After an hour, she nervously asked if she could leave. "I can't do this, Mom. I don't think I can take it."

"I understand. You have to go home and tell your dad and he can phone Matt in Madison when he decides it's OK to tell him. Matt has final exams to concentrate on. Making that call for me will be hard enough. You go. I'll keep you in touch with what's happening, honey. I love you."

"I love you too, Mom," as we hugged each other. "I'm sorry I'm not stronger to stay here with you." And she started crying again.

"There's nothing you can do except sit here and stare at him—and hope for the best, listen to him barely breathing like that, so quietly. I'll call you when I need you, dearest. You've done well by coming when you did. I'll let you know what happens next."

Later, my fuzzy mind registered some of the words that the specialist said. A blood vessel in my father's brain stem that coordinates his brain with the rest of his body has burst, an aneurysm, an ultimately life-threatening condition.

Bea had come and sat next to me as I signed a form that said, "Do not resuscitate." No life-saving efforts would be given to him.

After that, we followed his breathing self onto a bed in the new intensive care unit, but in his case, "intensive" was not a treatment option.

I began randomly adding up what needs to be done when this is over. We must find out what the State will do to his property to pay for years of hospital care for Mother. Dad's attorney Chester Johnson has all those papers dealing with claims from the State. That's why my dad didn't maintain his home and shop the way he should. He knew the State would take it all when he died. Where does that leave Mother Courage and our business in his building? Will we have to move? Or pay rent? That would do us in for sure.

What will it take to clear out the building? What a mess, except for the bookstore and where we decorated his office.

Everything else is falling apart. And we have to get rid of his old float figures that he saved, and boxes of artificial flowers, bric-a-brac, drawers full of old catalogs and statements, photos and letters, ancient tools, half gallon cans of paint, brushes, sign card and twelve-foot rolls of paper in various colors leaning against the dusty wall of his front hallway.

And his house.

Fortunately, Tony came to sit with me and interrupted those concerns. Then I went home to be with Bea to find out about tomorrow's program and rest.

Jan on May 9, 1981

I found a unique Mother's Day card by Ladybug & Company in the hospital gift shop and I sent it to Jenny. It says everything I feel about her.

> On Mother's Day to my beautiful daughter Jenny.
> "She who is my daughter,
> I loved you from the moment I saw you.
> In you I saw all my hopes and dreams
> For the future to blossom.
> I tried to teach you to believe in yourself.
> I gave you wings
> And taught you how to fly the best I could.
> When the day came for you to solo,

> You spread your magnificent wings and soared
> With our shared dreams, yet separate aspirations.
> You became everything I ever hoped for a daughter to be.
> How grateful I am that regardless of time or distance,
> You are still and will always be my daughter."

We visited Barney off and on during the day. Well, actually, we couldn't "visit" because he couldn't respond. We went home that Sunday night to make decisions about what to do next. Of course we had to postpone our camping trip indefinitely.

Chapter 6

Jan on May 12, 1981

Bea and Carolyn, Laura Williams and so many hospital people have been sincerely helpful during this closing chapter in my life. I'm not used to all the quiet that surrounds me, especially occupying a section of the intensive care area that's not currently occupied by other patients.

I sit and touch my father's hand or arm, holding on, letting him know as best as I can that I am here. I wonder if Alex has come up to see him. If he has, no one told me.

Last night, Bea stood on the other side of his bed, touched his hand and reached over him to hold my free hand. She told me to talk to him. He would hear me, she said, but when I did I would cry and I didn't want him to hear that.

She spoke boldly though. "Barney, I want you to know that I love Jan and that I will always take care of her. Don't you worry about that. I promise you that she will be all right because we will be together and I will watch out for her."

"Yes, Dad. We will take care of each other and everything will be good for us. Don't worry. Everything will work out."

When I was alone with him, I remembered all the years my dad and I took care of each other in an unspoken partnership. I knew he had been proud of the way I became a good student and athlete, then a teacher, a wife and a mother, and later a successful newspaper and PR professional. And I only disappointed him once, a big once when I hated his having a relationship with another woman. I couldn't stand to be with her and her damn dog, Chico. Still, I didn't let him down when he needed me to do anything for him. For my whole life, I didn't let him down, even when I was a kid.

I think of those years when I was living alone with my mother when he enlisted in the Seabees. The pain of servicemen and women leaving loved ones to go to war must have been terrible—and when he left, I never truly understood how damaging it could be. I suppose I emotionally disconnected from his absence even though he left me to be with my unpredictable mother when he didn't have to enlist to save the world from the Axis powers: the Italians, Germans and the Japanese.

In 1976, I stayed with Chico when he was last hospitalized and found and read the letters he had saved from my mother while he was in the Navy. Most of them are sad, especially when I could read between the lines and fill in the unspoken pain. He wrote positive and happy letters and V-Mails so she and I could exist in our own World War II until he was honorably discharged to come home to take care of us again.

Now I understand what pain he must have endured when they would be happy living together at home again, then she would become unstable and be hospitalized. Then he'd get hospital bills, have to sign for electric shock treatments, and finally give permission for an experimental treatment in 1950s that claimed to be the saving treatment for schizophrenics: a pre-frontal lobotomy. And then it didn't seem to change her behavior at all; years later my high school friend became Dr. Gloria Stevens who read from her medical records that the lobotomy had been aborted.

After he came home from the South Pacific, my mother became ill again and was hospitalized permanently. He found an escape with his involvement with the American Legion, worked hard to buy its own clubhouse, and served as a Post 310 commander until its politics turned him off. The Legion became his second home, but he never dwelled on the disillusionment and grief that caused him to separate himself from that organization. He continued his connection with the Veterans of Foreign Wars.

His veterans' benefits helped him buy 214 2nd Street. And here am I benefiting from that now. Somehow he was able to pay for my college because the university system set up extension centers for veterans so they could earn their first two years of credits at home before going on to their junior and senior years at a college or university. They made exceptions on college requirements, which also helped me get through without having to take a foreign language or math classes. I'd never get through those.

Most veterans who came home alive and well were better off financially, went to college, became owners of small manufacturing companies, etc. Those men who stayed home made big money by working long hours in factories during the giant war efforts to save the world from the Germans, the Japanese and the Communists. But not our self-employed and relatively poor independent sign painter Barney Anthony who enlisted in the US Navy Construction Battalion as a Seabee.

Years later, he had to fight with the State of Wisconsin's finance agents by saying he could either pay for his daughter's college education or his wife's bills at a mental institution. And he stuck by that, but he always carried the burden that his properties would be taken when the State claimed its due. Now it's up to me to pay what's due. Well, we'll get estimates on his two properties and see what they're worth and then sell them to the best offer. Or we'll fix up the house and then sell it. Hopefully that will cover what the State medical bills require.

I must have learned my positive attitudes, my optimism from him—and my work ethic from my mother.

What a good grandfather he became. We'd drive to Winnebago even when I was still nursing my babies so my mother could see them. We'd picnic or take Mother out for dinner and a drink, and he insisted to pay even if he couldn't afford it. Then she'd throw it all up. And how he loved to come to our house for holidays. He'd pick Mildred up at The County Hospital for a few hours before taking her back. How painful. No wonder he never visited her on his own nor took relatives to visit with her.

He could have divorced her and he told me that, but he said he never would. It would have given him a chance to be free from harassment from the State to pay her bills. He could have married again and start a new life with someone else. But he didn't divorce her.

What freedom he gave me. Both my parents did. They trusted me to do no wrong or to cause them any grief. I figured they both had enough grief to live with. When Mother was sick and sent away, I had the run of the house, and the neighborhood, the town and my world.

When I left Alex. I'm certain Dad didn't know why and didn't ask me; yet he offered me what help he could. I'm certain Alex told him about us, yet my dad gave me continued love and understanding without each of us saying one word about my new life. Since we opened Mother Courage, he was happy having Bea, Jill and me around—and some customers once in a while too.

I can't keep on thinking about this. I'll go over to my office for a while and see what's going on. Each time I'd leave for a break, I'd give him a kiss on the forehead and told him I'd be back soon.

Bea on May 13, 1981

Carolyn called me saying that Jan is at Barney's bedside. The nurse called their office and told her there wouldn't be much time left. I said I'd be there right away.

These have been hectic days and we have not slept well. We both continued going to work but didn't know what would happen and when. Our trip is in limbo. Matt had come to our home and eaten supper with us. He is to graduate on May 17. These are crazy days with Jan coming and going, in and out. She gave Matt her dad's blue 1966 Ford Fairlane with a powerful eight-cylinder with only 50,000 miles on it. Barney inherited it from his older brother Clarence after he died. It hadn't been out of Clarence's garage for several years and Barney kept it in the shop basement, but like most of our Wisconsin autos being driven in salted snow and ice, it too was rusty. At least Matt can drive back and forth to college without depending on buses or hitching a ride.

I arrived at Barney's bedside, and Jan and I held each of his hands. I talked to him some more; Jan was quiet. Everything was quiet, which made the monitor sound even louder. And so white—the hospital linens and those so-called privacy curtains with the late afternoon western sun glaring brightly through them. And Barney's transparent skin. You could see the veins and bones in his frail hands and arms and face. His chest barely lifted the hospital's cotton bedspread that a nurse had folded down neatly at his chest and under his arms placed parallel along his body.

He never opened his eyes since we found him on the floor at home on Saturday morning. Five days later and in his quiet manner, he stopped breathing and slipped away from us, the two of us with him. The nurses must have read his monitor at their station and slipped into our space quietly and quickly. We stepped outside the curtain to get out of the way.

Jan alerted the Veteran's Affairs office, which is what Barney told her to do when he passed.

Jan had seen the hospital's morgue cart disguised to look like an empty gurney with a sheet covering it too many times in her journeys through the hospital corridors. "They know what to do," she said to me after we checked out at the nursing station. "They don't need us here," and she picked up the nurses phone to call Carolyn in their office to tell her what had happened and that we would head directly for home where I poured us a drink. "To Barney," we toasted. Jan sat in her recliner when I started making the calls and stuff we had to do, including making an appointment for tomorrow morning to find out what Barney's papers revealed at the Veterans office.

Jan on May 14, 1981

Barney had his burial plans all arranged to be interred in the cemetery's World War II section. He may have considered his wife's, my mother's, do-it-myself burial, a bit too casual, but he never said so. I'd taken over my mother's affairs, especially when I felt I was the only one who cared for her. How insensitive he must have thought me to be, or else he was relieved to be free of that responsibility.

He had picked out what would be on his bronze memorial marker, and significantly, he chose not to have any cross or religious marking on his plaque. He never told us he wanted no religious symbol on his grave. I knew he was a lapsed Lutheran, but it must have taken considerable conviction to refuse, to renounce the customary cross on one's own grave marker. (Actually, he'd told me more about Chico's burial details.)

Philosophically, he was a Unitarian, but he never told me! Perhaps he never realized it. All these years he could have joined us in church, but he never talked about our faiths, except that he seemed to enjoy coming when his grandchildren were involved in church programs. He certainly never came when I was involved in a church service, but then, I may have never told him about them.

He had selected his burial location facing southwest, and Art McCallum, the Veteran's rep, made a copy of my dad's service card and took care of the last minute details received when he called the hospital after Bea talked to him yesterday afternoon.

> Block 15, WWII, Grave 110
> Charles B. Anthony
> PTR1 US Navy Seabees
> World War II
> May 3, 1904-May 13, 1981
> Born at 9 p.m., 5/3/04 in Lakeshore Bay, changes name on 8/5/27; died on May 13, 1981. Service record from discharge papers: MRS Milwaukee, Wis., 1/30/43 to 4/23/43; MCTC WIMVA 4/24/43 to 8/14/43; 100th N.C.D. 8/14/43 to 2/15/45; CBRD, Camp Parks, Calif., 2/28/45 to 4/18/45; NCCTC DAVRI 4/18/45 to 6/4/45. 29 months. Health conditions reported to Veteran's rep Art McCallum: Extreme fatigue, myelofibrosis, prostate, chronic laryngitis, bad sleeping habits.

Served in Majuro in Marshall Islands and was in a train wreck in New Mexico.
6/3/46 Vet Admin guaranteed $6,000 loan on 214 2nd Street .

We picked our city's most prestigious funeral home for him but his visitation room was downstairs in one of the smaller rooms. As we had agreed, Bea picked a modest casket. The directors helped us write his obituary. I hadn't even considered that; Bea helped me remember the details. I should have put "Barney" in his name. That's how most people knew him. I included immediate survivors: my name, Jenny and Matt, and chose to include their father's name, but I didn't think outside the accepted standards and include Bea's name. What category would I put her in? I should have said "Friend." There is no status for our relationship.

Fortunately, I remembered his older brother, Elmer; of course, my mother's preceding him in death in September 1976; his being a sign painter for 51 years until his last working day on Friday, May 8; and all his honors as Lakeshore Bay's foremost float builder. Bea and I added, "He will be remembered by his relatives, his many friends and business associates as a kind and friendly gentle man." It concluded with "Memorial donations to Orphan Critters have been suggested."

Bea was brilliant in selecting a memorial card with a Boy Scout image and "Scout Promise: On my honor, I will do my best to do my duty to God and my country and to obey the Scout law. To help other people at all times, to keep myself physically strong, mentally alert and morally straight." The funeral will be at 9:30 a.m., Saturday, May 16, at the Unitarian Universalist Church with the Rev. Dr. Tony Logan officiating.

He rated a separate article in the newspaper.

"Charles Anthony dies at 77 . . ." with details of the funeral service and the survivors and added homey details from friendships with individuals in advertising or garnered from their clipping files, including articles that I wrote when I was a reporter for the paper in the early 1970s.

". . . Anthony was best known as the person who designed and built floats for most of the annual 4th of July Goodwill Parades over the last forty-three years.

"Known to many as 'Barney,' he had a sign-painting business at 214 2nd Street and worked up until last Friday.

Anthony began sign painting in 1925 and worked on the first "Goodwill" parade in 1937.

"He continued working on floats for the parade every year after that, with the exception of the three years in World War II when he was assigned to the Navy Seabees.

In 1976 he built the float he was to ride in the parade after being named 'Mr. Goodwill,' and more recently the sponsors of the annual Independence Day celebration created a float trophy in his name.

Somewhere in past conversations with my dad, he talked about pallbearers. He said to be sure to ask his two black friends, Don Nobel and Doug Holt. Don Nobel is his friend and 2nd Street neighbor for many years and a frequent assistant when Dad needed special artistic work. He also helped us building floats. When I asked Don, he said he would be proud to do it. When I went to Doug's Downtown Pool Hall and asked Doug, he politely shook his head and said no. He explained that he wasn't one to be among my dad's people. I was completely surprised at his response as we stood facing each other with his old soda fountain and hot dog grill between us. I leaned forward on the counter with both of my hands open to him and tried to tell Doug how that wasn't the way my dad nor I nor anyone else felt. I asked him to please think it over again, that my dad had sincerely told me to have Doug and Don do that because my dad was grateful for their years of friendship. He wanted to acknowledge their friendship. Doug took a crumpled gray handkerchief from his threadbare suit coat to wipe his eyes, and then he agreed to be a pallbearer.

Our Tony Logan always spends a couple hours talking with family about their memories for the funeral. Tony conducts a funeral that helps the grieving celebrate the life of the deceased. I probably should have asked Matt and Jenny to join us for this gathering, but I didn't consider it. Alex's shadow always seems to hold power over them, and I didn't want to risk any conflict. Of course, Bea and I had enough stories to tell about my dad and his life—and his dog. Bea met with our organist and friend Em to pick out songs, especially patriotic ones.

Jan on May 17, 1981

It's time to run the gauntlet of funereal duties: first, the visitation.

I was late to the funeral home Friday night and somewhat out-of-it. People were sitting in chairs already when we arrived—right up in the front row in front of the casket. I'm not going there. I'm not going to stand with people and hear them say that he looks so good. I won't tell them that I searched around to find a spot-free necktie at the Junior Women's Guild resale shop for him to wear. I couldn't find his American Legion tie in his closet and his other ties were way over the hill. Holy Hubert Humphrey! I even found a tie that had "I Like Ike" repeated in a small letter pattern. I don't think he would wear that one with me around. I'd always considered him to be a dedicated Democrat until after the WWII when he liked Ike and became more conservative.

He didn't like protesting against the government and I'm sure he didn't like watching Chicago's 1968 Democratic Convention, which liberals, some media and I labeled it "a police riot." Dad seldom wore a tie anyway, unless he went to a funeral or took a lady friend out for dinner, but I couldn't find any of those in his closet. Why didn't I have him wear his floral Hawaiian short-sleeved shirt with the open collar, and his favorite brown plaid trousers and brown and white wing-tipped shoes that he wore on his float in Lakeshore Bay's 1976 Fourth of July parade? (Do you need shoes when you're to be buried?)

Upon entering the visitation room, I did stride forward and alone, quickly looked to see if he and his second-hand tie looked

OK, and turned around to pay my respects to the front row mourners: my dad's remaining brother, Elmer, his son, Dean, and my widowed Aunt Sylvetta. I'd only see them at funerals when my dad's relatives died. I paid my respects to my mother's oldest sister Ora and her daughter Marge with their husbands, and then I moved around the room after glancing only once more at my dad.

People had to come to me if they wanted to talk to me standing near the large doorway at the back of the room. An extremely tense Bea located herself with her Jill and with women from church, our Women's Network, former neighbors and women from work: Carolyn, Donna Durand, even Marian Brewer, head of the School of Nursing, Sharon and Marian who were with us when we found my dad on the floor last Saturday, Beth Johnson and Robin Witte, Anna Spence and Joan Rohan. I hadn't talked much recently with Marge Bookerman and her mother Nellie, Adelle McEwen and even Diana Dixon since they chose to take sides and be my ex-husband's friends, but they came to my father's funeral.

Some old dear friends of my parents were there too: Dave and Rose Robsen, and several World War II veterans and their wives; and even some of my high school friends with their families: Nazaly and her mother, Anna, who was practically like a mother to me; Joan Smith, her daughter, Sue, and her mother, Hazel, who was like a friend to me and who knew my parents "from the good old days."

I was surprised to see other high school chums: Sam Barmanian, one of Dad's photo customers; Dick and Gloria Larsen came too. Dick had lived on our block where I grew up. He was younger than I, but I gave the little kid his first tennis lessons and later he became a winning player in high school. We also called on him to join our float building team as our best carpenter. He helped us have fun and keep our perspective while we were struggling and sweating to create those July Fourth floats.

Other business customers joined to pay their respects, including those who were my peers like John Henry and Tom Vance who knew my dad through his business. There were others I didn't know. I wished I could have talked longer with them to learn more about my parents, but now wasn't the time.

Several of his neighbors sat quietly, including his best lady friend Mrs. Ella Keller, who lives two houses up the block, and her daughter, Bev. Mrs. Keller had lived there longer than we had, and I learned a lot when I was a kid from Bev and other older girlfriends. Mrs. Keller always seemed so German-Lutheran strict with me so I stayed out of her way, but she and Dad became close friends in recent years and I finally found out she had a pleasant sense of humor. I'm sure she'll miss him. They watched out for each other.

One couple that I should have known better was there—Hugh and Doreen Humphrey. Hugh sadly told me that Barney was like a father to him and he gave me a gentle, tearful hug. If that's so, why didn't we know each other better? He had become my dad's right-hand-man. I realized it was Hugh who did my dad's sign work in the later months—or years. I guess it was a secret between them, and now I realize it was Hugh who painted our Mother Courage sign with such perfection—and I never knew that to thank him. Dad always seemed a bit vague about taking credit for doing such a fine job on our sign. It was Hugh who had come to see my dad last Saturday morning and reported his lateness to Jill that started the events of this final week of my dad's life.

I heard sobbing along a line of empty chairs against the wall, and I guessed he was one of my dad's circles of pals who sat alone wiping his red face with his handkerchief. I sat next to him to meet him and touched his knee, trying to comfort him, and through his tears he mumbled quietly that he was the last of their old-timers' gang that went out for lunch every so often and had a couple drinks together. "Barney would set his dog on the barstool next to him." I couldn't understand him when he mumbled through his heartfelt tears and I didn't want to be rude and have him repeat it. I don't remember his name.

I was surprised to see Alex's brother Jack and his wife, and his sister, Var, and her daughter, Sona. That's the first time I've seen them since I ran away from home and Alex. They were polite, although I was still conscious of their Armenian anger at my leaving their brother and their rage at my infamous lifestyle. Anna Spence once described Var and Sona as "Hate Incarnate" when they talked to Anna about me. In contrast, Alex's cousins Sue and John Esegian, our coroner, are kind to me—always. Sue made this up and we appreciated her joke about all of us being "out-laws" rather than "in-laws."

Oh! Clark Young came too—my retired Lakeshore Medical Center administrator and his wife, Betty! How considerate of them. I was pleased and surprised that they cared that much to come to my father's funeral visitation.

I always wanted to thank Betty Young for recommending that we must visit Tintagel when Bea and I toured England in 1976, but never did tell her how important that place is in our lives. It was at Tintagel, at the legendary King Arthur's castle, at its chapel altar stone that Bea and I said our vows to love one another as we looked out over the roaring Atlantic below us, as we stood so solemnly, so defiantly together with Merlin's cave swallowing the tides beneath the castle ruins surviving on top of its steep rock cliffs.

And Doug Holt came to the Friday night visitation. Doug was the only Black person there. I don't think he knew about my being in a minority as well.

Matt and Jenny milled around the edges of the room too. Like me, they wanted to remember their grandfather as he was when he was alive. I introduced them to distant relatives and people who were fifty years their senior. I am proud of my son and daughter, but I guess we aren't organized for funerals. There wasn't a prayer or a ritual for this wake. We didn't even offer a snack or a drink. In closing, the funeral director gave details about the next day's services and that a luncheon would follow at Danish Hall. It wasn't until all had signed the memorial book and left that I saw that Alex had come before everyone else and signed his name in large letters on the book's first line.

The next morning at church, the family of pallbearers placed my father's flag-covered, closed casket at the front of our church sanctuary with flowers around it. I hadn't realized how difficult it was to lift the casket through the door and up and down our church steps. For mother's funeral, her body was being cremated in Milwaukee before her memorial service, and all we needed to carry were large green plants and potted chrysanthemums that would live on past the service.

Tony shared stories of my father's life as a newsboy delivering papers early in the morning before going to school and giving his widowed mother his earnings, his love of travel, falling in love, marrying and then having to cope with my mother's illness, his being a good father and grandfather, tales of our family's three-generations of float-building and parades, tales of his dog Chico, and Barney's kind soul and his living out his principles to be a good and gentle man. Em pulled out all the stops on the organ playing a medley of American patriotic songs.

It was a celebration of his life.

Bea and I, Matt and Jenny followed the casket from the church. I don't remember who was there or where they were sitting. But they followed us out and we made a parade of cars for my dad through downtown and to the cemetery and the World War II Veterans' monument and burial sites.

I was surprised when we arrived for the burial and saw uniformed American Legion veterans standing in formation with their rifles at their sides. My father had attended many funerals of his veteran comrades, but I don't remember his mentioning any gun salutes. As a Navy Construction Battalion sailor, I don't even think he even fired any gun during the war, except maybe for boot camp training and drills.

People gathered around us.

Tony spoke at the gravesite and gave me a copy of his edited words by UU writer and minister Kenneth Patton: "It is the same at the end as it was at the beginning. We come out of the womb of the mother to open our eyes, and we return to the grave with our eyes closed. The world that gave us forth in magnificent motherhood receives us back. The world is the rejoicing mother and the grieving woman, giving birth and suffering the death of all her beloved offspring. Humankind is one when as infants they are held to the breast. Humankind is one when in death they are given back to the dust. If we would learn it, humankind is also one during the few years of breath we call life."

Tony spoke my dad's name and nodded to the American Legion leader who spoke official words of my dad's service as a Navy Seabee, and then five or seven guns were shot three times. It was shockingly loud and echoed through the Spring's budding tree branches. Then uniformed veterans folded the American flag and handed it to me. I was again surprised.

As people began to leave for a memorial luncheon at Danish Hall, I saw Alex standing alone and away from everyone. I knew that he felt as if he had lost his own father because his dad died when he was twelve. I went over to him to give him a word of sympathy, touched his arm, and he twisted his body away from me and walked toward his own family's burial plot of his father, mother and our prematurely born infant son who died after his birth.

Bea's selection of Danish Hall was perfect for my father's final reception. State Street in the good old days was a thriving business street and it was once one of "the places" to go for Sunday dinners and wedding receptions. Most of the people who gathered together this day had been there in those days. A lot of my family's history happened not only on that street, but exactly on that corner where, before my birth, my eight-year-old half-brother, Richard, had been struck by a car and died.

Several others attended the church, cemetery service and reception than were at Friday's funeral home, including more of Bea's family which helped her cope with these events. Jill had to leave to open Mother Courage and Matt had to get back to Madison for his graduation ceremony tomorrow.

Long tables were set with Danish open-face sandwich plates, lots of smorgasbord servings, pitchers of beer, and coffee and sweet rolls for dessert. A round table off to one side held a tray of fine cordial glasses and a couple bottles of Danish Aquavit, or as Bea calls it, Danish kerosene. That was saved to toast my dad. It went over well with everyone. The various factions mixed together somewhat, as in Barney's friendly nature. People mixed together more so after the first Aquavit toast and succeeding shots of Danish kerosene.

Only two negatives emerged.

My cousin told me that she and Aunt Ora were surprised that we didn't even say "The Lord's Prayer" at my mother's or my father's funeral. It is what I would call "A Feminist/Unitarian Oversight," but I didn't tell them that. After learning about my father's choice of his burial plaque without a cross, I was confident in saying to her, gently, "I'm sure my father would be happy that we read 'The Boy Scout Oath' instead, which meant more to him as an Eagle Scout, and served him well as his life's motto."

Scowling Alex sat alone at that round table slouching in a wooden folding chair with his elbow poised on the table. He didn't take off his coat. Why did he even come? I tried to ignore him, but our friend Betty said she felt sorry for him and went to sit with him. I'm sure she didn't bring him any comfort, and you can't say Betty didn't try. With her having close proximity to the Aquavit, Betty's attempt to make him more comfortable alone in his misery on the fringe of the group perhaps motivated him to leave.

Finally, people said their good byes and we were able to go home. But I had to drive Betty home with Bea following in her car. Finally at home, my strong, invincible, "I can do anything self" let go. I could crash. Still I had to tell myself, "Take it easy. Rest up for tomorrow—my son's college graduation ceremony."

Jan on May 16, 1981

Oh Dear Bea,
Have I told you lately how much I love you.

You and my dad accepted each other but even more, you both grew to care for each other. He understood why I love you, you amazing woman.

You understood him and have never said one negative word about him throughout the long days you have shared at the store and in our lives at home. And at his end, you took charge of his funeral details and created for him an emblem of love and compassion for all of us to see and remember

When we first asked him to let us use his storefront for our bookstore, you didn't know what hostility could have met us, nor did I, and we trusted together that we could make Mother Courage happen. And it has.

My dad had a sad life – his tragic relationship loving Mildred and her son – but his compassion expanded as he took on the two of us with trust, understanding, acceptance and love.

And you made a better life for my dad and your Barney.

Blessed Be!

Me

Chapter 7

Jan on May 17, 1981

Bea woke me at 4 a.m. to drive us to Madison for Matt's college graduation. During the ride we tried to figure out all the places and strategies he experienced in his relatively young life. Since he was sixteen, he was always away on some adventure when he wasn't in the classroom. He started with canoeing around Lake Michigan's islands with three young adults. Right out of high school he became a counselor at a boys' camp and endured a huge storm with tornado sightings while sheltering his young charges. His father, Jenny and I drove him to Spearfish, S.D., where he had a college cross country running scholarship, and when we returned from that trip, I immediately left his father and moved one block away from 16-year-old Jenny.

Matt spent the summer there working for a forestry company, climbing up and down sides of ravines and chopping out brush and invading tree species. When he came closer to home by enrolling at Madison, he loved the liberal campus yet he applied himself frugally and soberly on a college campus known for its academic excellence and beer consumption. He had language requirements to fulfill and after walking into a section of German in Bascom Hall with 1,500 students, he decided to learn Indonesian. His first semester of Indonesian had eight students; the spring semester was down to only four. A terrible teaching assistants' strike on the campus made Madison a militant campus almost as bad as in the Vietnam era. No one would cross the picket lines, but his little group met off campus so he continued to learn more of the language.

His Indonesian instructor asked him that spring what he was doing over the summer. (The summer before he tried to sell encyclopedias to residents in Alabama and said he never needed another character-building experience after that.) So he took his teacher's advice and hitchhiked to California's Berkeley campus via Oregon and south along the Pacific coast.

He enrolled in second-year Indonesian with about eight students and Berkeley awarded him a scholarship. He told me it was because Berkeley thought he was a whiz-bang from Madison. But he has always been known to push himself. And he lived in an Indonesian cooperative and talked the language all the time. While others were struggling and quarreling, he had fun and even advanced to using slang with the best of the students, even those from Indonesia.

He told me he was interviewed by the CIA and the military to see if he wanted to join them, but he politely declined.

My father had hitch-hiked and hopped boxcars via the southern route to get to see his love, Mildred, at her parents' home in Berkeley. My mother-to-be and her young son, Richard, were escaping from her first husband by driving across the country with her two California-based sisters, Emmalyn and Louella and her son, Eugene. The women and children traveled in Louella's mid-1920s Chevy across all kinds of roads.

We parked Bea's car off West Johnson Street at Matt's co-op where he served us a veggie bagel breakfast in the two-story house's kitchen. His room was a closet off a sitting room. He could sit at his desk with the door open and slept above on a mat on boards resting on the closet molding.

We proudly waited for him to dress up and don his cap and gown for photos and then we drove him to Camp Randall Stadium for an outdoor ceremony on a sunny and comfortable morning. Good thing too because it took about three-and-a-half hours sitting in the stands before 1,500 grads walked past the podium to receive their diplomas. Of course Matt was among the last and the graduates were getting more rowdy as the time dragged on.

What a proud day for me to have my son graduate from my alma mater. And of course, I cried when we all sang "Varsity." With my dad's funeral only one day before, I was especially vulnerable.

As he finally crossed the platform to receive his diploma, Matt waved enthusiastically to the thousands in the Wisconsin Badgers football stadium including Bea and me sitting in one section and Alex and Marge sitting elsewhere among the throng. They were meeting Matt after the ceremony to celebrate with him—arrangements made to eliminate the tension of being in the same space.

Our reserved accommodations at a Madison motel included a heated pool and whirlpool and we checked in right after the ceremony, took a long nap, then swam and soaked. Bea savored her brandy and I my martinis, and the two of us found a supper club overlooking Lake Mendota and treasured the nautical ambiance and a delicious seafood dinner. After all we had been through, the luxury of the motel's healing waters and being served a first-class dinner with a lakeside view began to heal us.

Rather than returning home, we continued our road trip for a few more days to be away from the personal and legal decisions that needed to be made—and the enormity of labor that waits for us back home. We headed north for the Circus World at Baraboo and watched a muscular demo of how the working crew and circus animals unloaded the trains and helped hoist the tents. We cheered the Big Top clowns and more elegant performers. We swayed together on the back of a bristly-haired, scruffy-eared, colorfully costumed elephant; took a close look through the bars at the tigers and lions; petted safer animals and toured the museum's array of circus wagons and memorabilia. We hopped on the Ferris wheel and merry-go-round and cherished our private little picnic overlooking the circus sights with colorful banners flying against the cool, blue sky. Our gourmet luncheon included croissants, lobster salad and wine that we bought along the way and kept in our ever-present cooler holding ice cubes and various liquid refreshments.

We chose scenic roads to the Mississippi River and stopped to burrow fifty feet underground on a tour through an old lead mine. We checked in to a Platteville motel to swim again in a heated pool, but this time we practiced using our new snorkels and masks.

That's not all we practiced.

We also nurtured each other with joyful passion that had been neglected. Our love itself had not diminished with all this pressure, but for many weeks the pleasure of intimate ecstasy had been too exhausting even to contemplate. With problems and issues set aside for these three days away, we re-explored our divine woman's earthy shrines, performing our sacred rituals upon each other. At first impatiently feasting and tasting skin, face, arms and thighs, hollows and hills, lips, tongues and ears and other inside pleasures, we melted our salty, tearfully wet selves into orgasmic oneness. Then with slow, intensely tender touching, our laying on of hands and fingers salved my grief and our frustrations. We blessed each other with our Goddess sacraments. Our fingers fed each other in a communion ceremony as we sat cross-legged and naked from each other, placing in our lover's mouth our shredded strips of string cheese, crusty bits from a fresh loaf of bread, and sensuous sips of our jug white wine. "This is in place of that flask in your favorite *Rubaiyat of Omar Khayyam*," I smiled. Our bodies again melded like the pictures of the book's Persian delights, in blissful rest, until our desire for more gifts of erotic compassion transported us to the *Rubaiyat's* "Paradise enow."

Oh yes. We also visited Dubuque, Iowa, rode a stern-wheeler on the Mississippi River, drove on to Galena, Illinois, with its many renovated historic antique stores and then we headed directly for our home.

Bea on May 24, 1981

Sharon and Marian will be coming by for my birthday, but we're keeping it simple because we've been getting ready night and day for two Friday and Saturday rummage sale weekends at the shop. We've moved everything to the basement entrance, but we still have to climb up two long flights of stairs if someone comes in the front door of the store. And there's heavy office furniture for sale up there too. I hope we can sell it all. You can't imagine what's there, and how dusty it all is. Of course the remains of float paper and festooning and fringe will go with the Fourth parade people. That event's coming soon. The major tools will go too. But who will take the life-size astronaut, the huge chicken, a giant welded-wire peacock, a phone booth, an Uncle Sam's hat, heavy display panels and boxes of finely crafted artificial flowers and foliage that Barney bought before cheap copies were made and sold at every store in the U.S., even at gas stations.

I placed classified ads and we'll have to see who will come and what will happen.

We also had appraisals made of Barney's home and this place, and they each came to about $17,000. "Handyman Specials" they called them. The appraiser said the land was more valuable than the buildings they stood on. Barney's neighbors at each place asked us if we wanted to sell, but they wouldn't even pay that amount for the properties. We sent all that to Attorney Chester Johnson to settle Mildred's hospital bills in Barney's estate with the State.

Jan received many sympathy cards that she read when we came home from our brief vacation escape. I didn't know most of the people, but I thought I'd jot down some of their comments for her to remember someday.

From Carolyn's daughter Jane: "Please accept my deep sympathy and know you are in my thoughts. While I wasn't acquainted with your father, I know he raised a courageous, talented, strong, loving and admirable daughter. More fathers should somehow produce such daughters!"

On a card with children laughing sent by Joanne Zekas "I chose this card because it shows the joy and delight I feel your father brought to so many children in his lifetime of float making for all those 4th of Julys. What a wonderful memorial for a man's life! How proud and pleased you must be, despite your sadness and pain and loss. He will always be remembered joyfully by you and thousands of others!"

From Nick Dixon, of all people, on Lakeshore Medical Center's stationery: "Dear Jan, I am sorry that I was not able to be around to share your bereavement over Barney's death. Barney enjoyed life, and he also helped other people to enjoy theirs. Expressing one's condolences to a long-time friend who has lost a loved one is difficult, but my thoughts are with you. Sincerely, Nick."

I wonder if he does that routinely for all Lakeshore Med's employees.

Jan on June 6, 1981

It's good that I could leave work to be at the shop helping Bea bargain for all the absurd items in my father's unique rummage sale. During those days, people told us stories about the Fourth, the floats and parades they remembered and how their purchases will be used as they hauled elements of my father's past out of his building. He would not have been emotionally suited to part with all of this.

In Lakeshore Bay's early days, his historic building's front door was once on a lower street, level with the River Woods and its revolving bridge. Barney said the building to the west of us, with which we share a wall, used to be a whorehouse. He told us that my mother's father laughed when he saw the bricked-in basement-level windows on the west side of our wall. Grandpa told my dad, "The guys used to jump out of those first floor windows when the place was raided by the police."

In the sorting, I warned Bea to watch out for hidden treasures in his estate. We actually found a four-inch square booklet of fragile gold leaf that he'd used for quality signs and he once added gold leaf strips from high ceiling to the floor between rare wood paneling in a Frank Lloyd Wright home. Finding the gold leaf became a joke about our discovering greater wealth, perhaps a can of South African krugerrands in a cubbyhole somewhere. The cans we did find contained only dried-up paint.

The YMCA Indian Guides float chairman was overjoyed to find eight-foot floral feathers for them to make into a giant Indian headdress for their float in this year's parade. We gave them all of the remaining floral paper and supplies. Bea's son Josh wanted the life-size astronaut for a party that he and his wife were giving. Jenny's friend bought my dad's table saw and lathe and some lumber for his woodworking business. We kept Dad's heavy standing Craftsman drill press that Bea's sons carried into our basement workshop to go with the heavy-duty tools from her father's collection. We kept leftover boxes of nails and screws and hand tools, but especially the staple guns, staples and long bank pins—my float decorating tools that symbolized my labors for so many years.

We gave Don Nobel a generator and anything else he wanted to carry into his living space next door. Don loved getting the artist spray tools; Bea didn't want to deal with that. Don said he could use my dad's favorite tool, his Cutawl. My dad would stand for hours, bending over his workbench, carving outlined signs from heavy-duty cardstock to identify each float theme and sponsor. Dad often said that Cutawl made him unique among his profession, and I thought then of another local signwriter who pioneered neon, stayed home during WWII, adapted his shop to get government contracts, and actually made a lot of money for his wife and children—before, during and after the War.

The guys from the neighboring upholstery shop bought great bargains for the lumber and tools they could use.

One black-haired Chicano lady wearing bangles and beads adorning a strong red dress with matching wedgie shoes bought several boxes of geraniums, daisies and daffodils. She said she'd have an instant garden, "Mine didn't bloom right this year and my husband won't even notice the difference."

A young man from a local floral shop stopped by several times to buy window display fixings and decorative papers. On the last day, he hauled away all the remaining artificial floral boxes sight unseen.

Some of Dad's photographer customers came in to buy out his collection of huge paper rolls for commercial photo backgrounds. A bartender bought corrugated designed paper for his party room.

The owner of a dancing school bought out the lot of old float figures, treasuring each one. She would build dance routines around them for their recitals.

Gone was the dusty debris of decades of constructing displays, painting signs; sawing lumber; building floats like the one Jan made with their carpenter John Verbught. He constructed the mountain top of Iwo Jima on a farm wagon. Jan then used chicken wire lumps for the mountain and newspaper strips wet with wallpaper paste to cover Iwo Jima so Marine veterans covered in bronze colors could pose like the picture and hold up the American flag she recreated.

The space evolved now into wispy ridges of dirt as pieces of my family history went out the door. Outlines of departed objects remained as negative footprints from where they had stood for so many years.

Fortunately, I rescued a couple items that were precious to me. Bea was ready to finish a sale of a transparent blue bowl filled with shells. A gem of a memory hit me in the side of my head and I grabbed the bowl from the buyer, shouting "NO! That's my Shirley Temple cereal bowl and it's not for sale!" Yes. When I spilled out the shells, I saw Shirley Temple smiling at me like she did when I finished my Wheaties and drank the sugary milk from the bowl. Was I ever happy to have recognized it and add it to my meager collection of childhood treasures.

I also found Indian clay bowls, artifacts from 1936 when Dad, Mom and I took our six-week car trip to California. Mom bought these bowls, a turquoise ring and a beaded Indian headband from Indians at a roadside stand. We also saved two fake Indian headdresses that were used as float costumes. Who knows when you may need blue-feathered Indian headdresses?

Significant evidence of what transpired in my life reappeared when I opened a Kodak box of color photos and a roll of negatives dated from September 1977. Dad had appeared in my lost home on Lake Michigan. It showed our back yard that morning when we were packing for the trip to take Matt to college in South Dakota. Dad wore one of his Indian feather headdresses in honor of the wild west destination. Dad asked our neighbor to take a group photo that included my dad, minus the headdress, Alex, Matt, Jenny and me, plus his dog Chico and our dog Pepper. The photos and negatives ended in January 1980 with pictures my dad took before he and Matt buried the dead Chico in his red-lined, plastic-cushioned aluminum casket.

When the sales were over and the basement almost empty, we were able to sweep it out and replace my father's past with our little camper and our *Courage* sailboat.

Bea on May 31, 1981

We were to meet Jenny and Matt at Barney's house so they could have anything they wanted. We also needed to keep them up-to-date on what we have to do about the financial claims from the State. Matt was home for the weekend from his summer job in Madison where he routed auto trips for AAA members. He'll be off again in the fall to start his Master's program at California State College-Stanislaus. And Jenny quit being a college student and is working full time now as a cook at St. Agnes Hospital, a job she held part time since she was sixteen. She seems happier now. And she's put in her application to be a U.S. Postal letter carrier working outside, not inside as a clerk. It takes a while to get to take the exam because veterans gain access with a higher priority to fill new openings.

They could see how run-down the house was, especially the upstairs apartment with holes in the kitchen ceiling tiles where the roof leaked down the wall and floor, creating an impressive plaster blister on Jan's first floor bedroom ceiling. No wonder that door was always shut. Ceiling chunks had landed on both levels. The summer's heat in the empty upstairs apartment caused the tile flooring to curl up like giant potato chips. Each one would have to be broken and chipped off the floor by hand before carpet could be laid.

Barney kept the place where he lived clean but nothing was replaced or repaired. Wallpaper and draperies were faded and frayed. We dared not touch too much in case the fabric, shades, plaster or tiles would dissolve or fall off in our hands. The furniture, the carpeting, the kitchen were the same as when Jan moved into it when she was seven years old. We didn't even want to speculate at what was needed on the exterior of the house.

Almost as the soon as we opened the door to Barney's house, the neighbors started coming in asking about his furnishings. Jan told me later that she started to feel as if she were in the *Zorba the Greek* movie when the Madame died and all the villagers swarmed in to take her possessions.

Somehow an antique dealer showed up and Jenny phoned her upholstery friend to see if he would be interested in some scratchy mohair furniture from the early 1930s. Items that now seem to be antiques were the then old furniture her mother brought upstairs for the attic apartment she created so she could rent out the downstairs when Barney served in World War II.

We had an instant estate sale that cleared out most of the big items and we could start renovating the house either for resale or for rent until the State and Barney's attorney settled on the final figures.

Jan sold her dad's old Rambler to Carolyn's son for $100. A recycling handyman, he's the perfect person to keep it going. We'll have to borrow it from him on occasion to bring stuff out and around.

Matt and Jenny wanted nothing from the house even though they joked about when they were toddlers playing with a little lamp with a boy and girl kissing and the bureau that held little candies that they could eat. (Jenny would get all of Jan's china and crystal ware *before* she died because those precious pieces were left behind for her when Jan "ran away from home" to be with me when Jenny was sixteen.)

Jan filled a box or two with letters and papers to review. After Matt and Jenny left, she looked in a box and recognized Matt's handwriting on one Barney's envelopes. Jan almost cried when she read aloud Matt's letter in the scribbled handwriting on frayed pages of steno notepad paper.

Then she let loose and really cried when she found an unopened box with the new tape recorder she had given him for his birthday present on May 3. She said she should have sat with him and interviewed him personally rather than merely hand him the black recorder and tapes and expect him to talk into this mute piece of machinery—as if he wasn't lonely enough.

There's more work for us to do again: two of Barney's properties and our own home. Egads! I'm in the real estate, financing and rehab business now.

Bea on July 4, 1981

This year's Fourth of July celebration without Barney was bittersweet, of course. Our family and friends gathered on his front lawn that we claim by getting there before 7 a.m. to spread blankets on the grass to keep the all-night partying campers restricted to the parkway grass along the curb. Jan and I, like firefighters when the alarm goes off, jumped out of bed into our clothes, grabbed the ice cubes and filled the cooler, picked up the newspaper and pulled into Barney's yard before the police set up road barriers to control traffic.

We settled in to wait by reading the paper and enjoying a couple Bloody Marys before Jill comes with her traditional offering, a box full of donuts. This family tradition, takes place without our eldest member—Jan's father and my dear friend.

On the dot at 8:30 a.m., dozens of area rescue squads and fire fighters rev their motors and alarms starting a half-block from us to travel along the parade route. Reserve military heavy duty equipment follow with proud drivers of local manufacturer of heavy farm and earth-moving monster machinery reaping their way with every part turning along the city street rather than in some remote field or construction site.

At 9 a.m., the first band marches by to start the parade. The vibration of brass and the drums, the flashing uniforms and the flags trigger our tearful emotions and, when we glance at each other, we end up laughing at our tearful blubbering. Of course, we don't stand there crying all the time. It's that this year's loss has so much meaning. And we're both so damn tired.

Veterans follow local politicians and the American Legion marching band with Barney and Jan's refurbished and rebuilt many times Iwo Jima float and its bronzed Marines raising the flag that she had shaped with pins on chicken wire to match the original photo years ago when they first built it after The War. Every time it passes, people stand and cheer. So many memories for her.

When our family and friends join us or when there is a break in the parade, we'd take them into the house to show them what we've accomplished so far—and we absorbed every healing stroke of appreciation for our efforts.

As customary, the parade float judges awarded prizes with teenagers marching in front of the float, holding a banner for each award named in honor of former politicians, industrialists and major donors. Jan knew who all those people were because her parents were involved in the Fourth of July Goodwill events from the start in 1937 or some year like that.

This year there would be an honorary award banner for Carl B. Anthony for the best amateur float in the parade. Barney, and Mildred too, had helped so many groups build their own floats, giving them advice including printed how-to-do charts, selling them used materials at a bargain. This year, the Goodwill Committee decided it would be most appropriate to have his name remembered with all the big name wealthy dignitaries.

About an hour and a half passed before we saw his name in bold red letters on the white banner that came before his prize-winning amateur float—the YMCA Indian Guides float decorated with the giant Indian headdress feathers and the remains of all the float paper that we gave them in the rummage sale.

Tears welled up at that sight. What a celebration! And how appropriate! The last of Barney's float materials became the Carl B. Anthony prize-winning float for the YMCA Indian Guides with fathers, their sons and some daughters in their Indian gear, sitting together on the huge decorated trailer. Jan's Explorer Scout father would have been so happy—as we all were, standing in front of his house as Jan and her family had done for years, and now Jan's and my family are here too. All of us cheered, some of us cried joyful, deeply felt tears, knowing that his loyal, hard work would live on in this award, and with all the people he and Jan's mother have helped and have entertained in the past with their beautiful floats.

Our personal lives may have changed, and to some we may seem outrageous, but the proud spirit of Jan's parents lives on with hundreds of those who knew and remember them.

Jan and I embraced, jumping up and down in celebration. Then she whispered in my ear, "To me it will always read 'The Mildred and Carl B. Anthony Award.'"

Chapter 8

Bea on July 13, 1981

Somehow we're finding time to enjoy the *Courage*, our 17-foot National One Design with a bronze centerboard and rudder sailing from River Woods Marina. But it's tough not only to find the time, but also to fit the time we have to match the weather we need to sail on Lake Michigan.

    I listen to the weather reports each morning and afternoon to decide if it's worth launching her in the river and maneuvering her out to the chop on the big lake. Unlike little Braun's Lake where we first tried out the *Courage* and had to lift the 25-foot wooden mast, fitting its bottom end up and into and out of the mast step, before and after we launched in on or off the trailer—and that's not so damn easy. That's why we pay the marina $400 to dock and launch from there, using their rust-bucket towing cars to move the trailer to the dock on the river, and vice versa, almost asphyxiating myself when I'm twisted around to look over the trailer hitch next to the decomposing exhaust system while the breeze blows the fumes right up my nose.

    Jan stands, oftentimes out of my view, and waves a variety of directions so I don't know what she means and I go the way I want anyway. If she throws up her hands or pulls out her hair and hollers loud enough, I stop.

    Sharon and Marian, brave or naive souls that they are, helped us step the mast on Summer Solstice after we pulled out the smallest sailboat of all those in the River Woods Marina. Perhaps the regulars remembered us from last year. I'm sure if they saw any of our mishaps, they'd remember and laugh about us with the others in the sailing community and nearby yachting clubhouses.

When we do get the *Courage* in the river, we have to turn it east to get it out of the harbor, sometimes into direct winds, and onto the Lake with winds of its own. With sails flapping next to Jan's ears, she's stepping on lines and trying to hear and follow my commands. We'd drop the rudder and I have to decide whether to go with the sails or use power from the second- or third-hand, two-horse engine Matt gave us last year. If so, I'd leave the tiller to crawl three feet to the stern where the motor was mounted. I'd have to coil a rope around the top flywheel and give it a yank. All the while other boats would be coming and going past us up and down the river. "Fend off!" we'd yell when needed. Then after several tries, the rope could fly off into my hand, or it would finally start and then the engine would conk out right when I'd return to the tiller, so I'd have to crawl back and twist and yank the rope again.

Meanwhile the harbor rocks loomed closer, or the lake waves surged against us at the river's mouth, or motor launches and charter-fishing boats with their two or more power motors thrust wakes of waves around us. Yet we survived somehow.

Our best sail so far with Sharon and Marian was when we made it safely out to the Lake and headed north toward the Lighthouse with full sails giving us a rush. We jumped out and swam a bit at the Zoo beach before heading back because the flies were starting to bite.

Oh, the joys of boating!

Jan on July 21, 1981

My schedule at work seems easier than when I'm at play.

Randy and Nick are ignoring me. I wrote them a letter but I took the advice given to angry letter writers, which is to write the letters but then burn them. But that won't stop forward action and changes. That's not the way I handle injustice, but so far, having them let me do my work without their demeaning criticism produces results.

Besides, Nick's probably up in Door County and Randy's too busy running the hospital to bother about me.

After the last round of parties, I stayed away from work last Monday because of the flu. I actually stayed home for an illness for the first time in years, enjoyed the peaceful rest and I slept all day.

Bea on August 13, 1981

We're working as hard as we can to repair Barney's house and the shop area. We were bickering with potential buyers, but they want us to give away his property because they say it's so run-down, but we see its potential and have decided to make Barney's property our own.

As if we don't have enough to do. Jan had to buy that 13th Street flat and now the downstairs tenant moved out after getting battered about by her boyfriend. That's the end of that relationship and she decided to move back home. Now we have to pass a building inspection and I had to patch a big hole in the bathroom wall and then paint it when it was dry. Jan worked on other projects while I finished up that project. We never should have bought this damn property.

A year ago the person we bought it from left so much rubble in the garage and in the basement you could start a mushroom farm down there. We wish the realtor we used to close the deal had negotiated informed specifications that the seller should have repaired because we bought into housing code problems that we have to solve.

Jan hired a high school boy to carry junk to the curbing or to her dad's car to be taken to the dump. That old Rambler could have burst with trash when she drove it to the local dump. She paid her dues and they told her to follow the signs. Jan said she couldn't believe that she ended at the highest peak of Lakeshore Bay's growing mountain of junk, which she quickly unloaded more to the future ski slope. Some critters and a hundred gulls swarmed around her—and she's a bit phobic about birds when they're in the house.

When she finally cleared out the Rambler and piled into the driver's seat, she had trouble getting it started. When it finally did start, she realized its tires were sunk into the landfill. Visions of her climbing down through the trash, leaving her father's cherished station wagon as a home for scavengers motivated her to rock the Rambler out of its rut and steer a winding way out of the hulking remains of human consumption.

Honestly, between that mess, the shop and the house, I'm struggling against feeling like the whiskery old trash man in my Chicago neighborhood with his horse and wagon going up the alley calling out with a sing-song accent, "Raaags. Ooold clothes. Any metal to sell? Trrrash or Trrreasures?"

Jan on August, 15, 1981

From the physical labor that Bea and I have accomplished cleaning up our properties, it's no wonder her arthritis is bad. Still, we keep going at it, helped along by generous amounts of healing brandy for both of us.

Bea is amazing. The first job she tackled was to take a sledgehammer and radial saw to knock out and cut a doorway through my bedroom wall into my parent's closet that was between each room. Why hadn't my parents done that in my years of inhabiting my room with a makeshift, rough old 2 x 4 lumber frame for a closet that was draped with cheap plastic floral curtains? Bea took that sledgehammer and released years of frustration for each of us by knocking a hole in that wall. Then she framed in a new wall between the closet halves, trimmed a doorframe and set in a closet door in my room. I did the grunt work of disposing of the debris.

Then we tore off all the crumbling plaster on the ceiling and Bea figured how to install a hanging ceiling with tiles to hide the mess. And, wonder of wonders, she installed an electric light fixture in the ceiling and installed its on/off switch on the wall next to the door. No more string hanging from the dim, bare light in the ceiling. I'm forty-nine years old and I finally acquire my own closet and a bedroom ceiling light with a switch on the wall in my old bedroom that I'll never sleep in again.

When we pulled up all the old carpet, we could see by the floorboards that the house once had three narrow closet-sized bedrooms. Good thing we didn't have to remove any more walls because who would know what we'd find. No gold krugerrands, I'm sure.

We labored after work and every weekend to get the downstairs livable. Joanne Zekas helped us paint the woodwork and we'd sing while we painted away. Betty Willing brought Em over with her so we could have company while we worked. Our kids helped us move extra heavy items for the city's clean-up week.

Bea on August 17, 1981

I'm a grandmother and I held my day-old, red-haired grandson today. Jacob, 6 pounds, 13 ounces, and 21 inches long, is quite a grown-up name for such a cute little baby. I hope his parents know what to do with him. I've kind of forgotten with to do with little ones and can't believe I had four children in seven years. That whole gang filled the hospital room to see their first nephew.

Jan's kids came for supper last night. I'm cooking creative recipes from our productive garden veggies.

Her first-born Matt, now 22, is heading off to begin his master's degree in Indonesian studies in California. Matt can speak fluent Indonesian now after being immersed in the language while living in an Indonesian co-op in this special major program at Stanislaus. The course includes a trip to Indonesia in September, spending time in Java, Sumatra and Bali. We warned him to look out for tigers and stay away from volcanoes as he leaves us again for more adventures.

After dinner we watched her daughter Jenny, now 19, play baseball for her women's league team. Jan heard through her grapevine that Alex is worried that Jenny may become a lesbian like her mother because she's such a good baseball player. Hell, we heard that every women's team in town wants to have at least one lesbian on their team to win games.

And Alex is nuts. Jenny hangs with lots of friends, including a Country Western band that plays where she works nights behind the bar.

It's amazing how the years fly by. Jenny seems to be happy and content with her circle of friends and her work. Jan says that's all that counts. She's still living with her dad, but she has roommates to keep her company and share expenses because her dad's traveling so much for his company's computer network.

Bea on August 19, 1981

The Mall opened this month and our book business is awfully slow. Good thing I have the Lakeshore Bay Women's Network project to keep my mind occupied while I'm at the store, 'cause I'd go bananas waiting for customers to come in.

I don't usually involve myself with issues like this, but a woman's right to choose what to do with her body is critical. I'm thankful I have never had to make such a choice.

My talk was well received and without conflict during the question and answer session that followed. Also, our bookstore needs me to take a turn to call attention to what books it offers for women and others interested in women's issues.

Jan's feminist activism in the newspapers and at conferences is risking her job and our financial security.

I spent time researching that helped me with my talk.

"On April 6th of this year, a public hearing was held in Madison on two bills before the Wisconsin Assembly that would petition the U.S. Congress to call a constitutional convention for the purpose of amending the constitution of the United States of America to outlaw abortion."

(Using many publication resources that I brought from our bookstore, I briefly traced the history of the Constitution and the Bill of Rights emphasizing the 19th Amendment finally granting women the right to vote and citing that although an amendment may be proposed by state legislatures, it has been suggested from time to time, but it has never been done before.)

"This is a dangerous procedure coming before the Wisconsin state legislature that raises serious and unresolved questions that create doubts among legal scholars on the advisability of holding such a convention.

"From a human perspective, the outlawing of abortion poses dangerous risks to women and children's health and to the individual civil and human liberties that form the cornerstone of this country.

"If the congressional convention is convened and the so-called 'Human Life Amendment' is proposed and ratified, people everywhere need to be aware of the consequences of such an amendment to the Constitution.

"Several drafts of the Human Life Amendment have already been made public. It declare that fertilized eggs 'are persons entitled to complete constitutional protection.' Another portion reads, 'The paramount right of life is vested in each human being from the moment of fertilization without regard to age, health or condition of independency.'

"A possible consequence of the implementation of this amendment, if ratified, is that birth control devices that prevent the implantation of the fertilized egg in the uterus will be illegal. Women could be prosecuted for use of low-estrogen birth control pills and intra-uterine devices. Further, it is possible in the interpretation of this amendment to investigate women who miscarry to see if they had caused the miscarriage. Medical personnel who attend these women would also be open to this type of investigation.

"Other possible consequences could be that women would be forced to carry to term a fetus with genetic disease or congenital defects and that victims of rape and incest would be forced to bear a child conceived in those conditions.

"Women or girls who seek abortions, doctors, clinics, families and friends who aid them may be subject to prosecution for a felony or premeditated murder.

"Even those abortions necessary to save the life or preserve the health of the mother could be forbidden.

"We doubt if any girl or woman makes the choice of the legal abortion now available without complex and serious deliberation. The Human Life Amendment advocates would have us believe that females are incapable of making rational decisions about their own well-being and the well-being of their offspring. Responsible women have struggled for centuries for safe and accessible birth control and abortion rights. Women and men have gained the right, legally, to decide when to have healthy, wanted children that they may adequately care and provide for. Is this right to be taken away from us?

"And, furthermore, is this right to be taken away from us by an amendment to a document that was written by rational human beings to provide and guarantee rights and freedoms for citizens of this country?

"Although the female is deeply involved in the decision of whether or not to have a child, Human Life Amendment advocates tend to ignore the male's role in this decision. Not only the father who may be responsible for the child born under the circumstances of forced childbirth, but the male as a member of the society that will ultimately be responsible for the care and upbringing of these children.

"The proposed Human Life Amendment is not only a desperate threat to women, but also a threat to all citizens of this country, both male and female."

Jan on August 23, 1981

One rainy morning, Bea called me at work from my dad's house. "Jesus, Jan. You can't imagine how it's pouring here—it's raining right through your side porch roof like a waterfall."

When I lived there, we'd always enter the house from this enclosed side porch. We'd leave the doors unlocked or put the house skeleton key in one of the porch cabinets where all my friends or anyone could find it. Our dog Lady would bark at strangers or anyone who knocked. Otherwise she'd greet you like a friend if you opened the door and walked in. The side porch also served as locker room and changing area for my tennis buddies—and a place to neck if it was too cold to sit outside on the porch steps. Now rainwater was coming through its roof like a YWCA gang shower room.

Obviously we'd need a new roof on the whole house. Wisely, we decided that job was not for us to do and we hired out for that, but what about the gutters? We could save money if we hung new gutters ourselves before the free-lance roofers came—and we did. I was the up-top ladder person and Bea was the measurer and cutter below. To muster courage and strength, we had to be fortified with brandy, and I'm happy to say that I've survived some leaning, stretching and hammering of roofing nails and gutter straps into some far-reaching corners without falling to the ground.

Then I tackled the porch window glazing. I never realized how forty years of sunshine could bake the glaze. When I scraped what was left holding the glass in place, the panes were suspended in space. So back on ladders, I reglazed all the windows around the house. It's a wonder my feet didn't get to be bird claws after standing on ladder rungs hour after hour.

Fate blessed me when I moved from the late afternoon sun on the south side of the house to the shade in the front on the east windows. While I worked, I looked over my shoulder and recognized two old friends from my Lakeshore Bay Montessori School days. We parents started the school with Matt, age four, in its first class in 1963. The two women didn't recognize me on the ladder in my paint scarf and work clothes, but then I called out, "It's a wonderful sight to see that two of my old friends are still friends."

It was Alice Rogan and Mary Carson. We'd enrolled our children in the same first class. I'll always remember Mary Carson's three-year-old daughter when she understood the concept of reading. She was aglow when she told her classmate at a shared table, "It's like lighting a candle." I had volunteered to write the Montessori newsletter, so I remember stories like that.

I stepped down from my ladder and we had a cheery conversation about our lives and our kids. Then Alice told me that her daughter Heidi was to be married soon and would I consider renting them the apartment.

I said, "How can I not consider anyone from our Montessori school? They should be great! We'll meet and show them the place. Here's my phone number. Give us a call."

They did. And I enjoyed seeing this young adult woman from Matt's pre-school Montessori class and her soon-to-be husband, Ken. And they loved the place, even if it wasn't finished. It was a couple blocks from Heidi's mother's house. I explained that after we finished with the lower apartment and the basement, we'd be working upstairs and we'd be renting that out so someone. They wouldn't mind. The lower apartment would be perfect for them. And they agreed to move in as soon as we finished.

"But one thing," I pointed out. "We and our families want to be able to sit on the front lawn every Fourth of July for the parade."

"Absolutely. No problem."

We had our first tenants ready to move in when we're ready!

Bob Sawyer on August 25, 1981

Dear Jan and Bea,

Before we left Lakeshore Bay to go back to San Francisco, I came to your house to give you each goodbye hugs but I didn't catch you at home, so we'll all have to remember the last time we parted so much more. I really have fun with you two!

I have thought of you so often and meant to write many times since leaving Lakeshore Bay, and on last Friday I came home to find the Carnigians, Matt, Jenny and Alex, in my home with Louis doing a superb job of entertaining them.

But what I mean to tell you is how beautiful a time Matt and I have had together—and also Louis. The two of them like each other wonderfully. We have had a house full all summer and Louis and I have reached the unanimous decision that Matt has been our favorite guest. We've had such fun times, from the night we went to see Pat

Bond play Gertrude Stein in a lesbian bar here to the fabulous afternoon the three of us spent on one of the beaches absorbed in deep conversation and shared a sincere sense of community, for lack of a better word.

It made me think of the feelings and experiences I've always imagined to have been shared in the Mother-Daughter weekends you women had in Door County.

Truly, Matt and I have renewed a deep friendship and started something special between us that's absolutely delightful and fresh. Matt is beautiful. He is blossoming into such a humane, compassionate young man! We both have learned and experienced great things this summer.

Love to you and Bea,
Bob

Jan on August 26, 1981

I wonder what went through Matt's mind when he went to a lesbian bar with Bob and Louie with Pat Bond doing a take on Gertrude Stein? I'm sure he didn't know anything about Gertrude except maybe for "A rose is a rose is a rose" quote from someone making a joke about it. Only recently have I actually understood that she meant in the 1930s by "a rose" when I read her "Lifting belly can please me because it is an occupation I enjoy. Rose is a rose is a rose."

I also remember seeing Pat Bond in *Word Is Out*, a documentary film on PBS with stories about the lives of 26 gay men and women, and I looked her up in its published book that Mother Courage sells. Bond's a big woman like Stein and in her segment she said she "escaped into the Women's Army Corps. I thought I could go to Paris where Gertrude Stein had been."

Bond lived through the military witch hunts in Tokyo where five hundred WACs were sent home with dishonorable discharges after women were threatened to tell on their friends. "They got one of our kids—Helen. They got her up on the stand and told her that if she didn't give the names of her friends they would tell her parents she was gay. She went up to her room on the sixth floor and jumped out and killed herself, She was twenty."

Pat Bond lived through police raids on San Francisco bars in the 1950s. She reflects, "I'll miss the excitement of the old gay world, somehow—of belonging to a secret place that nobody knew about but you. I'll miss that. It was comfortable," she said, "Everyone knew the rules, who they were to be and what they were expected to do. It was more comfortable then." She described it as being more comfortable then.

It's different now without the old "butch and femme roles," but not that much when you still have to fight for fairness and equality and against intolerance and fear. Being a lesbian is a complex life not easily understood–even by Bea and me, and we have to learn without a set of rules. When I was straight, I had customs and expectations, rituals and rules to follow. My life is different now not because I have had sex with another woman, as in Gertrude Stein's "lifting belly," but that I *love* another woman. That love has profoundly affected our lives and in this society, except for an enlightened few of our family, friends, and church members, we've grown into a different species, as "a rose is a rose is a rose."

Jan on Labor Day, September 7, 1981

Rather than Labor Day holiday, it's another labor weekend for us. We've cleaned, spackled, sanded, wallpapered, brushed and rolled on gallons of paint—and best of all, we had a good time accomplishing the jobs together. We touched every square inch inside the downstairs, including installing new paneling, carpeting and linoleum.

Fortunately for us, Goldens Department Store was closing and had its final sale—another retail store more huge than our little Mother Courage Bookstore could not even couldn't compete with Lakeshore Bay's new mall. Near the end of one Saturday of our hard labor, strengthened with energy jolts of brandy, Bea and I measured all the rooms for carpeting and linoleum for the kitchen floor. We took our penciled figures to Goldens and sat on carpet rolls to pick out a simple pattern with the best price and Bea computed what we needed. We also found a carpet-cutting electric hand tool that looked as if it would be easier than using our box-cutting tools. After the heavy day of working and drinking, I was plastered inside *and* out. I was never good at math, especially fractions, square feet, algebra, geometry, etc. Bea was figuring all this out and comparing it to what was available. It's up to her—and we found good bargains.

They loaded the goods in my dad's Rambler station wagon and we parked it in the shop to protect the twelve-foot rolls from rain.

The weather was sunny and dry on Sunday when we backed the Rambler into the yard and unrolled the new carpeting on the lawn. We'd saved the remains of the crumbly old carpeting for a pattern but Bea measured it all again. "Measure twice, cut once," has become her favorite motto. We used our new tool that cut through the new carpeting like a fine electric scissors. I was astounded when we carried the new rolls into place and they fit exactly against the wall, ready to be edged with the floor molding. But when we sliced our final cut, all that remained was a twelve-foot ribbon of carpet less than four inches wide! What a celebration! We did it! Everything's coming together!

Bea did carpenter work too, enclosing the antique cast iron sink with a well-build cabinet to hide the pipes and all else that lives under there. Fortunately Bea's Jim did the electrical work for us. That saved us lots of money and all we had to do to repay him was to have his little family join us for Kentucky Fried at our house, after cocktails, of course.

We've labored for weeks when we weren't working or at the store. We chipped away at the brittle kitchen and the bath flooring that snapped into pieces with age and layers of rusty-red paint that my dad had applied over the original Armstrong pattern installed before my mother raised enough for a down payment to a mortgage toward the $2,800 asking price and my parents and I moved there in 1938.

When I was washing out the refrigerator to be moved so we could replace the flooring, I stood eyeball height to the Frigidaire logo and noticed a pencil mark in front of my nose. It was "6:10" in my father's handwriting that I knew so well. Why was that there? My dad wasn't in the habit of adding snapshots and magnets to blank, white appliance spaces. It took some meditating on the 6:10 image to recreate in my mind that perhaps he had come home to make his supper, turned on the TV for the news, maybe he began to fix himself a cocktail, felt the initial pain in his brain stem as he was getting ice cubes from the tiny freezer inside the vintage appliance, looked up at the clock, grabbed a pencil from his shirt pocket and wrote the time on the white enamel door before he headed to the dining room to make the phone call for help. But before he could dial a number—What number would he have chosen?—he passed out, fell and lay there unconscious, I guessed, until we found him before noon the next day.

I showed Bea the 6:10 before I wiped it off the white enamel door. If it was the last note my father wrote, I could hardly save it for posterity. Yet it will live in my heart and in my memory. The 6:10 of his passing, alone, yet still in his own home, having worked up to the last day of his conscious life.

We put old blankets under the heavy appliances to pull them out of the kitchen so we could install the new one-piece linoleum that Bea had measured and marked so well and we had cut out so carefully. We towed the refrigerator and the unique vintage gas stove on skinny legs with shelves built on each side covered with curved doors, all enameled with a yellow marble finish. You had to light its iron burners with kitchen matches. The new linoleum fit so neatly into the space and we tacked down the freshly painted molding at its edges. We admired at the kitchen and bathroom floors with such pride

We were so tired we should have called for male muscles to help moving those appliances back in place. The stove was dragged back in its corner, and then the refrigerator. We had to allow for space away from the wall to remove the blankets and, when we pushed the refrigerator back into the alcove made to hold the refrigerator's coils, the rusty front foot leveler clung to the new flooring and gouged out a hole—right where you'd put your foot to open the door.

Hearts stopped when we heard and felt that tiny but significant gash under our feet. All our perfect work was accomplished and then to have a scar, a small one, true, but a scar as prominent to us as a boil on a nose. Ugh! We needed that brandy jolt to ease that pain, especially when we felt so high because of what we had accomplished.

When we recovered from our shock, we pasted down the flaw as best we could. Bea and I had tackled each room, corrected long ignored flaws and turned the house into desirable a living space for the young couple who would move in soon.

My father would be proud of how Bea and I rebuilt that old house left decrepit by his intentional neglect and/or lack of motivation to repair because of what the State would take to pay for thirty years of his wife's mental illness.

We made his house whole again—at least the first floor, the basement, gutters and the roof. We sat in the backyard looking at the place for a while, then we'll rest for a week before we tackle the second floor attic apartment.

Jan on September 9, 1981

I remember the back steps leading to the upper flat where my mother and I lived while my father was in the Seabees. The paint had been peeling off for years, hanging brittle chunks, warped and dangling, leaving the original old wallboard exposed. I was living up there with my unpredictable mom, showering in the basement, peeing in a bucket upstairs because we couldn't afford to install plumbing, carrying the bucket to the basement to empty it or, if it had shit in it, asking the downstairs tenant to let me pour its contents down their toilet.

I walked up and down those back steps in my strange life as an early teenager during World War II. My father left me for thirty months to take care of my mother. That's what I thought I was doing during the duration of the War; but actually, I was caring for myself and coping with what was going on around me.

The back steps led me up to who-knows-what when I'd come home from school or from bumming around on my bicycle or from Lakeview playground across the street.

Much of the time I found love and laughter motivated by my mother's friends who helped us during the War. Most of the time we worked out our issues, like any mixed-up teenage girl struggles with her mother. But in this case, it could be my mother who was mixed-up. I never knew what would happen next, but I always knew that she loved me.

I'm finally correcting the flaws up those back steps, renovating and renewing the passageway up to that little apartment that now has a complete bathroom while Bea struggles with its plumbing, floor tiles, and its tiny rooms, making them cozy and livable again.

Two nights ago we ourselves exploded in one of those angry, weird full-moon crazies that I used to fear as an adolescent. Bea always says I start those off during cocktail hour. But, of course, I know that she's been drinking during the day at the store while I'm at work and then again with me when I concoct and consume my compulsory two, oversize martinis before we eat supper. I want to feel the buzz, so we don't eat until late. I need to feel the buzz to block out the burning sensations from letting myself get angry about work. Hell. I also drink because I want to drink. No excuses.

We have a wonderful love together, but sometimes the behavior that we express is not Bea's or mine—it's alcohol.

Of course, we're both overworked. All this bone-weary labor of fixing decades of the sad disappointment of my dad's loss of his wife is getting to us. To me, at least. And of course, we're both stressed out financially, yet we're spending money in hopes of future successes that may never be fulfilled.

We've been so good to each other, but two nights ago, the calm that I try to maintain exploded at some small statement, an edgy criticism that I don't even remember. And then I got angry at her.

It's crazy. It's weird. Why do I let myself get sucked into this? I should know better after all the years I've dealt with craziness.

After we settled down and ate supper, we went outside and made a fire to burn up some of the ancient lath scraps that we brought home after installing my bedroom closet. We've planned to have our own full moon ritual and symbolically burn away the past. So, we started our ceremony off key and on edge. I pulled the garden hose close to the fire pit to be ready should we need it. That lumber is generations old and desert dry dusty tinder with slivery, sharp broken points. Our outdoor iron pit stands on stubby legs with an iron band to fit under the rim and the lid.

I volunteered to feed the flames, but Bea was determined to do it, and as I watched her, I don't feel responsible for these outbursts. I love her. She's the person I've searched for all of my life. Why do I feel as if I'm the only one who is best for her, especially when she—when we lose control.

She was breaking lath over her knee, staggering a bit on one foot while she brought her knee up to meet the sticks cracking apart as they came down on impact. I anticipated what happened too late. She reached into the dark pile of wood, pulled out a long lath and in one twist before I could shout out, she drove a long, rusty nail into her thigh above her knee.

She pulled it out as I shouted and ran to her. We had some ceremony all right—a bloody full moon rite that would need tetanus shot. She wouldn't go to the ER as I urged her to do. I put the lid over the flames and followed her into the house. She barely let me wash it and put antiseptic on the wound.

After tending to her, I doused the flames. My emotional self, my weary wounded heart seems to leave me when we have these explosions. It takes a long time to heal from an attack from her—or from anyone. I thought, *"This is a role you've been acting all your life—your role to be responsible when others lose control. Remember, Jan, you have a tendency to catastrophize. But it's easy to do when you love somebody, not to separate what that alcohol does to you and the one you love and what that's all about. Alcohol makes some people crazy. Am I always responsible for what happens to us? Do I always have to work and keep cool even when I don't feel like it? I don't know what's going to happen next. I've been lucky so far. I guess I just feel the fear and go ahead and do what must be done."*

I try to take another deep, cleansing breath and move on to put out the real fire, clean up the ashes—and dispose of the rusty nails.

Jan on September 12, 1982,

We made tender love last night. After her tetanus shot yesterday morning, Bea's body was whole enough and free from enough discomfort to have me hover gently over her in my most suspended and elevated kissing of all the areas that aren't hurting or healing. Then she put herself on top of me toward a smooth and rhythmic vibration of our loving orgasm together.

Thankful for that and wanting it to happen often, we lay together in the breezes from our windows and peacefully traveled off into sleep, my favorite kind of satisfied sleep, my face happy from having brushed itself upon her, my mouth happy from her tasty response with hers, my breasts rejoicing with the touch of her mouth still singing upon them, my genitalia joyful from the fondling and the gratification, my skin celebrating quietly the memories of the incredibly intimate moments. Blessed Be because I did not have to beg this time for love. I was not rejected. I had not even asked, but I was wanting after so many summer weeks of waiting. Will I have to wait long again? I know she loves me even more since I exploded in frustration at her grumbling, growling disposition brought on by years of discomfort and pain.

Her threat to me of separation and my cool response to that possibility may have made her realize how dependent she is on me for her well-being. Though she is the Alpha person in our practical partnership, I am the Alpha person in our stability and in our inner supportive relationship. Yet I know that I have freed me from the word that I hate, the label of "co-dependency." Why is that word so hateful to me? Because it puts me down and makes me feel stupid for caring for and loving her so completely all these years. Was it at the cost of my own personhood? I think not, but yes, I suppose it's true that I have put her needs first before I consider mine. I'm not doing that as much as before, and I'm doing that only when I want to. And why not? I love being polite and considerate of my primary person's needs. I love doing things for her and my family and friends, but now, only when I choose to do so and when my needs: physical/body, intellectual/mind, emotional/feelings, and spiritual/soul are in balance. And I do have control over that.

When I feel that balance, I walk as if on air, like a teenager free from worries and responsibilities and disappointments. Yes, even like a kid who brings a good report card home to her parents, like a toddler playing in the warm sandbox or splashing in the tub, like an infant seeing her reflection in the face, in the eyes of her loving mother.

Abandonment. I know that is my recurring stress from childhood, tracing steps back to my past of losing my mother to schizophrenia over and over again until she was institutionalized permanently.

Choices. What games do we play with fate—with life? Who makes choices based on what? Looking back at choices made, how routine some of them were and how seriously they affected my life. Yet how courageous many of those "choices" were and how formidable are their repercussions.

Does one choose to fall in love with another woman? Who cares! I did it and I'm glad—Blessed Be!

Chapter 9

Bea on September 13, 1981

I had a tetanus shot at Lakeshore Med the first thing this a.m. and then we went back to paint a second coat in the upstairs bathroom. Our raven-haired lesbian apprentice plumber Sue came over to advise us on our plumbing problems. We had a beer while she told us some hazardous stories of women in construction jobs.

Now that the roof is finished we're able to tackle one of biggest nasty jobs in the upstairs apartment—the soggy, saggy suspended ceiling panels where most of the rainwater dripped into the north side of the house. Jan stood by to grab the panels or to hand me tools and I climbed to kneel on the kitchen sink and wrestled out the nearest panel above me. Down poured a flow of vermiculite insulation particles right on my upturned face with dust and probably asbestos fibers filling my mouth and nose. In my shock, I gasped for air and inhaled more toxic crap. The ceiling's loose insulation installed almost forty years ago started piling up around me, dropping on my head and shoulders when I curled up like a ball to protect myself. Who knows what else could be up there? No South African Kruggerands, that's for sure.

Spitting and sputtering, I jumped off the sink and looked for fresh air by unlocking the barely used fire door and I stepped out onto the aged little wooden porch propped up to comply with fire codes for second floor apartments. I'm lucky the porch didn't collapse under me. That's where I threw up all the insulation from my mouth and nose. I can only imagine how much I inhaled into my lungs.

After I recovered, Jan suggested we quit, but I'm such a mess I kept on going to rid ourselves of all this crap. Fortunately the summer's heat up there must have dried up any mold, and the suspended ceiling and its World War II insulation particles were only in the area where Jan's mother had built the dormer so they could stand up in the kitchen. But we put bandanas over our faces and covered our heads and finished off one of the worse jobs I've done in my life.

Fortunately, brandy is readily available to comfort and cure.

It also gave the two us the determination to rip out the old air conditioner from the little window in the living room. The heavy monster has been hanging there for twenty years and when we finally wrestled it loose from its sun-burned cemented fittings, we both held it with our hands while dragging it bodily inside the room before it could plummet into the landscape, perhaps twisting and bouncing off the first floor front of the windows we'd finished caulking and painting. Why don't we learn to wait until we can rustle up some muscles among our male offspring?

Fortunately, Jenny's been helping us by chipping off the foot-square vinyl floor tiles that have curled up from the summers' heat and years of neglect. They're damn heavy too, as we carry boxes and bags of the scraps down the back stairway and out for the rubbish collection.

Compound all this with work on 13th Street where I installed new door locks and lay new bathroom tiles while Jan painted the porches and front door exteriors to make it at least look better.

The wooden soffits on this old brick house were rotting out because the gutters were "built-in" as part of the roof itself. That concept may have work fifty years or more ago, but all that wood and tarpaper and metal has cracked and rotted out the fancy "heritage" architectural wood on the brick house. Don't ever buy a house without finding out what the roof is like. And of course the former owner didn't warn us about that. She sold herself out from under a bad situation—and we bought it.

Now Jan often climbs a ladder to reach the roof above the first floor kitchen. Then she hoists gallons of sealant and tools and that ladder so she can prop it up again to climb to the second story roof to fill those cracks in the broken shingles and old-fashioned, built-into-the-roof decomposing gutters with tar paper and black, gunky, oozy sealant. She actually hangs over the edge two stories in the air with a spackling tool full of tarry crap!

How did we ever get ourselves into these messes?

Jan on September 18, 1981

I almost enjoy the quiet view while I straddle the roof peaks of our 13th Street property and overlook the treetops surrounding me. If I fell, I'd be dead. It would be quick. And someone else would have to finish the work I still have to do. My death would be peaceful, except for the terrifying heartbeat time it would take my body to reach the ground. I'd be free of all this anxiety in my life, at work and at home. How long has this been going on? If I hadn't learned to live with an unstable mother and an absent father when I was a kid, I probably wouldn't be able to handle it now. The stress at work and at home, Bea's mood swings, I never know what I must deal with as each hour passes. Why do I let them bother me so much? Why do I become depressed because of her depression? At least it is peaceful up here, even though I hang over the edge of the tired old roof that's rotting around me. If I fell, I'd at least be close to my new Lakeshore Med's emergency center. That is if I were found alive.

What was in my mind when I wanted to buy this old house? I convinced myself that it would be a good investment, one that I could afford and perhaps we could parlay it into more as the time goes by, especially when inflation is decreasing our savings and real estate seems to be increasing at fifteen percent. Bea and I certainly haven't been making money on our other ventures and my paycheck makes me angry every time I get it because I know that what I do for the hospital is worth so much more than my salary.

But as I sit here alone looking over the south side of the city with my Lakeshore Med and the Catholic high school only blocks away, I realize the underlying reason that I wanted this property is to have a safe haven in case something would happen between Bea and me. Sitting above it all, resting next to my tarpaper rolls and adhesives, I realized that I needed a place to fall back to if our tensions, made worse with alcohol, caused Bea and me to separate. She walks out on me now when we argue. That's so damn frustrating; nothing gets resolved. But so far, she always comes back because there is nowhere for her to go, and we never pick up where we left off to solve our issues.

If the worst happens during one of our alcoholic confrontations and we split, I could have the upstairs tenant move so I could live in this pathetically tiny upstairs apartment, continue to rent out the first floor apartment and walk to work. I would survive. The solitude would be healing. I could finish writing my novel.

My widowed grandmother survived by making her upstairs into a rental unit. My unstable mother and I lived in our attic and rented our downstairs home to someone during the War. I'm too old now to be sent by social workers to summer camps and a foster home. I have to provide for myself even if I've given control of all my money to Bea to manage. I didn't even do that with my husband, but I wasn't the sole wage earner in my home then.

When I was a kid coping with my mother's craziness, I tried staying out of the way when she was that way. But Bea's mood shifts are driving me crazy, yet I don't want to stay out of the way. Again, I feel that I never know what I'll find when I come home. This time the booze is driving us both to madness. Yet we drink to heal our wounded expectations—or to celebrate our accomplishments. Any excuse. I drink because I deserve it after all of my hard work. I drink to try to keep up with her, damn it, to be numb, to try to play. Two double martinis before supper and several glasses of wine every evening plus Bloody Marys on weekend mornings.

I deserve it. What's Bea's excuse? She wants it. Who knows what she drinks during the day. Her dreams are fading: the bookstore bores her; the customers, when they do come in, bore her; waiting bores her. It's that trite metaphor: for her the glass is half empty; for me it's half full. Ironically, "the glass" in the saying is usually being filled or being emptied. Yet when she decides to work on a project that she wants to do, she's at her best and nothing can stop her.

I'll fix this roof even if she is furious about my doing it before I leave home to work on it and after I return home from making a dent in the task. We can't afford to pay to have it done and we can't let it rot away.

My expectations have always been that we would work happily together, as a team, two creative, happy women producing and achieving together.

It's not working.

I should be able to rise above it and shine, make jokes and be light. But Bea's depressions scare me. She mumbles words hinting at suicide. And when I ask her what she said, she replies, "Never mind."

It's scary and I don't know how it will end. A suicidal threat—that's real. What will I find when I go home? What am I going to find? What or how? It's not knowing—and when everything's good it's wonderful and that means that you have so much to lose when it goes bad.

I've had to face that my whole life. When my mother was home, I never knew what I'd find. I played or worked on the playground across the street. It was good for everyone. Close to home to help her; to be there if I was needed.

That damn 4th of July holiday has always a factor in my life. I was twelve or thirteen and working with my mother on those July 4ths without my dad to help us. Work and work. It was terrible. Really bad. Fighting with the crew. I was afraid they'd quit on us. She wasn't strong. She'd drive us crazy.

Now I'm forty-nine years old and this year we rid ourselves of all that leftover float paper and dusty old float fixtures. It's all gone, even the spaceman. And now, Bea is talking about closing our bookstore.

Yet I won't fail in my endeavors. I must succeed. I will endure.

Bea on September 18, 1981

I mailed a letter on our ship's life-ring logo that's made it look like the scientific female symbol. I say it stands as a life ring for women. We don't publish our *Courier* newsletter anymore, so this is the first time in a long time that our old circulation list received any news from us. I hated to do it, but it's what I had to do.

"Mother needs your help" was its bold heading.

Mother Courage is now looking for volunteers to work in the store. Volunteers will receive discounts on books and could earn book credits.

We would like to be open more hours, especially in the evening, to be able to serve more women in the community. We also need help during the day. We have been open for two and a half years and are still operating in the red. Therefore, we would be unable to pay someone to work these times.

We feel strongly that the Lakeshore Bay needs a women's bookstore and we are committed to staying in business.

Jan and I have contributed all we can financially, not to mention time, creative effort and grinding hard work. Given the realities and the rules of the small business game, like the IRS rule that says you must show a profit in at least two out of five years or they may question you about the nature of your business. (It could be classed as a "hobby" and you can lose all your tax deductions.) Then we might have to consider closing.

I am not doing a "poor me" routine; I'd like to tell you some of the financial facts of the business. For my five to six days a week, fifty-two weeks last year, all I was able to draw from the business was $1,753, and that included $708 in paid health insurance. I accrued no Social Security benefits and contributed to no pension plan. And I am a single woman with no husband to support me or to put me on his benefit plan. I am saying that if I had any sense and interest in it, I'd get a job with a regular salary and some fringe benefits. But I feel we must keep our women's bookstore open.

So we need your help. If you could volunteer your time, please contact us. Call us at 632-3120.

If you can't volunteer, please give us your business.

Sincerely,

Bea

We never got a one.

Jan on September 24, 1981

A lot of hard work to prevent a scare among Lakeshore Bay families could have been compromised yesterday by the Bay View Times front-page smart ass headline spread with a three-column story and photo under the headline, "Lakeshore Med's recalls 180 babies." The large, square photo taken in my presence by my BVT photographer friend Mark Hanson showed a nurse's firm hands holding an infant's foot with tiny toes. The foot is being injected with a shot of gamma globulin. The cutline says, "The foot of a recalled baby feels the needle at Lakeshore Medical Center."

"It must have been a slow news day," I explained to those coming into the office waving the newspaper in their hands. "If you read the story, it's good for us."

Randy often faults me for being a reporter rather than a public relations person, but this time he climbed on my fire engine and helped me prevent a possible four-alarm blaze.

Physicians do not want to admit to any error, misjudgment or negative condition as individuals or as a group, and it took a couple days for me to collect the facts that started on Friday, September 11.

Perhaps if I hadn't have to placate officious and secretive Dr. Olander and relevant physician department heads, hospital administration and the dedicated delivery and nursery staff, I could have composed a concise story. Instead, the six-page document was rewritten and revised and finally approved after two days of my scrambling for everyone's approval.

No matter how cautious we strive to prevent a crisis situation when we see potential hazards and correct them, events occur beyond our control that may change the hospital's image, intimidate hospital employees and our supporters, and leave misunderstanding and misinformation in the community.

This "recall" word used in the lead came from my *Bay View* medical reporter colleague Gurda Jensen. She actually summed up the whole situation in one paragraph. "About 180 babies born at Lakeshore Medical Center's since August are being recalled for tests and shots as the result of a hospital nurse and a Lakeshore Bay physician contracting infectious hepatitis."

A smart-aleck page editor took that word and made the most of it, adding a sensational front-page placement and its headline. Those who read the rest of the story would understand that Lakeshore Medical Center's was responding to a situation in a responsible manner.

From the start, I should have played the devil's advocate with greater advocacy. I should have been more aggressive and not have assumed that Randy knew of this on Friday. It wasn't until Tuesday that Randy found out about the problem and then he actually helped me get the facts and make plans to solve this problem. He had the power to immediately call briefing sessions of hospital staff to plan and prepare answers to concerns from other sources and audiences.

I was stunned when he and I sat in the empty meeting room, waiting for at least ten minutes for other staff to join us. "Jesus," he spurted out impatiently. "Are we the only two people who consider this a serious problem?" Hospital staff finally came in to tell us what they knew, but it took us until almost 4 p.m. on Wednesday before I had in my hand the information that I needed for a media release that I could distribute.

It was strange to be on Randy's side of an issue, and that gave me the authority to reach physician chairmen and break through to our bombastic infection control and laboratory head, Dr. Olander, a barrel-chested, loud and powerful man who is accustomed to having complete control.

But you can't control the health of a new physician joining our medical staff, an expert neonatologist specialist who moved to Lakeshore Bay from Wisconsin's premier neonatology unit started in the late 1960s by faculty physicians of the Midwest Medical College at the Midwest Center's Medical Complex. I didn't know his name and I didn't ask because I knew he wouldn't tell me.

It was he who brought hepatitis A to our new intensive care nursery, and somehow a nurse came down with it too. Olander did not want anyone to know that a physician could be vulnerable to disease. Of course, we would honor the confidentiality of the two who have the virus. Dr. Olander's opinions and suggestions were relayed to our team by his staff. It was not easy to deal directly with his intimating personality.

We collected nursing administration and directors from infection control, obstetrics and neonatal care to plan our screening and inoculation program and how families would be notified to bring in their infants without alarming them any more than what would be natural. Our staff anticipated all the emotional implications, and we planned in detail the best way to help keep the situation in proper perspective. Getting nursing staff involved gave us valuable information. As hospital insiders, they were invaluable in solving this dilemma and they felt valued as part of the solution.

We held daily briefings each morning and afternoon and told the insiders the nature and dimension of the situation and what the hospital planned to do about it. Our hospital president and Randy's boss Nick Dixon kept the physicians informed. The information exchange was invaluable. It helped to standardize the answers and eliminate fear and confusion among employees and "outsiders" who were looking to the insiders for informed answers. Each person became a more informed, consistent and confident hospital representative.

Randy King and I, with the advice of many, prepared the judiciously written statement to anticipate every angle and cleared it with physicians and administrators. Though it may have been too long, I had to please everyone and I would rather be faulted for having too much information than not enough. It was also comforting to staff who wanted consistent direction.

By the time the story finally broke, our hepatitis screening and inoculation program showed the hospital as responsible and positive. If the story had broken earlier it could have left serious negative images reflecting physician and hospital employee neglect and the hospital's complicity in keeping quiet about it.

I included within the printed newspaper story some of my media release to show the difference in reporting news and in telling the story from a PR point of view. As Bea says, "Jan's job is to make shit into sunshine." Most of the background information in the news story came from our media release that also included phone numbers of relevant physicians, including Dr. Olander. From his quotes in the news story, he must have spoken politely to Gurda when she called him.

"Lakeshore Medical Center's recalls 180 babies"
by Gurda Jensen

"About 180 babies born at Lakeshore Medical Center's since August are being recalled for tests and shots as the result of a hospital nurse and a Lakeshore Bay physician contracting infectious hepatitis…"

But my media release headline was, "Lakeshore Medical Center's tests to identify potential source of hepatitis A in the community."

My lead paragraph was, "Lakeshore Medical Center's began a testing program on September 15 to identify potential sources of hepatitis A in the community.

"In addition, as a precautionary measure, the hospital has recommended to inoculate all of the babies born at Lakeshore Medical Center's between August 11 and October 11.

"Two cases of hepatitis A have been confirmed by Lakeshore Med/Medical Center that may be related to cases reported recently in Milwaukee.

"One case confirmed by Lakeshore Medical Center's involved a Lakeshore Medical Center's nursery staff nurse.

"A Lakeshore Bay physician is reported to be the second case.

"As a preventative measure, Lakeshore Medical Center's has chosen to conduct a thorough screening and gamma globulin immunization program for newborns and those employees who may have been exposed to the virus.

"The hospital's precautionary response to this situation is being directed by Dr. Claude Olander, chairman of Lakeshore Medical Center's infection control committee and medical director of Lakeshore Medical Center's laboratory.

"Dr. Olander stressed that no newborns have developed the disease.

"Normal precautions taken every day in handling youngsters in the newborn nursery and our nursing cohorting system make it highly unlikely that any infant will develop the disease," he said.

"An isolated case like this is not uncommon in hospitals," Olander explained.

"Health professionals risk themselves to the dangers of exposure of infection every day by caring for the people who come to us with infections needing to be treated."

"We have high standards of infection control to protect our patients and employees and we are conducting this through screening not only to prevent the spread of the disease but to do a complete investigation to track down how this happened so we can work to prevent this from recurring."

"We're actively pursuing the source of the infection," said Olander, "which could have come from outside the hospital. Lakeshore Medical Center's in Lakeshore Bay is one of more than a dozen hospitals which sends newborns in need of intensive care to Milwaukee units…"

And on for five more pages, some of which was used in Gurda Jensen's overdramatic news story itself.

Though Randy faults me for being friends with my newspaper contacts, he should know that it's more than our friendship that they value. It's trust and respect for my integrity that make our working relationships invaluable.

Gurda told me she had heard about the babies being recalled for screening and inoculation from a grandmother at the *Bay View Times* on Tuesday afternoon, September 15, but she was assigned a story that had her attend a day-long conference at the Lake View Conference Center. When she called me after deadline time on Friday, September 18, we were ready with an appropriate media release.

She told me that if she had called me Tuesday when she first heard about it, and if we had nothing to give her of a specific nature that would satisfy her requirement, she would have interviewed mothers who were "fluttering and wondering." And she would have phoned Nick Dixon for a statement and printed whatever he said with the available information he had.

Gurda and I agreed that it was better for both us—for her to be working with me to help get the story written on paper with more accuracy than a phone interview.

She also told me she too was appalled at the story being placed on page one and the wording and large type size used for the headline.

On that Friday, September 18, our area experienced a tremendous thunderstorm with flooding rains. I had been running around the hospital for several long days and had been worrying and dreaming about the hepatitis scare through these nights. What if I can't get all the approvals and have time to rewrite the releases? What if they found an infected newborn?

The administrative secretaries would take my typing and hand-written changes again and again to give me clean copy to get physician and administrative approvals. Copies were made and distributed to relevant hospital staff. By the time the last version was typed before they went home for the weekend, I had to drive in the downpour north to Dr. Wilson's residence in Lighthouse Point for his final approval. He is an OK guy, easy to get along with, so I wasn't too worried about having him make lots of changes.

(If the *Bay View Times* doesn't call during the weekend, I plan to drop off the final media release to Gruda on Monday morning.)

<<<◇>>>

Every hospital communicator has thought defensively during national crisis events, for example, when President Reagan was shot that "I'm relieved that he wasn't taken to my hospital."

Imagine the overwhelming job that public relations people from Kansas City's hospitals faced last July 17 when suspended concrete walkways packed with spectators collapsed on the Sunday afternoon ballroom tea dancers in the lobby in the Hyatt House Atrium. Over a hundred people were crushed to death and 200 were injured. Hundreds of their family members rushed to area hospitals searching for their loved ones.

Several years ago, I wondered what we would do if the Shah of Iran came to see our internationally renowned Digestive Disease Center.

Should one of my hospital PR colleagues ask me to speak on my experience with crisis communications, I would probably ask, "Which crisis?" and think of hepatitis in the Birth Center, or a mother of a chronically ill psychiatric patient speaking against Lakeshore Med's facilities, or a nurse being raped, a psychiatric patient drowning in a bathtub, or a six-week hospital strike.

Hopefully, the communications skills acquired over the years to meet "crisis" times may help to produce more positive, productive results as we live and work through difficult and interesting times.

Thinking all this through again, I drove east off Main Street in my rust-bucket Toyota, into this exclusive residential neighborhood. Behind me, the west wind blew the rain clouds from the skies above me and out over the Lake. Suddenly I pulled my car to a stop on the side of the street. A breath-taking image radiated in front of me—

the most awesome, glowing, overwhelmingly colorful complete double rainbow arched over the water and gratefully blessed me with its radiance.

Chapter 10

Bea on October 1, 1981

We haven't settled Barney's estate, but our young couple is moving in today while we work upstairs finishing the bathroom floor, caulking the tub, installing plastic tiles and plastering the chimney that runs between the kitchen and living room, an integral part of the remodeled attic.

Our child sexual abuse therapy book is shaping up and we're meeting with Rachael to pull our ideas together. She calls *Something Happened to Me* a partnership, but I often feel like I'm her employee.

We took our second Gateway class to learn word processing techniques, but there's a shortage of equipment so there's little chance for realistic experience. Before we know it, the classtime is up and we need more practice. We have to take turns and Jan says that doesn't help reinforce her memory processes. She's a hands-on person all the way.

Speaking of which, we gave ourselves a vacation over the weekend and went to see Kathleen Turner and John Hurt burn holes in the movie screen in *Body Heat*. After resting from our rehab labors, that movie was enough to turn up our own body heat for some passionate lovemaking. We must have built up some muscles doing all that physical labor on our properties because we were strong enough for two days to make love, drink and eat during this cool autumn weekend.

We released months of tension bouncing together on our bed with pillows flying and vibrators humming under the sunny open windows with Mother Nature's breezes kissing us. The only trouble was that Jan makes so much noise during those climatic bursts of passion that we have to close the windows or the neighbors could call 911 for a rescue squad. Or if she'd repress herself and stay quiet, she'd burst a blood vessel or two and we'd have to call 911.

Yes, we'd calm down some and go to sleep, eventually. But on our little vacation together in our home, we'd wake to nourish each other again.

Our focus is fun—like children. No responsibilities. No worries. Playing and creating with pleasure gives more pleasure. We have done much for others during these six months. Now doing for each other is a most appropriate reward. A great gift. We are more than alive. We are music. We are mystics. We are miracles because we found each other and we have rediscovered what a precious treasure we have—in each other and in our togetherness.

> Small wonder it takes another
> to understand the raging passions,
> the sexual tensions of a woman.
> Soft elasticity, tactile, sensual undulation
> yielding a breath at a time.
> Smoldering pulse beats pound progressively
> into a conflagration of raw power.
> A tender tightness that shakes to the marrow.
> The wild high mewing explosion.
> The rest of rests.

Jan on October 19, 1981

I called Bea on Thursday night from our Hospital Public Relations/Wisconsin (HPRW) conference in Madison to tell her that I won another award but, except for last year's Fellowship Accreditation, this one tops the bill. It's the Carol Mehlberg Award of Communication Achievement for my comprehensive submission of last September's "It Takes People," the Clark Young Building Open House event. This morning at work, Carolyn and I compiled all the awards that we, Bea when she worked with me and now

Carolyn and I have won. It's the third time in five years that Lakeshore Med's won top honors for a major PR project, plus twelve additional awards garnered in ten years from the Wisconsin Hospital Association and HPRW.

Last year I returned from the conference as a HPRC Fellow, one of seven members ever to have "demonstrated outstanding professional growth and achievement." Yes. And my professional group honored me—a lesbian. I know most of them know it because of local members sharing tidbits with their State colleagues. And so far, those who know me have been sincere and supportive. I have not sensed any changes in their dealings with me.

My oral interview before a panel of two business PR professionals and one journalism professor must have gone all right but I don't remember much of what they actually asked. It was intense. I'd prepared a thorough portfolio and seemed to keep cool as they talked it through with me. A key factor asked by one of the panelist was if I am a member of the hospital's marketing committee. Marketing is the wave of the future, he proclaimed, and I was able to sound as if I knew what was going on as a member of our marketing committee.

I really don't believe that anyone else on our Lakeshore Med marketing committee knows any more that I do. All they seem to do is sit around and stroke their mustaches. It's good that I had paid attention to HPRC speakers at past workshops so I could survive the panel's questions. At my hospital, my part on the marketing wave of the future hasn't crested yet, but at least I'm in the water with the sharks.

My Wisconsin public relations peers were excited for my having been selected "for the highest professional honor our Council can bestow," wrote Project Chairman Marty Jameson. "The selections process was intense and competitive. The panel set high standards and developed exacting criteria for its selections. You can be truly proud to have met those standards. There will be no general announcement prior to the luncheon so I ask that you keep these results private until then." But Carolyn and I couldn't stop jumping about throwing papers in the air and Bea and I celebrated in our own way at home.

But that didn't mean that Carolyn and I couldn't jump around and throw papers in the air and that Bea and I could celebrate at the bookstore and at home.

Nick also received the announcement from Jameson as did the others who wrote letters of support, and Nick scratched a note on it and sent it through inter-office mail, "Jan—Again, Congrats. Nick."

For this year's award, Carolyn wrote a hospital newsletter story thanking all the people who helped make the open house a success: photographer Bob Haban, free-lance writer Tessa Nichols, *Bay View Times* ad consultant Lorry Hansen, and we'll submit a media release to the local papers.

I invested a lot of time preparing that winning submission. It included a five-page review of our competitive hospital environments, the project's goals and purposes, its audiences, timetable and budget, unique factors and an evaluation of its successes. Included in it was a functional five-page Special Event Planning Form listing every possible requirement: who's responsible for each factor; a cost estimate from advertising, publication handouts to requests for food; and a mundane but invaluable list of maintenance requirements from coat racks to microphones and more.

Also, I've managed to chair the HPRW's Fellowship program. I guess that's what they do when you win the year before. Now the young, new president asked me to take it on again because I've been so well organized for this year. It's a highly diplomatic assignment easing potential fellowship candidates through the review process. This year one worthy candidate didn't make the grade because of charges of unethical practices from some HPRW members. That was not fun, especially when I respected the individual and her work—and I empathize with a victim of judgmental people.

I spent precious hours on the phone listening and calming troubled persons. I worked hard to keep this accusation quiet while I tried to stay neutral. I guess I'm lucky not to have crossed one of my HPRW colleagues.

I wish someone like me could serve as a neutral advocate to defend me to *my* hospital administrators. As my mother used to say, "Wish in one hand and shit in the other and see which fills up faster."

<<<>>>

Last weekend I spent a day with over 3,000 women attending the 7th annual Women to Women Conference at Milwaukee's Red Carpet Inn. I was overwhelmed at all these blooming feminists taking a couple days to energize themselves through keynote speakers and workshops.

Rachael Sandler told me about it and that she would be a workshop leader, so I wanted to hear what she said and how she would promote our book which would be out in a few weeks. Too bad we couldn't have had it now.

Another writers' panel shared their experiences, but only one fashionable author in a floppy, flowery hat to match her flowing feminine gown owned up to actually making money off of her romance novels. But she said that money wasn't her motivation because she was married. That's great news for the rest of us who have to earn a living and find time to write. In a jammed cocktail bar after the session we gave each other pep talks on being strong women and achieving our goals.

Bea on October 24, 1981

Judy Chicago's *Dinner Party* has come to a Printing House Row warehouse south of the Loop for a fourteen-week run in Judy Chicago's hometown, and Mother Courage hired a school bus for our customers to see it for $10 a piece for the bus, exhibit and accompanying movie on the making of *The Dinner Party*. It was great to be able to introduce others to Judy Chicago's monumental work. It took her five years, $200,000 and the help of over four hundred artists. It was good for us to see it again—and hopefully to sell some of her intensively researched books with concisely conceived paragraphs on international women of achievement, including her introducing us to an unfamiliar bevy of lesbian women from Paris, as in Natalie Barney's salons of lovers and friends, American authors and other women who openly lived with and loved other women. That part of their lives was hidden until women scholars and writers looked at their history from a feminist point of view.

Jan continues to search for books to read more about these women. I guess she needs the affirmation of their lives to bolster hers. She read about gay personalities as well and tells me all the gossip. American Natalie Barney was a lover of many, and Paris was her home base with other Americans like Natalie's dear friends of over fifty years, Romaine Brooks, Gertrude Stein, Alice B. Toklas and other English and international lesbians. Most of them had inherited money and traveled around Europe and back and forth to the States. It would have been difficult in the 1920s to have lived Natalie Barney's artistic and free life in America, and especially in London because of the criminal laws that restricted gay behavior for which Oscar Wilde was imprisoned.

The conservative English lawmakers were going to add an amendment to that law stating that lesbianism should be illegal as well. They were going to pass the amendment until they determined that the law would inform women about their options, tell women who have never heard of that lifestyle, or affirm women's thoughts if they had dreamed of their sexual alternatives. The Torys decided to be quiet about lesbianism, but a Lord Chancellor was quoted to have said that if these debauched women ventured out of their closeted circles, they did so at their own peril. That didn't slow down Vita Sackville-West and her lovers, including Virginia Woolf, among London's sexually liberated intelligentsia, the Bloomsbury Group. Jan had read about Vita's escapades in *A Portrait of a Marriage* right before our relationship started.

This lack of information was true in our lives. The "L word" was never spoken except as derogatory labels in our adolescent years: queer, dyke, butch—and even that was rare. But we knew if we fooled around with girls, it was to be kept a secret—and there may be something wrong with you.

Judy Chicago pledged to make the awareness of historical or mythological women's lives more available to all. She writes, "Sadly most of the 1,038 women included in *The Dinner Party* are unfamiliar, their lives and achievements unknown to most of us. To make people feel worthless, society robs them of their pride; this has happened to women. All the institutions of our culture tell us—through words, deeds, and even worse, silence—that we are insignificant. But our heritage is our power; we can know ourselves and our capacities by observing in this grand style that other women have been strong. To reclaim our past and insist that it become a part of human history is the task that lies before us, for the future requires that women, as well as men, shape the world's destiny."

Jan had written about our viewing of *The Dinner Party* when we saw it in San Francisco for our bookstore's *Courier* newsletter. It took Chicago two years to find another exhibit area for the work—and it's hinted that this could be the last chance to view it. Both the Art Institute and the Museum of Contemporary Art in Chicago declined to show the piece and other offers were cancelled. It took a woman's organization, The Roslyn Group for Arts and Letters, to make it possible. Because its dinner plate images seem symbolic of female genitalia, critics and established art museums deemed it too controversial.

The work consists of a huge triangular banquet table fifty feet on each side with thirty-nine table settings, each symbolically honoring European and American women and the eras they represent from the Primordial Goddess to artist Georgia O'Keeffe.

Jan said that if she ever won big money in the lottery, she'd build a permanent home for this monumental work: "This is like the Pyramids of Egypt. It's women's first Wonder of the World."

Bea on November 1, 1981

Everything's good between us. Jan loves it when we have Sunday afternoon interludes instead of working our butts off fixing up old buildings. I'm planning Jan's fiftieth birthday party while we're still working on her dad's house. Marian has a young male associate at work who's looking for his own apartment and he may be our upstairs renter.

Yesterday we worked at home and at the shop. I installed a TV antenna on the shop roof and threaded the band through the back window that's two floors plus off the concrete sidewalk below. Now I can watch some TV programs when it gets too dull around the store.

While I was hanging out off the roof, Jan was at work screening for Halloween Trick or Treats bags again. This year they hired some kid entertainers so the line would seem to go faster. What a drag for her again this year. It's too bad children and their parents have to go through this fearful exercise. What happened to having Halloween fun!

We'll we made the best of it 'cause when I got home to warm up the pumpkin soup I'd made, I found his proud parents and my little grandson dressed in the Halloween suit that I gave him. After offering them soup, Jan came home and Jenny and her friend Beth stopped by, then Marian and Sharon. We all celebrated with my pumpkin soup and we had a grand Halloween evening with everyone.

This afternoon the two of us enjoyed another little interlude, changed clothes and worked at Barney's estate, then went on a "Take Back the Night March" through a high-risk, inner-city neighborhood that's near our church and the City Hall. Some redneck white guys tried to intimidate us women and our parson Tony who played his guitar at our kick-off rally. We had flashlights and something new, green light sticks that you crack to create the glow, so the march took on some of the Trick or Treat fear that haunts us. Undaunted and inspired to tough it out, we marchers chanted louder and gained more strength because of their demeaning remarks.

Bea on November 15, 1981

About thirty people came to Jan's tremendous birthday party last night. Wine flowed at our Mermaid Inn. Good food and a rainbow birthday cake with flaming candles kept the crowd happy, singing, sampling instruments, playing charades and making mischief with our variety of young and old, gay and straight, women and men friends who mix well with each other in our home.

I bought Jan a silver champagne bucket, but the best gift of all came from Print-Line when they delivered boxes of *Something Happened to Me.*
Rachael Sandler couldn't make it to the party but she sent a card where she wrote, "Your friendship has warmed and encouraged and is a truly centering thing for me. Happy, happy birthday and let's give 'em hell for the next 50! Love, Rachel—"
We called Rachael this morning and she came right away to see the finished product. It's beautiful and I'm proud of what we have accomplished. Our bookstore has one mainstream paperback book by a victim of incest called *Kiss Daddy Goodnight: A Speak Out on Incest* by Louise Armstrong. This deeply disturbing book was written for adults, and it broke the insidious silence that has blocked public awareness of the problem for so long. Our book may be the first of its kind published to help children. Others have done children's books using vague terms and teddy bears, etc., for illustrations. But our book is real and honest and important. Now all we have to do is to have it reach the right audience and see a return on our Mother Courage Press investment.
Jan showed Rachael the mailing list labels and we started stuffing envelopes with books and the media release to mail tomorrow.

Jan on November 15, 1981

Jenny came over to wish me a happy birthday and brought Matt's letter from his study trip to Indonesia for me to read. He intends to stay on after the tour heads back to California State College-Stanislaus to live in a small village to do ecology research toward a Master's degree. He said he'll be back home in January.

Dear Dad and Jenny,

It's now between 2 and 3 a.m. and I'm too keyed up to sleep. We're leaving at 5:30 a.m. for Sumatra.

The northern industrial countries are flailing away with their domestic troubles, and a lot is planned to develop Third World areas. Big companies from Singapore are realizing that they can't exploit large areas of land like they used too.

I learned about tropical ecology at a micro level and I don't know why I even enrolled in the course, but I'm sure glad I did. These huge corporations are consulting with my professor's recommendations so that the people aren't getting fucked over: i.e. getting moved without compensation, cutting the forests without considering the rivers, and introducing development plans that might not work at all. Communication now is too good to get away with it. These companies want people who understand the ecosystem and yet see the potential for development. He has invited me to return and study at the Institute of Ecology, but he has given me all the room to decide.

As for me I am fluent in the language.

Bandung is located between the mountains and is more temperate: i.e. in the 70s. Hell. A few nights there I put on a long sleeve jacket and had some hot corn on a street corner! Bandung is a university town and it is also the center for government in West Java. I will be teaching English in the meanwhile, and most of the technical texts are written by Americans.

I don't want to stay in Indonesia for long. Heck life in the States is great! I see this as a real opportunity to get paid well for doing a job I want to do—helping people.

Our plans are well thought out. Take care 'cause we're bound for Sumatra!

Love Matt

Jan on November 24, 1981

On Thanksgiving Eve, we joined a crowd of women for a fundraiser to support the lesbian production company that sponsors Milwaukee's women's music concerts. Tonight's concert with Erica Glasner on her autoharp drew many into a little bar off the main street. Because of Bea's musical talents and our Mother Courage connections, we've been invited to attend a few meetings with the Milwaukee group, so we've become well acquainted with women like Erica who has an earthy quality to her voice that matches the folk twang of the autoharp that she holds across her chest so she can walk, dance and move around the stage.

I went to buy Bea a drink during intermission and when I looked for her, I saw her in deep conversation with Erica at a table with only two chairs near the back wall. I took her drink to her, offered to go back to the bar and buy one for Bev, which she appreciated. Those two were head-to-head conversing, listening intently to each other over the din of women's voices. I put Bev's drink next to her and, not wanting to interrupt their obviously intense exchange, I returned to stand at the bar.

Another women's group started playing and Bea and Erica kept right on talking. Bea rejoined me when Erica returned to her place near the sound control panels. Bea suggested the music was getting too loud and wanted to go home. On the way she filled me in a bit on how Erica was getting a divorce and wanted Bea's advice. Erica was married to some big-shot doc and she didn't want to have to go to court or have the divorce and child custody in the papers. Bea said she didn't know why Erica picked her out for divorce advice except maybe she needed someone who wasn't aware of all the issues. And I added, "And someone who's not only been through the mill herself and with me, but is smart about struggling to keep your kids and your career and your financial security."

Bea on November 26, 1981

I cooked an awesome, tasty turkey dinner for Thanksgiving today. Jill came for a bit in the morning like a good daughter visiting her mother on a holiday, but she has to be with her boyfriend's family for Thanksgiving dinner. Jan and I always defer our holidays to the other side of our children's families who have only one or two offspring and their spouses or boyfriends to feed.

Fortunately, we have other friends who have become our family, like Marian and Sharon, and we make sure we're not alone on holidays.

We're still painting, wallpapering, paneling, building cupboards and installing carpets to hide the floors. Jan seems to be taking days repairing and painting the back stairs and hallway passages, nooks and crannies, but I guess it's like a rite of passage, being rebirthed, regurgitated, or something from her past. She returns to 13th Street a lot, too. Her wanting to buy that damn flat must have been something from her past.

I tried to fix the upstairs plumbing on Barney's place, but I finally gave up and called a plumber. So far we've only hired the roofers and now a plumber. When spring comes around we'll get the house painted. Barney only painted one side of the house at a time. True, he always painted each side well, but it took decades and Jan said she doesn't know if he made it all the way around.

With all of the work that we're doing on our properties, you'd think I wouldn't be bothered by my crazy menstrual cycles, but I must be getting close to menopause or having what is now called "Pre-menstrual Syndrome" or "PMS." We're getting information on this at the store in women's journals and newspapers, something that "the experts" didn't know about or didn't care to find out: mood swings, tension and irritability, headaches, bloating.

Like last week when I slept a lot during the day and evening, I dozed off where I sat—and was depressed and cried, too. But now at least I know something of what's happening to me. I read the women's advocacy articles criticizing the medical profession for not recognizing this condition, supposedly caused by a hormonal imbalance. I still think PMS is misunderstood and mistreated, but at least the condition now has a name.

When I read a PMS article to Jan, she knew exactly what the symptoms are, she said, "because I experience that in you. I always wondered what did I do wrong to prompt those abrupt changes in your attitude. Maybe I can learn to understand what's going on and not respond in kind to those mood swings that make me crazy too."

Damn it! I'm always to blame.

Anyway, one of the solutions they suggest to alleviate "this wretched condition that makes them unbearable" is to lay off alcohol, but that's what helps me get through that time of the month. Some women lust for chocolate. Fortunately, craving chocolate is not my problem. They write about PMS being connected to unresolved emotional issues, "especially with issues you might be reluctant to deal with. Most women are surprised to learn how much our emotional biography impacts on our health." No shit! That's something new?

Besides, I'm too close to menopause issues now to worry about the popular new syndrome—PMS.

Jan writes on November 29, 1981

My mother thought she might not be around when I had my first sign of menstruation and prepared me for that event. And she wasn't around. And I handled it. I have never been intimidated about having a period like my friends. They called it The Curse, Aunt Flo and the boys would joke about On the Rag. They'd sit out gym class games, even mild exercises. I'd never forfeit a game or a chance to dance. And I'll take on menopause whenever that comes.

Bea on December 14, 1981

We're done! Last week Jenny came to help Jan finish the hall and I scrubbed the floor and stuck the kitchen tiles in place. We worked late that night finishing carpeting too. Today we finished the last little details, finally painting our way out the back door after carrying out all the tools. Our young tenant John will start paying rent on January 1.

I'm sorry to report that the extended Christmas hours have started at the shop so we're back to boring, dark times there again, including Sunday afternoons. I was so tired when I got home after that, I wiped out in my chair after our cocktails and eating the emotionally and physically warming chili supper I had made. Though I finally went to bed, I was restless all night but woke Jan for a sweet interlude.

Jan on December 19, 1981

Fortunately I have Bob Haban to help me take pictures at one of the two hospital Christmas parties. I used to delight in attending when our benevolent Mr. Young was our administrator. He never needed any help with his annual employee morale booster Christmas party speeches, and he even had his own chin whiskers. This year Nick asked me to revise the hospital's annual report for his Christmas speech. I'm the one he asks to boost employee morale? Is he aware of my feelings towards the decisions made by him, and how he condones the decisions made by Randy and Chuck? Oh well, put on your Nick Dixon hat and try to imagine what may be going on under it.

I admit that after all these years, I still enjoy posing employees for special photos and capturing their personal histories when they received awards for years, many for decades of work. We always post them so staff can order photos. That takes time to process and distribute, but it's rewarding to know that they'll appreciate these photos when they're all dressed up and with their husbands, partners and friends having a good time together. And they'll always have the person who took those pictures in their memories and remember that they were smiling at me when I captured their happy faces.

Our new neonatologist, Dr. Steven Glasner, represented the physicians at the dinner. Nick Dixon introduced him and Dr. Glasner offered a quick apology for bringing hepatitis to Lakeshore Medical Center. He explained the infection control's analysis of the event. He caught hepatitis at his own going-away party from eating a handful of popcorn from a bowl brought by one of the grateful fathers of an infant cared for at the Midwest Center Medical Complex's leading neonatal intensive care unit. He thanked everyone for their positive handling of the situation and said he was happy to have come to Lakeshore Med and to Lakeshore Bay .

Of course, I now recognized his name and will double check with my Milwaukee contacts to see if he truly is Erica's ex-. Because of their young children, it would be difficult to move too far away. Do other lesbians' ex-husbands feel as if they have to move so they don't have to deal with issues they must deal with on their side of "the closet?" Alex seems to feel that way. Is that why he and Marge have been traveling to Alaska, Australia and New Zealand with the pretext of finding him a different job? Is Australia far enough away from my notorious self and my nefarious partner?

Bea on December 26, 1981

I have so much to celebrate. My family's Christmas party at Josh's house was perfect—healing too. The whole family was there and everything was super. Jan's niece Kathy and her Jenny came for dinner on Christmas Eve. The store hours will be back to normal even if our year's end totals dropped $7000 from the year before from, about $20,000 two years before that. That's a depressing fact that I have to deal with. Every spare minute we've had has gone into fixing Jan's dad's properties, but we'll have it all rented soon, and we don't have to do any more physical labor at Jan's dad's house. And our Mother Courage Press book is out there finding its market through our mailings.

Last week Jan and I helped my Jill and her boyfriend Tom move in to their apartment. We all helped: Josh, Joel, Karen, and Tom's parents and his brother Tim. It was strange having his parents and me make up their bed after the brothers carried it up to the apartment. Jan stayed in the kitchen unpacking boxes to keep out of the way. We did good work. Then we all went to Jake and Angie's for sloppy joes and the rest of the family joined us, including my baby grandson. What a grand day. What a grand holiday season!

Chapter 11

Jan on January 11, 1982

Our staff-made "For Your Health" TV production for Lakeshore Med will be premiering on Tuesday, Feb. 2, and we've been creating promotional details and TV programs that should please everyone from the logo to the theme song with a balance of healthcare subjects so no one department feels left out. Well, hardly no one. And if so, we'll try to include them in another year.

Our own creation, our TV logo incorporates a stylized drawing of a crowing rooster perched on the top of the last "h" of "To Your Health." It's fitting to celebrate with a proud rooster calling out to all about how grand everything is.

(I remember the first time I went to the First Unitarian Society in Milwaukee in the early 1960s and saw their crowing rooster on its steeple rather than a cross. Yeah! Our church has a shepherd's crook to go with its original Universalist name as The Church of the Good Shepherd. Our UU founders have used powerful symbols to represent our church principles.)

I suggested an inexpensive solution for royalty-free program theme music and asked our Rev. Dr. Tony Logan to play one of his tunes. I knew he'd help us and he said he would be happy to do it. Laura Williams had met Tony earlier after she asked me to suggest someone to speak at her Parents Caring and Sharing support group's December meeting.

"It's always hard at holiday times to deal with the loss of a child," Laura explained. "I don't want a speaker who would stress his own religious views and neglect grieving parents with other concepts of what the holiday means to them."

Of course, I suggested Tony who spoke gently with universal spiritual concepts, played his guitar and had people singing. He made every hearts feel better.

Ever since that, Laura joined with Carolyn among my spiritual church and Moon Group friends.

We've been busting our buns putting together thirteen shows—and we've learned more about the process after each program. We've written some good scripts by making an extensive worksheet for each topic so everyone working on it, including our special guests, can anticipate what's needed and how best to make it educational—and entertaining. Usually Laura and Pat Holman pull together the main points and then Laura, as the program host, goes after the docs and asks them to show her and the audience how to zero in on topics like avoiding winter emergencies, learning safe and sound advice on taking medications, exploring the meaning of life via the new hospice service, managing stress for high level wellness, and, of course, amazing newborns and their potential that includes an ultra-sound of a preborn moving in its mother's womb.

Our new camera guy, Mark Bertini, gets better with taping and editing every program. I get better at pulling scripts together based on all our ideas. Carolyn holds down the fort in the office. We choose various locations in the hospital and bring in all the props to each scene. I've been known to grab an empty wheelchair to transport heavy pots of foliage to add greenery to a site. Our committee meetings are wild and fun. The stress is high as well. There are times when Laura can barely express what she wants to say, but when the camera starts to roll, she comes across like Barbara Walters—and the doctors we ask to participate love doing the programs.

Actually, we should have known better than to start TV productions with all the other events we have on our schedule, plus those projects that we can't predict.

Matt's now pushing interoffice mail cart around Lakeshore Med until he gets a professional job. I always surprised to see him here. Our Human Relations person, our Marge, now ignores the unwritten hiring rule that a supervisor and a subordinate can't live in the same house, the 'rule' that had Bea dismissed from here rather than continue working with me after we bought our house and were outed as a lesbian couple. Obviously, Ha! I'm not bitter. It's not Matt's problem that Marge and his dad are in a serious relationship.

Matt's learning computer skills to get a good job. In spite of our shaky economy, you would have expected Jefferson Medical to hire him with his being one of the Japan-Jefferson high school students chosen to represent Lakeshore Bay and travel to Japan as their bicentennial gift in 1976. But more important, he would be invaluable to the company with all of his Indonesian experience to utilize with Jefferson's international markets. If they do hire him, he probably would be living in foreign countries most of the time and we'd never see him. Of course, we don't see him much now anyway. That's why it's great to bump into him when I'm dashing around a corner at work helping produce our TV shows, or even better, to have him come into our office delivering our mail.

And speaking of computers, Bea is itching to get one. She's studying up on all the technical magazines and shopping around for something that's pretty basic. I'll probably learn to play Pac-Man on it. It's a good thing that Lakeshore Med installed a word-processing center so we can ask those typists to produce our reports and the in-house publications. We have to be careful not to ask for too much work and get our requests in with plenty of time because we're not too high on their priority list, unless it's our newsletter deadline.

Our technical work seems to be less, but the other assignments expand.

Jan on March 30, 1982

The Bay View Times columnist, old friend and newspaper colleague Frank Tower wrote an item in yesterday's paper.

"TV surprise: Through the magic of television, Joan Beach didn't have to wait until she got out of Lakeshore Medical Center to see her new granddaughter Mary Ellen. By unhappy coincidence, Joan was admitted to Lakeshore Med as a patient the day after Mary Ellen was born. But that gave RNs Karen O'Grady and Mary Patterson an idea because along with audio-visual technician Mark Bertini, they had been filming a "For Your Health" sequence on newborn potential starring Mary Ellen and her parents, Paul and Pat Stevenson.

"So Joan and her husband Ned got to see Mary Ellen's gray-blue eyes peeking at them from a small TV monitor before that particular segment of Lakeshore Med's health series had been edited."

I responded today to Tower's column.

"Thank you for your reference of our opportunity of letting Joan Beach see her grandchild on our TV equipment. It certainly showed how caring our staff could be. Unfortunately and ironically, Mrs. Beach's death at 61 was announced in the paper the same day. That was moving for those involved in her care. I'm sure the family was moved too.

"I'm enclosing some background information on our TV series for your information. A news brief was printed in Sunday's paper. We were quite naive when we started this TV project and our expectations for "Emmy-award winning" productions grew as we became more involved. We've done an excellent series for amateurs and we hope we can do another next year, especially when we have spin-off benefits like the Beach incident and when we can acknowledge physician and staff expertise in another media, inform the community of our services in an entertaining way, and provide healthcare information—all at the same time.

Bea on May 6, 1982

I'm packing up our books to take to another Accent on Women weekend at UW-Oshkosh. I hope we sell as many books as last year.

For her workshop presentation, Jan decided to spice up her speech at the conservative meeting she gave at the Business and Professional Women's group in November 1980. She added music and slides in reworking her speech, but she's continuing to find out that she's not strong unlike Helen Reddy's anthem, "I Am Woman." Jan's not invincible. She is busting her ass while I sit here waiting for business at the store or waiting to fill *Something Happened to Me* orders. At least the UPS guy and the letter carrier come in.

I do get entertained by the unique Mary Virginia Devine. I like to call her The Divine Virgin Mary, but not to her face because she is anti-Christian, pro-Wiccan and an eccentric genius. She's a Ph.D., but her parents keep her close to home so it's difficult to imagine her going away to college. We wanted her to come to our full moon group but she said her parents would never allow that. She has a manuscript, *Brujeria: A Study of Mexican-American Folk Magic*, that's going to be published by the esoteric and occult Llewellyn's World Magic Series, a New Age publishing house specializing in the old ways—magic and pagan books and magazines.

She does travel on local busses during the daytime wrapped in a long cape, barefoot in sandals and she wraps her bounteous brown hair in a disarrayed bun with snarly curls falling around her face and neck. And when she comes in to the store, she usually brings a box of chocolates or she buys some books. My knowledge of parapsychology and my research in the Goddess attract her, and I think she loves it that Jan and I are a couple. One day she swooped into the store and started talking in her rapid lingo that turned into a one-woman Gilbert and Sullivan operetta original performance against Catholicism, the priests and the Pope, or Poop, as she calls him. I don't know what prompted the anger that she vented in verse, song and humor, but it was fabulously entertaining for both of us and worthy of a much larger audience.

The Bay View Times picked up UW-Oshkosh's Accent on Women's promos and printed Jan's workshop intro. I wonder how that will go over with Randy and company.

"Women and Energy; A Resource to be Re/Mined" is the workshop led by Jan Anthony, partner in Mother Courage Bookstore and director of communications at Lakeshore Medical Center.

"The workshop's concept stresses that the greatest loss of natural resources is the waste of women-energy, and that women can empower themselves and others to use their resources as sparks to ignite new awareness and positive change.

"She will describe the dominant power system, women's loss of self-esteem and suggestions for connections to create more systems to gain equality of women.

"To make people feel worthless, society robs them of their pride. This has happened to women as a group. All the cultural institutions indicate through words, deeds and even worse—silence—that women are insignificant.

"Knowing about the power system that subordinates women, elevating their potential by seeing that other women have been strong, and enhancing each one's self-esteem by connecting with personal hidden strength and with the energy of others will give women the power to insist that women, as well as men, shape their own lives—and the world itself."

Jan's multi-media presentation in a windowless classroom on May 8, 1982

(Meg Christian's recording "Hello Hooray" as an introduction: "Hello hooray/Let the show begin/I'm ready…/So we will sit and we'll act so prim/And we will laugh/after all these years of crying/And self-denying/And lonely waiting/And fears and hesitating/Yes we'll laugh,/ Yes we'll laugh,/ and we'll laugh/As we see this thing/Finally, finally, finally begin, /And begin, and begin.")

"I received a strong, fundamental education during my years in parochial school: a valuable basic beginning in reading, writing and arithmetic—and in the traditional, basic Christian faith in God the Father, God the Son and God the Holy Ghost. But I was always considered a troublemaker even then because I kept asking questions and challenging or observing and remembering the teachers' violations in fairness and adult members' and classmates' compromises in ethics in daily living. I did not answer Yes to many of our class promises spoken in chorus during the litany of our communion vows and I never returned to that church after I graduated from eighth grade.

"Fifteen years later I became an active member of a liberal church in Lakeshore Bay because of my need to expand my spiritual dimension with the camaraderie and energy from like-minded persons in my life.

"Some of this personal information about my religious journey is to help explain why I was in my church a year ago listening to a service on eliminating sexism, which in this Reagan era of returning to fundamental traditions of the 'right' may be a topic that's hard to find in a traditional religion. And here I'm today asking questions, challenging, observing and remembering violations in fairness and compromises of women's role in religious ethics and in daily living."

(I told them in 1969 I wanted to read *The Second Sex* by Simone de Beauvoir but I couldn't check "that reference book" out of the library. I had to wait for my book order to come so I went to the library to read that book every day for a week. I continued reading Adrienne Rich, Kate Millett, Betty Friedan, Mary Daly, the angry but scholarly writers of The Second Wave of Feminism who researched into hidden history or "herstory" and created a new awareness of women's lives.)

"Simone de Beauvoir wrote about the particular frustration of the independent woman 'because she has chosen battle rather than resignation.' Perhaps less strident anger, the kind that does not sap energy from our lives and specific battles, will make us more understanding and supportive of each other's goals toward independence and equality.

"And that means "connections." (Write word on the right side of the chalkboard.) There are other concepts I hope to share with you today. In addition to 'connections,' I want to speak of 'patriarchy' and of 'self-esteem.' (Write 'patriarchy/male system' on the left, 'self-esteem' in the middle, and add 'female system' next to 'connections.')

"Since we opened our Mother Courage Bookstore three and a half years ago, I've been able to select and to read among the varieties of women-oriented subjects about what we as women have lost and for how long—and how far we still have to go before we can reach equal status if not for ourselves, then for our daughters and sons.

"I heard radical feminist Mary Daly, a theology professor at Boston College, speak at UW-Whitewater on January 31, 1980. She described male-oriented scholarship that has dominated our cultures for centuries is nothing more than 'scholar shit' and that existing university systems are like boxes of cat litter with 'scholars' scratching around in the same old litter over and over again.

"She's the writer who, in *Gyn/Ecology*, dis-spells the mind/spirit/body pollution that is produced out of man-made myths. She strives to free women by strengthening their powers of hearing and seeing, sensing and understanding their environment.

"'It is,' Daly writes, 'a complex way of perceiving the inter-relatedness of seemingly separate phenomena. It is also a pattern-detecting power that may be named 'positive paranoia.' Far from being a debilitating 'mental disease,' this is a strengthening and realistic disease in a polluted and destructive environment. Derived from the Greek terms 'para,' meaning beyond, outside of, and 'nous,' meaning mine, the term 'paranoia' is appropriate to describe movement beyond, outside of the patriarchal mind set...where dormant senses become alive...more aware not only of the blatancy and interconnectedness of the male power system, but also of its reality. The positively paranoid woman is enabled to detect and name its implicit presence, and therefore to overcome roadblocks in her dis-covery of being. Empowered with positive paranoia, she can move with increasing confidence.'

"I don't know how this happens, but an independent idea—something subliminally worked inside of me during a significantly down period in my career. I realized how paranoid I was becoming. And justifiably so! I started writing down the reasons why—and I started laughing at them and sharing them with other women, and they shared their paranoia with me.

"When I started sharing them, others from the Lakeshore Bay Women's Network contributed to my fearful evaluations at work and in relationships. For example, 'You know your days are numbered... (Pull out a card.) '...when your first written job evaluation in ten years is a three-page document, typed, single-spaced, concluding, 'The only reason you're getting a raise is because there's hope for improvement.'

"'And...when you wake up in your apartment on the morning after the party you hosted and remembered that your boss was the last guest to leave—and then you remembered why.'

"But back to the beginnings and scholarship—

"I remember how hard it was for me to find one thought-provoking book on the condition of women. Then I searched for *The Second Sex* in 1969. Compare that to today when thousands of books, journal articles and anthologies are being produced—or waiting to be printed in this depressed economy. It is exciting and strengthening to watch our resources grow and to learn from their messages.

"New scholarship is piecing together the fragmented dreams we were brought up to ignore, the sexuality we were taught to deny, the language with words that ignore our existence, the pride and esteem we were supposed to give to others but seldom to receive or to provide for ourselves.

"It also makes us aware that even our women's sense of time—cosmic time, 28-day cycles with the moon—our daily, weekly, monthly calendar system has been molded by patriarchy.

"In Charlene Spretnak's most comprehensive, important and readable book, *The Politics of Women's Spirituality, Essays on the rise of spiritual power within the feminist movement*, she explains that the Christians revere the 1,982 years since the birth of Jesus. The Hebrew tradition signifies the year 5,743 at their year. Feminist scholars now count women's heritage starting from 9980 years ago as the dawn of civilization when women had power.

"This truly momentous event for the human race was the development of agriculture by women who had been gatherers of plants, seeds and roots 9,000 to 7,000 years Before the Common Era (BCE). Since that radical shift in our ancestor's way of living, there's been a continuous, though not always wise or truly progressive development of technology or culture.

"Rather than count from AD years, or the BC era, or BCA, if you count the years by the ADA system (After the Development of Agriculture), that brings us now to the year 9,962 and makes us aware of that important women's contribution to our heritage.

"This date is based on the Neolithic era when tribes roamed the land with males hunting and throwing stones at possible food and at each other. They were in awe of the female power of birthright. This was when women, tired of grubbing around for roots and berries on the trail, started planting seeds to begin the agricultural societies around the world.

"Consider this—(Darken the room. Turn on the slide projector.) 'In the beginning was the word,' wrote John 1.1 in the Bible, but whose word? And which beginning? Our earliest artifacts those from the Paleolithic area, 35,000 BCA., consistently treat a single subject: reverence for and awe of the female.

(Venus of Willendorf slide.)

"Our ancestors regularly observed woman's body as the source of life. She bled painlessly in rhythm with the moon. Her body miraculously made baby people and then provided food for the young by making milk.

(Other primitive goddess slides.)

"Paternity was not recognized for a long while. In a primitive culture, copulation is not usually associated with the miracle of new life. A further mystery was woman's androgynous nature. She could draw from her body both female and male.

"Perhaps the oldest Paleolithic statues were expressions of the female body as living microcosm of the larger experience of cyclic change: birth, renewal, nurture and death. In time these energies became embodied in the sacred presence of the Great Goddess in many cultures. She was revered as the source of life, death and rebirth, as the giver of the arts, divine wisdom, just laws, and as the protector of peace and the nurturer of growth. (Slides of Diana, Athena and Nike.)

"But we lost this reverence thousands of years ago—after males discovered their biological part in the process. Women were forced into property rituals like marriage to sustain inheritor rights of fathers to their sons. This father-right also created in most religions a set of rituals to supersede and subvert what women did naturally, a religious one-up-man-ship that has usurped women's place as a spiritual being and made her dependent, isolated and subordinate.

"For example, in Christianity the rite of baptism subordinated the awe of birth; communion superseded loving food/breast nutrients; life after death judgments supplanted maternal love that accepts children trustingly and without exception.

"In a scholarly footnote that I've found impossible to find again in my research, one women 'herstorian' theorized that women who grew grain and made bread, grew grapes and made wine, offered their bread and wine in ceremony to warring and cannibalistic males as substitutes for their hunting and destructive practices.

"Transforming power, not power over others, was the truly significant and essential power and was known by women to be their own. And it can be today.

"We lost our history, our spirituality, our mythology. Centuries ago men broke into our symbolic sanctuary of power. They emerged with pious foreheads and with stolen gowns flapping around their thin legs. Then they issued from pulpits, from thrones, blinders for every person and a freshly devised history to change civilizations.

"1. God created Eve from Adam's rib.
"2. Women brought sin into the world.
"3. Woman is virgin, wife or whore.
"4. Woman's blood is unclean.
"5. Every woman should be overwhelmed with shame
at the very thought that she is a woman.
"6. Rape and child abuse teaches women humility.

"7. A proud woman should be beaten or burned.

"Centuries of persecution as women and isolation from re-enforcing sisters, mothers, friends, independent women of years past, who gathered like this Accent on Women program, were broken down, and we were separated from each other.
"Here's a list too painful to describe in detail, yet it documents the systematic breakdown which makes it hard for us to recover and to re-energize ourselves: a list that reveals the historic, powerful and inhibiting pogroms women have endured."
"Abuse of women and girls. (Slide of a hillbilly-type male holding gun to terrorized wife's head.'
"Indian suttee: Long listed in history as a custom where millions of Indian wives of all ages were burned alive on their husbands' funeral pyres. Today they have 'kitchen accidents' or 'dowry murders' for wives who do not obey."
(Close-up slide of contemporary women walking on five-inch-high wedgie footwear with straps around their ankles.) "Chinese foot binding: The thousand-year-long horror that crippled millions of girls so they could be made marriageable and sexually desirable to Chinese males. Their mothers and sisters were forced to repeat the torture on the young as they had endured it."
(Slide of a medieval-era woman with hands folded in prayer and bound to a log catapulting by men into a bonfire.) "Witchburning. To the peasant, the witch was often the independent woman who spoke her mind, the healer, the pharmacologist, a woman with property coveted by others, the midwife who dared to challenge the Curse of Eve and lessen the pain and lower the death rate at childbirth as best she could. Mary Daly estimates that nine million European people were burned as witches during the 15th, 16th and 17th centuries."
(Slide of African girl staring at camera.) "Clitoridectomies and other forms of genital mutilation have been and are still being performed on Third World women in African and Arabian regions."

(Slide of a Muslim woman in a burka.) "Montaigne wrote, 'There is no torture that a woman would not endure to enhance her beauty.'"

(Slide of drawings of a Victorian woman standing fully clothed with a male doctor with his hands up her billowing long skirt and one of partially covered dead woman on a mortuary slab with a doctor holding up her heart as a specimen.) "Procedures of altering genitalia were also performed in Victorian England and America by the then emerging male gynecological establishment as a form of behavior modification for 'troublesomeness,' 'attempted suicide,' and 'erotic tendencies.'

"Male gynecologists then viewed female sexual responsiveness of any kind as pathological, along with natural female life cycles. Natural processes like menstruation, labor and childbirth were treated as 'illness' and enhanced the myth of female frailty, which haunted the existence of middle- and upper-class women. To them, menopause was almost terminal.

"They calculated that the human body only has so much energy and if men were to be educated in professions, they would have to control their sexual needs more than the lower class person because sexual activity would subtract from mental achievement. In contrast then, because women are vessels for reproduction, if they used their brain, they would weaken their reproductive organs. It was even proposed that continued higher education would cause a woman's uterus to atrophy."

(I move about when I talk, yet stay close to my script as possible. But it got stuffy and hot from the closeness of the audience crowded in the room and the heat of the projector. I opened the door. When I returned, I tripped over the projector cords but regained my posture with a smile.)

"Combine this myth making of historic, though modified, current medical thought that women are basically sick with psychoanalytical thinking that compounds this theme and you may be able to understand how our power, creativity and energy had been channeled into domesticity.

"And what was left?

"We became passive. We lost our will power. We lost our connections, our energy with the past, with the present, with our hopes for the future.

"Traditional religion enforced the view that female initiative and women's will are evil through the juxtaposition of Eve and Mary. The story goes that Eve caused The Fall by asserting her will against the command of God, while Mary began the new age with her response to God's initiative, 'Let it be done to me according to Thy word.' And the husband assumes the same godly rights.

"Faith Wilding's poem 'Waiting' from which I will quote only a short segment, sums up women's sense that their lives are defined not by their own will, but by waiting for others to take the initiative…

… Waiting to menstruate
… Waiting for him to make the first move
… Waiting for him to give me an orgasm, Waiting—
… Waiting to grow wise, Waiting—…

"For many women, that waiting is over in their personal lives, if not in the professional or political lives. Many more women are joining in the great search to find out who we are and to know from new scholarship that our heritage is different and more positive that we were led to believe.

"Imagine how our lives would be different if—" (Slide of a Humphreys Bethlehem stable under a starry night sky with a bright star shining over it and someone shouts out from its shelter, "It's a girl!")

"A new consciousness, which was once crippled and confined…" (Slide of three nuns lying prostrate on the altar floor.) "…may now grow with the awareness of our true selfhood and our potential.

"What is our potential?

"Adrienne Rich concludes: 'We need to imagine a world in which every woman is the presiding genius of her own body. In such a world women will truly create new life, bringing forth not only children, if and as we choose, but the visions and the thinking necessary to sustain, console and alter human existence—a new relationship to the universe. Sexuality, politics, intelligence, power, motherhood, work, community, intimacy will develop new meanings; thinking itself will be transformed.'

"It will take a long time to accomplish this—and we get burned out and frustrated because of our serious setbacks. We need to remind ourselves that The First Wave leaders Susan B. Anthony and Elizabeth Cady Stanton both died more than a decade before women won the vote. And The Second Wave is only ten or twelve years old—and it was born of rage at what was happening to women. The fire of that rage helped to ignite others. But is that fire still productive?

"Being angry is a tough life and a lonely one. Others will not join you through confrontation, and anger can and is exploited by the system." (Slides of drawings of a Victorian matron with a knife in her upraised hand chasing a horrified man while a woman screams from a second story window, and a slide of an Amazon woman warrior on horseback with an ax raised menacing above her head, ready to attack.)

(The women snickered in wonder for the horrified man running from a large and furious matron. I paused again and took a sip of water.)

"We can only guess what he did to her?"

"But that's wasting energy in frustration. It's turning anger into despair, despair into depression—and then, why bother getting out of bed in the morning.

"Real power is the ability to move one's self and others to think and to change. Energy is what fuels us, propels us toward making that change. Energy is what keeps us going. Take advantage of energy boosters that are available to us like programs here today. Go to see Judy Chicago's *The Dinner Party* that celebrates our heritage and our power." (Slide of Chicago's triangular *The Dinner Party* table.)

"Read, learn and pass our wisdom to others.

"As women, we must not burn ourselves out fighting with each other while we're spending valuable fuel to survive in the larger world." (Slide of two elderly matrons, one Black, one white, arguing with each other.)

"As women, we must not waste valuable fuel by not accepting our differences, refusing to support each other because we disagree with each one's survival methods." (Slide of young Middle Eastern women line dancing on a beach.)

"Listen for the common thread that unites us. We have more in common with each other—with other women in most of the rest of the world. And that is going to make a big difference in the next few years.

"We must recognize women for their skills and for their gifts. Tell them. Appreciate. Care. Respect. Admire. Support." (Slide of front line of marching women at the First National Women's Conference in Houston in 1977 with Billie Jean King, Bella Abzug and Betty Friedan and American flags waving behind them.)

"Talk with women about their lives, visions, hopes, pain, passion. Accept women's choices however different from our own. Share your power.

"Reach the middle-ground man who wants to understand." (Slide of soon-to-be-father grimacing with his wife in labor as he supports her in the delivery their baby.)

(A sigh of relief for the birth of the baby and empathy for mother and father gave me another chance to move about in front of the desk.)

"Men do not want to get yelled at, to lose face, to admit to wrong. Most of them do not even know about the dominant power position they inherited. Their power is never, nor hardly even going to be handed to you or given away. Yet there are persons out there who can be open to learning more and accepting new values.

"Save your energy and put it to work to touch people with potential for understanding and change. Take advantage of discovering alternative sources of strengthening inspiration. Look to yourself and the strength and power within you."

(I opened Ntozake Shange's book of her play, *for colored girls who have considered suicide when the rainbow is enuf* and read, "I found god in myself & I loved her. I loved her fiercely.")

"And to close, I share Charlene Spretnak's conclusion on the dynamics of women's spirituality and the women's connections in our own system. 'I have come to know, to feel, oneness with all the millions of women who have lived, who live, and who will live. I contain those millions. Each of us does. Every moment. Such power cannot be stopped.'"

"Thank you," (I expressed with a sigh of relief and a smile of appreciation with applause from the women.)

"Thank you. Can you imagine where I found all those images? Most came from a Dover Clip Art catalogs." (I waved my copy at them. A friend shouted out, "And the other books she used must have come from Mother Courage Bookstore and Art Gallery in Lakeshore Bay.")

The one request I asked for from my speech to the Business and Professional Women's group was to read their reactions from their evaluation forms. I called and asked again, but no one ever responded to me about that. I must assume that the responses were unfavorable or they would have sent them to me.

The Accent on Women did send their evaluations to their speakers. Not everyone in the workshop responded.

The comments from those women who did are:

Workshop 28: "Women and Energy: A Resource to be Re-Mined" with Jan Anthony

How would you rate this workshop: (8 highly informative to 1 not informative. 11 responses with 6.6 average.)

The quality of instruction provided in the workshop. (8 being excellent to 1 being fair. 12 responses with 6.9 average.)

Comments:

    A good closing to our keynote speech. Asking us to go one step further.

    Have these workshops more often than once a year.

    Good lecturer.

    This was an excellent presentation—it showed much, much preparation.

    Extraordinarily well-prepared presentation. Not an uninteresting moment. Ask Mrs. Anthony again.

    Sincere, concerned, inspiring.

    Great research and good presentation—loved it.

    Went very slow, was disappointed.

Oh well. You can't please everyone.

Chapter 12

Bea on May 22 to June 1, 1982

Jan is finally taking a break from her troubles, including news of Alex moving as far from me as he can find a good job. Would Jenny go with him? Would Matt stay there forever? What would happen to the Door County land?

    We went almost first class to Door County, staying at a B&B run by two gay guys rather than invade Jan's lost acres further north. She didn't have the strength, she said, to battle Alex if he would show up—nor would I.
    It's been quite a year with Barney dying and the two of us doing all of that rehab work on his properties. We still don't know what the State will do to claim the money Barney's estate owes for Mildred's decades of being institutionalized. Barney's attorney friend told us not to worry and not to rush them into a decision.
    We spent time touring boat launching sites in case we wanted to bring our *Courage* up to sail around Green Bay and Lake Michigan some summer weekend. It would be easier sailing than launching on River Wood and overcoming the currents to get on Lake Michigan with its high winds and waves or its lack of wind for sailing.
    It surely was good to sleep in a comfy bed rather than in that barn on a canvas cot, eat in good restaurants and enjoy the flame-up fire of the fish boils—like the tourists.
    What a unique delight it was: being catered to by our handsome hosts, Barry and Ben who are a bit older than our sons. Ben invited us to sit with them at the barn overlooking fruit trees and sunsets, but we chose our own company after our day's travels. Blessed by a

balmy evening, we lounged about in the upstairs porch off our bedroom, drinking our cherry wine and enjoying the starry Door County night. And when we surrendered to the fresh, clean, cool air causing goose bumps off our moonlit bodies, we retired, refreshed, renewed to celebrate our oneness once, resting, whispering and celebrating again and again as when we were young and gay.

Barry knocked gently in the morning and set a tray in front of our door. The fragrant aroma of fresh coffee lured me away from my woman in our sweet and soft lovers' nest. I was hungry! Behold. It was a silver breakfast tray of freshly baked croissants, cherry and blueberry jellies, lots of butter, crispy bacon slices and spicy sausages surrounding a fluffy cheese omelet and sweet, warm Danish pastries; just what we needed after last evening's prolonged night of erotic pleasures.

Jan smiled and wondered if the buzz of Valarie, our vibrator, was heard from our room.

Of course we tromped around our old Door County haunts—my parent's log cabin fronting the Green Bay side of Door County. They made the cabin from trees that they felled on their land. We stopped at Jake's father's place on the Lake Michigan side near Bailey's Harbor. The drive past Jan's Woodridge made her shudder with Alex leaving his job and looking around the world for a different one. He could be up there so we drove on the gravel road slowly enough to see how her family's planting of 4,000 evergreen saplings survived. More than half are growing strong, their roots grappling through the shallow soil covering the acres of rocks and limestone beneath.

The next weekend we drove to Chicago and the annual Memorial Day convention of the American Booksellers Association (ABA) trade show. We'd paid a distributor to display one book, our first and only *Something Happened to Me*. It was shelved, thank goodness, with the cover facing out among hundreds of books he represented. We can only hope that the sad little girl on the cover could actually catch someone's eye in this giant glut of books and displays from around the world. That's a tall task for a little girl, drawn in black and gray who is only about five inches high sitting on a white cover saying, "Something Happened to Me."

Now as publishers and ABA veterans when we were not only book sellers. We brought a shopping cart with us this time—the first day to collect books, bags and other freebies, but after waiting in long lines for expensive convention food and drinks, the next day the cart also carried our gourmet sandwiches, a bottle of champagne and plastic champagne glasses. We found a rare quiet corner and set up our luscious luncheon under the exposition's expanse of ceiling beams and hanging banners.

Trapped birds that lost their way into this man-made cavern would tweet from above. That was the extent of Mother Nature's element at our picnic. What made us all jump was the explosive noise when we popped the champagne cork. Busy booksellers and buyers in our area were silenced by the gunshot sound of our bubbly bottle. When they searched for the source, we raised our glasses to toast to them and enjoyed our creative solution to the drab and pricey food and drink alternatives that others were forced to consume.

Between those trips, we rebuilt our garden into boxed raised beds and Jan set in tomato plants, peppers and eggplant, lettuce and radishes. But the biggest job of all was to rebuild our chain-link fence wall that was falling into our neighbors' yards. When we bought our house, we never noticed the physical problems that this house and lot would have, elevated above three neighbors by corrugated sheeting. We only saw what we liked and wanted.

Our able-bodied offspring tore down the entire chain link fence on top of a corrugated metal wall to keep our yard from eroding into the neighborhood. Our gang dug a deeper trench and reinstalled it all in a straight line. Various helpers volunteered, and did we need them, especially with the rented power posthole digger. I pictured Tom, Jan or me grabbing the handle, flying in a circle, hanging on for dear life, until the hole digger stuck and stopped in solid soil. When Josh came to take a turn, he wore rubber flip-flops and we visualized flying toes spiraling into the air. Joel and I pulled out the concrete corner post and then helped with the concrete work. Of course it rained and when Jan's niece Kathy came to help, she insisted on doing her share by digging on her knees in the mud with a trowel and a bucket.

Then Josh and I used the "come-along" towing tool to stretch and reset the chain link to align with the posts. When we were almost done, Jan's Matt came over and finished some of the details of this tremendous task.

We no more than finished that accomplishment than 13th Street needed a new furnace. Jan was depressed about this because not only did she need a different car than her rusty Toyota, but she's neglected her teeth and had to choose between the new furnace and perhaps dentures. She'd returned to her pre-divorce dentist when she qualified for insurance. Now her dentist had relocated into his new building with a staff that surrounded her mouth. She felt she'd have to help pay for all of his new employees' salaries plus the new building. When they gave her the estimate of the cost, she never went back.

She chose to install a new furnace and did so with Tim, a young Lakeshore Med maintenance fellow who did a great job for her. Then Jenny told Jan that some of her underemployed friends suggested a dentist who did good work and also took installment payments on his dental work. He also happened to be the brother of one of our lesbian circle of friends and now Jan's beginning to get that problem solved—and he rescued her saying that she's is a long way from needing dentures.

Jan on June 1, 1982

It was great to get back to work and find so many of our plans coming to reality. Several weeks ago, St. Agnes PR told us we would no longer have the space of two rooms at their health fair for our multi-department information and testing tables. We'd have to settle for one room and it would be again at the end of a dead-end hallway in the opposite direction of past years' displays.

After we gloated about being too competitive and too good for their event, we decided we were lucky they invited us in the first place. Still, we weren't going to be put down or out. Our TV team, now down to the reliable core members, Pat, Laura, Mark and me, met with Carolyn in our office to story board a new campaign to outdo our competition again this year.

Why did we need that entire staff to educate others about our hospital when we had our TV programs? We'd set up chairs and show "The Best of For Your Health" on a large-screen TV.

But who's going to walk down a hallway to watch TV?

"We'll entertain them," said Pat, of course. "And I volunteer to be Miss Piggy, in costume, of course, and walk around and hand out Video Theater tickets with a continuous showing in Space 21."

"Miss Piggy! Pat. You'd make a great Miss Piggy!" as we fell over laughing.

"Well thanks!" she exclaimed and then snorted and imitated Lily Tomlin doing Ernestine, the bra-strap grabbing, snorting telephone operator. "See! You thought I couldn't act!"

"The kids will love you and they'll bring in their parents. Let's make a Lakeshore Med video theater with a movie house marquee out of foam core and a display headlining our topics. We'll hang it from the ceiling tile braces, prop the display on the hall railings and use double-sided tape and a prayer to hold it all up."

"Right," with a note of sarcasm, "and we'll give them popcorn, too."

"Well, why not! We'll rent a popcorn wagon and hand them popcorn that they have to eat inside the room. We don't want St.

Agnes to have to clean up any spilled popcorn all over the hospital. They have to *eat it all in our video theater*."

"And the smell will lure people from the entire fair. Maybe we'll even get some patients and hospital staff. They can smell their way to us, especially after Miss Piggy here hands out tickets with 'Free Popcorn' printed on it."

"And don't forget to tell them that they can take a load off their feet sitting in one of our chairs to watch the show."

"If I'm going to be Miss Piggy, you have to wear circus-striped red and white jackets and straw hats and bow ties as ushers and popcorn poppers."

"And we'll stick Lakeshore Med logos in our hat bands."

We climbed about the mess of the past Blue & Gold Run debris and the future Lakeshore Med's Video Theater filling our office. Carolyn cut out our three-dimensional foam core scheme and painted it blue with gold spots to look like Broadway theater lights. She shaped yellow tag board to highlight our impressive hospital staff photos on the display panel. The costumes and the popcorn fixings had been ordered. What a team!

We drew standing-room-only crowds to our exhibit in the heart of St. Agnes Health Fair for five hours. Popcorn sizzled and popped in a red, gay-nineties popcorn wagon parked near photos on our Video Theater marquee. The tantalizing aroma permeated the fair, attracting people to the source.

On the supersized TV screen loaned from the library, visitors saw a twenty-five-minute tape featuring nine selected segments from Lakeshore Med's "For Your Health" TV series.

Laura Williams, the show's host, welcomed visitors via a video introduction, but she remained in the room to answer questions. People coming into the room would settle into watching a show and suddenly turn around and do a double take; Laura was upon the screen and she was right there in the room, too!

Topics selected for this continuous showing covered hypertension and stroke, vascular disease, fetal ultrasound showing a moving picture of a preborn, the famous Digestive Disease Center, help for arthritis patients, the new hospice caring, amazing newborns and hemodialysis.

Our goodwill ambassador, Miss Piggy, was there to mix and mingle with the crowd. Resplendent in lavender taffeta, a black feather boa, silver shoes and a full-head mask, Miss Piggy was the total "star" as she posed for photos with wide-eyed children and magnanimously gave away hundreds of tickets for Lakeshore Medical Center's Video Theater and free popcorn.

Carolyn and I wore red and white striped blazers and matching "pork pie straw hats." Jan never stopped popping corn. Carolyn handed out eight-hundred-fifty bags to visitors as they went inside the "theater." Mark, who did the technical editing as well as filming of "For Your Health," kept his video production glowing from the "Theater."

When everything was being packed up for the trip back to Lakeshore Med, some St. Agnes professional staff stopped by and said, "You people from Lakeshore Med always do a good job."

For three years, we've asked many of our hospital staff to represent hospital departments on a Sunday afternoon at a fair. This year we sustained a similar standard of excellence in presenting our services to the community through our TV resources, a contemporary way to educate and to communicate."

Cost containment is the focus for this season—as if it hasn't been an issue forever? That's the end of our *synergy* magazine. That's OK. We have new ways to get across our messages. All that means we have to do more for each other and as a team.

Bea on June 20, 1982

My daughter was married yesterday. She was aglow with happiness and I am happy for her. She and Tom kept everything simple with Tony Logan marrying them at church with the reception at Tom's parents' home. Jan was the official photographer. The day was beautiful. They already are living together in their apartment and they will finish college this year so they have to keep their expenses to a minimum.

Again, it's strange having my ex- married to my former best friend and all of us standing together for photos. Jan's behind the camera taking the pictures so I'm standing without my partner next to me. Josh had to lead both of Jill's "mothers" down the aisle while Jake stood waiting to "give his daughter" to another man, her husband.

Jan said she liked being behind the camera and moving about so she wouldn't have to have deep conversations with others. We took the film in for one-day service and found out that Jan would make an excellent wedding photographer.

(That reminds me: Tom's brother is gay. He's a nice kid, still in high school—but he gets around. When he found out that Tom's new mother-in-law had a life-partner, he wanted to talk with us on his own. He took the initiative and we followed through, except that Tom's mother had to come into our house before she deemed it to be safe to leave him alone with us. It was as if we needed to be checked out before she'd leave her son in our questionable hands. He only needed to talk to non-judgmental adults who would understand him. We were good listeners, but we may not have understood why he takes the risks that he does in this scary era of HIV and AIDS. When we finished our conversation, he called his mother and she came and drove him home.)

Jan on July 5, 1982

It's appropriate that my dad's estate with the State of Wisconsin and County of Lakeshore Bay finally was settled right before the Fourth of July. We could celebrate officially owning his estate's properties at the parade, especially when his name on a wide banner came down the route for the Carl B. Anthony award for the best amateur float.

It was good that we put in all the work and rented both units at his house because we still have them as ours. My parents' home did not go to pay for my mother's years of hospitalization, nor did the shop. It's in our names now. The State subtracted monies owed from the time my mother died in 1978 to the date of my father's death and that left a debt of $10,000, which we can pay off when we sell the properties or in installments. So we didn't need any cash to pay off the debt, but we did take money out of Mother Courage Press to pay for the repairs and the attorney.

Jan on August 15, 1982

Bedraggled-looking Pat and Andrea came to Mother Courage late Sunday afternoon and plopped down on our store's window cushions. They'd returned from their first pilgrimage to the Michigan Women's Music Festival and, before they parted to their homes, they needed to stop at Mother Courage to transition into their other reality.

They looked stunned and sunburned yet they were giddy when they told some of their experiences on Women's Land in Michigan: acres of wooded, liberated women's land where no men are present, except at night when men in huge trucks are escorted on the land to clean out the "PortaJanes." They compared the big names of our women musicians playing to several thousand partially dressed women or sky-clad under the sun and the stars and they showed us the tattered paper program with workshops on everything from learning to live with patriarchy, choral and instrumental music, even a workshop on living with facial hair—with some women having beards.

The glow they shared—and the warnings of freezing water in group outdoor showers; four-hour work shifts; vegetarian food served in a huge food tent; and threatening weather didn't change my mind. Nor would the stout, middle-aged white males shouting and heckling the women from the behind the barrier fence deter me. The area was guarded by the festival's women guards.

Nothing would stop me from getting us there. Fortunately, we can skip the facial hair workshop when we go to Michigan next August.

Bea on August 15, 1982

"Calm down, Jan. Yes. I can see how happy we're finally going on our well-deserved two-week camping trip but we're headed to the Atlantic coast not to Michigan and I've been busy training Betty Willing to be responsible for the store on weekdays with Jill staffing weekends and being available for Betty to call if necessary. We have to trust the Goddess to keep Betty as responsible as possible. Jill may drop in on her when she can. I'm also preparing our little trailer for following us out east starting with Labor Day weekend, the trip we were preparing for when Jan's dad died on May 13 last year—that is if Jan survives the stress at work and stays healthy.

Chapter 13

Jan on September 12, 1982

Nothing's like a motor trip to take your mind off your troubles, except for the troubles you meet on the road.

We were packed and ready before dawn for a jump start to avoid traffic on Friday morning of the Labor Day weekend, driving through Chicago on the Eden's and Dan Ryan expressways and around the steel smelting factories and smoke stacks lining the edge along the bottom of Lake Michigan on Interstate 80 and 90, the industrial pit of northern Indiana. Our little brown camper bounced cheerily behind us and we felt freer as we unwound further from work. As we made our way along the seedy route, a trucker roared by and honked at us. We saw him give us some sort of hand sign as he flashed by, but we dismissed it as a macho reaction to our trailer's bumper sticker that said, "Women do it better." We would have pulled off to see if something was wrong, but my "Chicago-wise" girlfriend said that this was no place for us to stop or to exit and get lost trying to get back on to the toll way, so I didn't argue and we kept speeding right on until we pulled up for gas at the Indiana/Ohio rest stop to fill up and zip back on our way to our New York, Boston, Cape Cod and Niagara Falls adventures.

I ran to the women's room while Bea dealt with the car. When she put in the gas pump, she noticed wet and greasy droplets on the back of the car and the front of the trailer. Those spots were even on the back of the trailer, even on our "Women do it better" sticker.

Whoa! And she raised the hood of her '76 Olds Cutlass that she inherited from her dad and found more oily splatters. By the time I returned, she was head-to-head with a mechanic; both were shaking their heads and pointing to the Cutlass's guts. We'd blown something in there and were on the last drops of completely dehydrating the transmission, or whatever. Nothing could be done here. We had to be towed, he said, and he called the nearest AAA service. We were lucky. If we had gone another few miles, the entire transmission would have been destroyed and we'd have to sell the car for scrap.

Ah! So that's what that trucker tried to tell us when he gave us hand signs back between Hammond and Gary. He had seen the first splashing of the fluid.

The attendant helped by calling the nearest emergency services. It's Saturday afternoon and where do we go with the tow truck pulling the car pulling the camping trailer. Well, the driver dropped us out of his cab at a mom-and-pop motel on an almost abandoned road. He maneuvered our camper into a parking lot and we watched Bea's car get towed off into the distance as we stood in front of our little room of the one story, ten-unit motel with rabbit ears on their TVs.

I've always known that Bea was a worrier, but this was unlike any situation she'd been in before. She had no wheels and we were in the middle of nowhere. At least we were on land and not on one of her boats. I could sense her blood pressure starting to max. All she had was the trucker's business card in her hand. She had swapped his card for her car and we didn't know precisely where we were on some little road somewhere in Indiana or Ohio. He must drop stranded motorists at that rest stop at this place frequently as he radioed ahead to get a reserved room that was waiting for us with an open door.

Fortunately, we had grabbed our large cooler and provisions from the car before the Cutlass disappeared down the road dangling behind his truck. Books! Books! We grabbed them too so we could read away the time. As is my custom and ritual, I quickly found some ice and we fixed ourselves our drinks. After calming down via Bea's brandy and my martinis, we went to meet our hosts and found out where we were—in the middle of nowhere and close to Mother

Earth. "Well. It could be worse," I said in my Pollyanna fashion, which, as usual, wasn't well received.

We didn't have to starve or rely on our snacks for our supper because the Goddess planted us right across from a little golf course and restaurant. The rest was acres of farmland. So after fortifying ourselves with booze, we crossed the deserted highway, entered the cozy restaurant and ate a filling Midwestern meal with meatloaf, mashed potatoes, peas and carrots, gravy, a lettuce leaf and a candied apple on the side with sherbet for dessert. While we ate, we explored options to rent golf clubs and a cart and play a game the next morning. We had never played golf together, not once. I didn't even know Bea could golf.

We stalled about in the restaurant as long as we could but there wasn't much business so we went back across the road, tried to watch TV and Bea paced the floor. I had been able to open the little door on the camper and pull out our suitcases with fresh clothes and then sat outside to look at the stars rather than the wavy TV. We drank, but we had to ration ourselves for an unpredictable future—stranded without a liquor store nearby. We finally went to bed and fell asleep on thin mattresses covered with scratchy sheets, wash-worn and faded yellow cotton blankets covered by thinning white and yellow tufted chenille bedspread.

After a fitful night and early morning rising, Bea waited impatiently and finally walked to the motel desk and phoned the number on "the card." Someone at the other end told her they had to order parts from Detroit and it could be late on Saturday or even Sunday. Detroit! The voice told her that it was a good thing they found someplace open on the holiday weekend, but we would have to spend another night or two where we were planted.

Our first time playing golf together worked out all right because we both cheated. Why count the swings you take when you don't even hit the ball on that swing, and why not take "overs" just because the ball only went a few yards or into a woods or a bunker. The important thing was to have fun even if I was always concerned about the foursome behind us. So we'd let them pass us, which meant that we had a longer time to play the game and to pass our lost day in the middle of nowhere.

Did you ever play bounce the ball in the parking lot or do tight-rope walks on the concrete parking bumpers to pass the morning while you're stuck waiting for your car; and you can't go golfing because they will return your car and can't find you while you're on the fifth green, or if you don't leave your base of operations, they will never return it and you're stuck going crazy with another crazy person?

Finally, at about three p.m., we were informed that our car is on the way. Now we have to charge the extra expenses like the motel and the golfing, plus the parts and labor on the car. Bea said the car expenses were out of sight, but didn't give me any details—and I didn't ask. Fortunately, our credit account is OK, but we still have the remainder of our trip to go and we're not even out of Indiana.

Bea's relief at reclaiming her Cutlass was almost equal to the time she found her four children after worrying that they had all drowned. She charged the motel and auto bills on our credit card and drove out of captivity to the east, stopping only at the nearest town's grocery and liquor store to replenish our supplies.

It was dark and I was driving when we reached the massive Interstate exchange where I-80 and I-76 meet. Because of the Labor Day weekend campground rush, I had made reservations in Pennsylvania on I-79 and hoped that the campground would honor that for us even though we were a day late, so when I saw a highway sign marker directing us to I-79, I confidently chose that direction.

We got off I-76 at I-79 and started looking for the directions to the campground. The exit signs to Warrendale looked strange, but so did the Pennsylvania lap seem contrary to our AAA guide that Bea hauled out of the glove compartment. It took us about a half-hour driving through in the dark night before we stopped at a little gas station and discovered we had driven on to the Pennsylvania Turnpike headed eventually for Washington, D.C. What luck to have exited at that time. Following new directions, we headed due north for about one hundred miles to stay at a campground as close as we could to I-80 and hoped that nothing else would go wrong.

We pulled into a campground so late that the office was closed, opened our trailer on an empty wooded edge and woke up so early that no one had returned so we could pay for what was left of our night's stay. I apologized to Bea over and over for making that wrong turn. I was confident last night when I chose that turn because the last time I drove it was in my previous life as a new wife driving east on the Pennsylvania Turnpike to meet my new first lieutenant husband after boot camp in Camp Peary near Williamsburg, Virginia. That was several "previous lifetimes" ago, and President Eisenhower had conceived a complete interstate highway system which had been finished in the three decades since my lonely but highly motivated auto trip in 1953.

<<<>>>

We seemed to have wings now, flying along I-80 through and over the beautiful green mountains, across long, new bridges over rivers whose names I remember from my history lessons about the pioneers heading west. When we crossed the Delaware River and entered New Jersey, my excitement level started rising. It would be only another little state and we'd be in New York City—or at least on the western edge of the Hudson River where we'd planned to camp north of the George Washington Bridge, driving along the Palisades Parkway.

Northern New Jersey has so much natural beauty compared to the frequent commutes I made in 1955 over weedy swamps, oil storage tanks and smelting plants into New York City from Long Branch where Alex and I lived when he was at Fort Monmouth.

I-80 lanes heading for New York City became doubled as we approached the George Washington Bridge. I gripped the steering wheel with white knuckles, knowing if I made a mistake now we'd end up on the bridge rather than heading north. Bea mumbled in her worried way about not being able to cross the bridge because we had a propane tank on the trailer. Heavens! How do mobile homes get across it! Don't worry. Just help me find the correct exit around Fort Lee and to any city large enough to be named on a sign or any reference to Palisades Parkway north. Of course "North" doesn't always mean "North." It could be "West" too.

I could see George Washington's towers looming closer and I surely didn't want to drag that camper back and around in New York City traffic, but I would if I had to. We were getting closer and I still couldn't judge which lane I should be in when Bea spotted Palisades Parkway north in time for me to slip to the right without losing the trailer or causing a gridlock traffic accident—and we had made it just in time.

What a peaceful ride on the parkway surrounded with landscaping bushes on the boulevard and the shoulders, hardly any cars and no trucks. We made good time again after such a long day's drive. Once a car honked at us and the driver pointed to the trailer. Oh, no! And we pulled over to check the transmission, but everything was sealed tight so we revved up to speed again. Then Bea and I read a road sign at the same time that restricted use of the parkway to automobiles. No trucks or trailers allowed. Damn it. We're headed in the right directions and we're not going to make a change now.

Following the campground directions, we did get off near the grim fortress walls of what looked like a prison on the Hudson River, found our way up the Hudson and pulled into Harriman State Park. Yes! There was space for us, said the camp ranger, and we followed his penciled directions on the camp map to pull up and ahead into a tall tree-lined spot overlooking most of the campground.

It was hardly that, more like a tent city with smoking campfires with an occasional whiff of some other substance. Of course! It was Labor Day weekend and those families in the cities headed for the woods, large families with little kids and grandparents, and we could hear the Babel of other languages, primarily Spanish from what we could tell. Of course! These people couldn't afford to take long vacations spent in fancy hotels and they brought their own entertainment and celebration. "Life is so fine in America. OK by me in America." We found ourselves in the Puerto Rico ghetto of "West Side Story" and as we started unfolding our camper for a well-deserved rest, lovable Spanish-chattering toddlers wearing footed sleepers came around to watch us two gringo women managing their camping gear on their own.

After we were settled in, enjoying our drinks and a little supper, we applauded our cross-country adventures, the "not-crossed-over George Washington bridge" accomplishment and finding this cross-over culture twenty-five miles up the Hudson from Manhattan. We enjoyed hearing the beat and joy of the music and laughter of people of another culture, relaxing and escaping from the harsh city—the city we plan to take on tomorrow. When it was time for us to retire, I flaked out completely as if we were alone in the woods. Bea, with her Chicago-wise ways, could have kept somewhat alert to the atmosphere around her.

<<<>>>

"Could it be? Yes, it could. Something's coming. Something's good," rang through my brain as we pulled away from our trailer on the hillside and headed back towards the bus terminal and a parking space near the George Washington Bridge. "New York, New York! What a wonderful town. The Bronx is up and the Battery's down. The people ride in a hole in the ground."

I was ecstatic. Bea and I are going to New York, to Manhattan together.

We parked at a gas station and bought round trip bus tickets from the New Jersey station to cross the bridge. I get a high on bridges. And this one transports me to my exciting city with my lover at my side. It made me tingle and bubble inside. So many places to go. So many things to do and in only one day. No wonder I'm emotional and excited! I love New York!

Stepping from the bus, almost skipping to land on Manhattan, we transferred and headed south between the river and Central Park on Broadway past Lincoln Center where we decided to walk on Central Park South towards the Plaza Hotel. I wanted to treat Bea to a carriage ride, but it seemed too expensive after our Indiana car troubles. Maybe on the way back uptown, we'd be able to work that into our agenda.

I had to take Bea to the Museum of Modern Art to refresh my memory of what I had seen before; if we had time, we'd do the Guggenheim on the way back. We actually held hands walking through Rockefeller Center gardens. I was full of stories about what it was like at Christmas and more tales wherever we went, and she had her stories too from when she came alone as a college girl to see the Big City and visit her big brother Calvin when he lived in Manhattan.

Breathtaking Times Square seemed seedier now, especially in the daytime. Most of the movie houses were X-rated. We didn't have time for a play, but we did walk through Schubert Alley and around and about. Bea did not like the panhandlers and clusters of strange-looking characters on the street. We shifted gears and hopped the bus headed to Greenwich Village and Washington Square where so many of my favorite authors had lived. We could have breathed in a high from the smell of pot smoke around the Square and the shops catered to tourists wanting T-shirts.

OK. We're off to the top of the World Trade Center, the highlight of this trip with spectacular September clear skies giving us a vast overview without the gritty details of a city—the city we've both visited in better times. This mighty height elevated us to a place of wonder. We could see the entire cityscape, bridges crossing rivers, and the Statue of Liberty in the Atlantic harbor with boats of all sizes dancing around her beneath us. One day I would like to walk across the Brooklyn Bridge and relive the era of Thomas Wolfe's life and novels, but not this time. We ate our late afternoon lunch before we headed toward the South St. Seaport museum and later, a trip on the Staten Island Ferry at tip of Manhattan. We always have to work in a boat ride on each trip, the more times the better.

Bea loved the seaport museum and harbor with its tall ships harbored there; even the faint but distinct smell of the Fulton Fish

Market added a natural touch to the old New York area's nautical charm. We always seem to photograph her at a ship's wheel, but this time we had the Twin Towers looming above the masts and rigging and her head.

I had Arthur Frommer's guide to find us a leisurely French restaurant in the neighborhood that we could afford and then we found a woman's bar advertised in one of the periodicals we get at the store. I had cut out the ad and carried it in my wallet. When we finally found it, Bea was a bit tense. "Where are you taking us, Jan!"

I wasn't sure myself, but I found Ruby's Place and when we opened the door the room had tables but also it was lined with women sitting on benches attached to the walls so we felt as if we had to pass through the gauntlet for inspection as we made our way to the bar. We ordered beer and looked around the dim and stark dance space and pool tables. The jukebox was loud, of course. On the way to the women's room through the cigarette smoke, we found a quiet sitting area in a back room for more intimate conversation. Women here were definitely not friendly to us, an obvious couple, probably tourists.

It was time to head back to our bus terminal at the Washington Bridge. Our buses stopped at so many places as we made our way that we gained a better view of the city than if we had taken the subways. Bea hated subways anyway, after spending hours on them every day while a college and art student in Chicago.

One George Washington bus to New Jersey had just left the station when we arrived. Because of the evening schedule, we'd have to wait about a half hour before the next bus left, so we decided to buy a drink at the nearly deserted, red plastic and fake white marbled-tiled luncheonette.

Bea was fidgeting, clutching her shoulder bag and camera case in her hand. Like a hawk, she surveyed the area when a young, mustachioed male left his group and headed toward us as if he wanted to strike up a conversation. I answered his greeting, and then I heard Bea bark, "Buzz Off, Buster!"

That shocked the both of us as he reeled back, his hands in a defensive mode against his chest. "Buster? Wow? That's a good one!" And as quickly, the counter waiter came right over to ask if everything was all right. The caught-off-guard male backed away laughing under his breath, and Bea thanked the waiter who watched over us until we boarded the bus; then I started laughing because I was so surprised at her reaction.

"Buster! That's a good one."

"Well, why not! Who knows what he and his gooneys wanted. Honestly Jan, you're so naive."

Then I could imagine how much tension she probably felt as we wove our way, lead mostly by me, The Tarot Fool, on an adventure without seeing or even looking for any pitfalls.

"I'm proud of you, Bea, for taking care of us and our bus fares and food and tickets, handling all our money today so I could soak in all the fun stuff. I hope you enjoyed your day."

"We'll see when we get back to our camper. I wonder if that's still there."

With the few passengers at 11 p.m., the driver maneuvered the bus back to the New Jersey terminal and we'll head for our car.

Our car! I have no idea where it's parked! Jeez, Jan! "I'm following you, Bea, putting all the responsibility again on her.

"It's a good thing I wrote it down in my little notebook here," and she had the location all written down. "Be prepared, Jan. Remember? Your father was an Eagle Scout."

With the seeds of doubt about what we'd find when we returned to our campsite, the journey home in the dark was long.

Our headlights scanned over our camping area and we realized that the entire tent city had vanished, except for our little brown camper standing alone on the hill between its tall trees. The entire campground population had packed up from its Labor Day weekend vacation and headed back to the city.

And we packed it in for a silent night in the woods after a remarkable fifteen hours in New York, New York, where Bronx is up and the Battery's down. And we never rode in a hole in the ground.

<<<>>>

Our drive across the George Washington Bridge through the Bronx, heading east and north, made us realize how distressed New York's decaying remains of apartment houses and buildings were along the Interstate. People would have to be quite desperate to have to live there. Or perhaps it was deserted, waiting for urban renewal projects to fix the damaged areas.

I-95 quickly turned into green trees surrounding our path near the Long Island Sound and affluent suburbs on a direct line through New London and to the Mystic Seaport Museum, a 19th century town with costumed residents, tall-masted sailing ships, quaint shops, a massive boat repair and building workplace, and a seafood restaurant where Bea ate fresh oysters and I had shrimp. As a sea captain in a former life, Bea was in her element.

Our next destination was to show Bea the awesome Newport, Rhode Island, so we drove close to the shore and crossed more bridges, huge bays, sounds and harbors. We stopped to eat at a colorful little restaurant with signs advertising homemade Portuguese food, which was deliciously rich and filled with an unidentifiable mixture of seafood and veggies. The beer was good too.

Newport, the home of American's Cup, has its own Land's End which we had to reach because we go to the end, as in England, and to the top, as in the World Trade Center's Twin Towers, the Eiffel Tower and more. We stopped and peaked through the giant gates of The Breakers, the opulent home of the Vanderbilts. This and other mansions of American's millionaires didn't appeal to Bea. I'd been through them in 1970 when Marge Manley and Adelle McEwen and I toured here so it didn't matter to me.

We discovered something better when we got into Newport, an in-the-water boat show with the most expensive yachts and sailing vessels for private boat owners this side of Onassis and Monaco.

"That boat even has baggywrinkles," she remarked.

"What's a baggywrinkle?"

"That what they call those fuzzy barrel-shaped balls on the rigging. They keep the lines and the sails from chafing."

"Great. I need to know that word. I'll use it all the time now."

And then she went on to name all the sails, ropes, rigging, spars and other trappings of ships. That left me breathless. I knew she was right when she said she was a sea captain in a previous life, and she could have sailed into her homeport right here.

So we went into a popular nautical bar where the sailing crowd met their friends and we drank rum in Newport with the rest of the rich and famous.

Unlike living next to Lake Michigan, the sweep of the ocean surf, the immense expanse of beaches and the ever-changing tides that I had never felt before flowed into a deeper appreciation of the cycles of the moon and the spirit of the Goddess. Even though we transported ourselves along human-made bridges and highways, we felt closer to a nature of vast power and natural beauty as we circled the edges of Buzzard's Bay on to Cape Cod.

We decided to drive to the Cape's middle to camp at Nickerson State Park and we could then slide up and down along its hook of land dependent only on time and pleasure. As after-Labor-Day weekday campers, we had the park to ourselves and after setting up our gear, we ventured to find some bay or spit of sand along the ocean so we could commune with the sea. We found the spot at an abandoned dock overlooking a cove that led to the ocean. We pulled two beers from our cooler and sat on the edge of the dock to feel the dusky edge of the day where the sky meets the cove's evergreens and the water.

Two men in a small rowboat entered our cove and we watched them maneuver their way to the rocky shore a few feet below us. "Hey," one called out. "Maybe you don't know it, but it's against the law to have alcoholic drinks outside of a tavern."

We waited until they drew closer and answered no as we put down our bottles which now were empty, and we asked permission to take a picture of their catch of the day while the boat passed below us. They had buckets of muscles and their craggy faces broke into smiles as Bea photographed them and they could see that I had picked up the illicit brown bottles and put them in the car.

The weathered boatmen rounded the old dock as we continued sitting, looking out to sea again without any interruption in the scene. Soon one of their bearded faces appeared below us from the waterline of the dock. "We were wondering if you'd consider swapping two beers for a bucket of freshly caught muscles? Do you have a place to cook them?"

"We sure would and we sure do," Bea said as I jumped up to get a couple of cold beers and a container from the car, and Bea bent down to pick up his bucket, empty the muscles into the bag, give him back his well-worn bucket and the beers, and shook his strong, weather-worn hand.

"Thanks! We'll enjoy this at our campsite. By the way, how do we cook these?"

"Just give them a good rinsing and throw them into a covered pot of boiling water," he laughed and said, "You can add some beer too if you like, but you might think you're wasting it. Shake up the pot some for about five minutes until the shells crack open. Then you pull them out of the shell with a fork and dip them in melted butter. There's nothing better and you can't get them any fresher than these.

The other muscleman added, "Don't eat the whiskers though. Pull them off. And thanks for the beer."

After our short drive to camp, we cooked the muscles as they told us to do. We had our before-dinner cocktails and were all aglow with the full day's drive, the salty environment, the generous drinks and the fresh, steamed mussels generously given to us by thirsty Cape Cod Yankees who harvested gifts from Mother Nature's ocean shores.

<<<>>>

I was anxious to get to P-Town, the gay and lesbian East Coast Mecca mixed with straight tourists too. It had its artistic, historical and seafaring influences, but I was on another pilgrimage as we drove past the surprising rows of identical tiny beach houses and into the town I had read about in my culture's magazines. We drove passed famous women-only bed and breakfast accommodations, but I could barely wait to park the car, walk and window-shop and watch the people come and go. Artistic Provincetown actually approved of who you are. It was freedom. Unlike our visit to San Francisco on the night of the Harvey Milk riot, we felt true liberation here as we watched straight and gay couples holding hands and families with children laughing and shopping, sunbathing and playing together.

The playfulness meant openness, a haven for anyone who had felt artistic, creative, political or sexual oppression elsewhere. I savored a favorite sighting of two young women looking across the harbor as they sat, squeezed tightly together between pier timbers with their arms around each other's shoulders and holding hands. We also found a row of old storefront doors wide open with busy shoppers of pornography. The window displays flaunting sexual toys and pictures could have shocked other middle-aged Midwestern lady tourists, but we women of varied experience and curiosity decided to visit our first porno shop, went in with a cosmopolitan air to look around and decided the merchandise did not appeal to us at this time. However, it was educational to check out what strange items and books are available and to know how to find them if you want them.

Of course, all other kinds of shops and galleries welcomed visitors on this beautiful September day, but we decided to sail out to sea on a colorful schooner that beckoned my sailor lover. A jolly bunch of women and men crowded together on deck. I picked up a distinctive sense of humor among the crowd and then recognized the gentle edgy playfulness that we'd experienced with our gay friends at home.

Soon after we left the harbor, we were completely enveloped in fog bank so thick we could barely see the skipper at the wheel. The sails barely moved. Of course, humor prevailed with double-entrendre meanings underscoring the songs we chose to sing and the jokes that entertained us all. While becalmed, we shared the snacks and drinks we all had brought as if we were one family having a party. Thankfully, we didn't have to paddle our oars to sail back to port because a blessed wind came right after a stunning sunset to send us back to port.

As soon as we landed, we headed to line up for a dinner at The Fish Factory, a crowded seafood restaurant on Commercial Street. Our $10 lobster dinner with corn on the cob and salad gave us an authentic taste of what lobster should be. And the warm bread was heavenly after our chilling boat outing in the fog.

We sat close together on a Commercial Street park bench under a leafy autumn tree surrounding an antique streetlight that filtered shadowy filigree upon us as we savored the immediate memory of our lobster feast. We were enjoying the night's harbor view, but we couldn't help but notice women in couples and in groups passing us in an informally happy but urgent parade heading to our right.

After the number of women and their pace to reach their destination grew more intense, we had to find out where they were going and what was going on. Of course! We found the Pied Piper, "The Best Women's Bar in America" according to a *Time* magazine quote on their flyer, which didn't identify which *"Time"* it could be. What else could entice so many to its lair. But what a pleasant lair it was. It was to be the last time Linda Gerard and Diane Marchal would perform together, they said. We were lucky to find a windowsill to lean on because the place was jammed with women eager to be entertained.

Russell Lamb, a female impersonator, opened the show for the comediennes and singing performers who came out on the stage ready to give their hearts to the audience in song and joy. And the women cheered them on into the night. How fortunate we were to have discovered this show by taking a chance and following the throng down an alley just off the beach at 193 Commercial Street.

Bea and I do not often "follow the throng" but we were pleased to have done so this time. We helped them close the show at 1 a.m., walked to our car parked on the outskirts of town, drove back along the two-lane road to our park and into our little pop-up trailer and slept soundly through the night with the glow of being welcomed for being ourselves.

Bea is happy photographing lighthouses, like the one in Chatham, and ships of all types for future paintings; but I considered casually stalking Kennedy sites and other celebrities as we meandered the seashore to Hyannis Port and boarded the ferry to Martha's Vineyard. Though we didn't go out of our way to find the Kennedy compound because Bea was driving and I was too cool to admit to being curious about their clan.

We passed smart shops and expensive-looking sidewalk cafes on the way to the ferry. I knew this wasn't my style. But when we joined the mix of Martha's Vineyard passengers on the ferry, we felt at home among the rich, the travelers and summer trekkers. Seagulls immediately aimed their hard and sharp beaks at those passengers who knew to bring bread and snacks for them. Not being a bird fancier, I stayed back while Bea took photos of people feeding these feathered dive bombers. No one was even nicked by their sharp and pointy beaks.

As day tourists, we felt at home as soon as we landed. The weathered houses with huge porches suggested an historic welcoming atmosphere and the shops' merchandise ranged from the chic to the cheap. Each of us rented a bright yellow moped, a brilliance that would warn other travelers that we were inexperienced moped tourists. On this island, I didn't have to be Bea's passenger as I was in the Bahamas; I could control my own fate as we meandered about the island with sandy roadside lanes and beaches. The bridges we crossed had no railings; they seemed to hop up and over the waters below. I couldn't avoid remembering the Ted

Kennedy/Mary Jo Kopechne tragedy at Edgartown and Chappaquiddick, and the other deaths that the Kennedy family—and our country—experienced with their losses. But I kept those thoughts of their grief to myself, thoughts of their epic saga of sadness and loss that even happens to the high and the mighty. Who needs a morbid travel companion?

Before we left, I actually bought a Martha's Vineyard T-shirt. Not too many people I know have been here, and I'm proud of being one who has. I cherish the idea of living on an island and would love to return sometime when I can experience staying in the antique white houses during the non-tourist season, become friends with those who live here year 'round, and perhaps find writers and other creative friends who make this their home.

Of course, we always keep Bea's big red boat cooler in the car with us, and it's usually filled with snacks, ice, beer and cocktail fixings. After returning on the ferry, we found the last of our day's supply of ice had kept a few beers cold for us, but we needed to stop for supplies on our way back to our campsite.

When we bought ice and assorted cheeses and cold meats—and more beer and cocktail mixers, we discovered a glass tank full of fresh lobsters crawling over each other. Each had one claw clamped with a rubber band. As we watched, we imagined how much we'd enjoy eating lobster again before we left Cape Cod. Why not buy fresh ones and cook one on our camp stove like we did our divine fresh mussels supper.

"Okay!" Bea questioned. "If we buy one now, how are we going to get it back to camp?"

"We need to get ice. We'll keep it in the cooler?"

"Do you know how to cook one?"

"Here's a recipe we can follow."

"But we have to put it in boiling water while it's still alive."

"We can manage that after our cocktail time—while the water's boiling."

"I heard that lobsters scream when they hit the water."

"I would too, wouldn't you?"

"Well, let's give it a try."

So we bought a half-dozen ears of corn and a big pink lobster. The tolerant, patient and friendly butcher who helped us pick out a female, two-and-a-half pounder, also gave us some cooking advice. "Females are more tender," he advised, and he explained us how to spill her out from her bag into the cooler and where to grab her when it was time for the boil. Before he gave her to us, he grabbed her and showed us how fresh she was by stretching out her tail and how quickly she snapped it back. "That's what I would do too under similar circumstances," whispered Bea. Then he rinsed her claws and body in the sink behind him.

While I drove back, Bea reached into the cooler and had to use devious hand maneuvers to distract the lobster long enough so she could pull out a beer. "Sheesh! I never thought I'd have to fend off a lobster to get a beer!" But undeterred, she pulled a beer out from the ice without getting attacked or having the lobster escape her confines.

Our campsite was fragrant with pitch pine and spruce that blended with the snappy, fresh aroma of an icy, dry martini—or two. The simmering pot began to boil on the Coleman camp stove on our picnic table, and we cooked our half-cobs of fresh corn in the salted water.

Then we had to decide who would drown our lobster in boiling water.

"You do it, Jan. I want to cover my ears in case she screams. I almost feel like a cannibal—and I wish he hadn't told us she was a female."

Armed with a long fork in one hand, I turned up the fire to make a rolling boil. "Bubble. Bubble. Toil and trouble, " I cackled as I grabbed her by her back with my free hand and thrust her into the cauldron using my fork. No screaming! Thankfully, there was no screaming. And after simmering for about ten minutes, I reached in with my kitchen tools to remove the blazing red and steaming hot critter and set her whole, lying on her back in the middle of the table, ready to be torn apart with shells flying, her tender morsels dipped in butter by guiltless, ravenous savages. We even broke off her legs and with slurping noises, sensuously sucked out their contents.

Naturally, we were covered with melted butter, corn nibbles and major whiffs of lobster essence when we were finished feasting under the starry night, free from city lights. After a quick stashing away of cooking gear, except for the wine, we grabbed our beach towels and teetered together to the slightly warm showers to bathe and rinse ourselves in the deserted campground. We dried and wrapped each other's nakedness with our towels, walked up the path, grabbed the rest of the wine and entered our canvas shelter to savor each other—like gourmet cannibals—until we, now fully satiated, surrendered to sleep.

Casually, we packed up our gear to meander through more of Cape Cod heading for Boston. I was confident about driving because I'd been there three times: once in 1942 with my father taking me on trains to Washington, D.C., New York City, Boston and Niagara Falls; then on a similar route with my husband in 1953 where his Armenian relatives in Boston escorted us on a grand tour through Concord and Lexington, Harvard museums and Boston when the highest building was stubby compared to today's massive, fifty-two story Prudential Tower. Adelle McEwen, Marge Manley and I drove here and New York City in 1970 to see if Adelle's daughter was okay living in Boston. Now I'm driving about New England with my lover.

We planned to follow the Interstate through Boston and camp north and close enough to find tomorrow after a full day in Boston. Yet while driving on the edge of Cape Cod Bay, we found the old Brewster Mill that still grinds corn, mostly for us tourists, but it was a green, peaceful place of history, built in 1663, and I cherished the sound of the rippling stream powering a creaky old grinding stones turning since before the Revolutionary War. Lush willows and flowering bushes line the pond with lucky ducks making it their home.

Of course, we had to stop at Plymouth and visit the Mayflower II, a reproduction of the original boat with people in costume telling us about the 1620 voyage and their first winter in the New World. We took our time and wandered about historic Plymouth sites. The area had a charming but haunting atmosphere that made me appreciate what these forebears endured to settle in this northern, harsh climate.

Early the next morning we headed toward the heart of Boston and parked our car as soon as we could in underground parking beneath the Boston Common. We emerged from the giant underground lot to be almost standing at Boston's Visitors Center where we picked out our map of the of the Freedom Trail, and we set off to walk each step of the almost three-mile trail, conscientiously entering every significant historical site, especially King's Chapel, which became a Unitarian church after the Revolution.

And I have a thing about those old graveyards and their primitive winged angel heads, the weatherworn inscriptions and the amazing tipsy slants of those tombstones surviving time and the elements.

In contrast to the old, we skirted around the cautionary barriers around the contemporary John Hancock Tower where glass was known to drop from its sky-scrapper windows from time to time. And as usual, we had to go to the top Skywalk Observatory at the Prudential Center where we could look down across the Charles River with small sailboats and rowing skiffs from today to the pre-Revolutionary era sites—all in the same vista. We also looked at The Commons and realized how far we intrepid travelers had walked—and we had still more walking to do before we were to reclaim our car and drive north out of Boston.

The renovated Quincy and Faneuil Hall Marketplace recaptured the 18th century era with its playful zest overflowing today with many languages, especially Italian, produce stands and restaurants, including an indoor deli food feast where we munched our way along on a variety of seafood and international delicacies. We enjoyed the sunny, fall day watching street performers, costumed Revolutionary War characters, and lots of street people, including us tourists.

We had talked about visiting our UU Vatican at 25 Beacon Street and traveling to Concord, Walden Pond and Lexington, but I'd been there before and I knew Bea would not be interested in my lecturing her about our UU authors: Ralph Waldo Emerson, Henry David Thoreau, Louisa May Alcott, and one of my favorite women in history and perhaps our earliest feminist, Margaret Fuller. I was right; Bea wasn't interested.

We took a chance and bought theater tickets to *Shear Madness*, a new mystery comedy in the basement of the larger Charles Playhouse. It truly was shear madness with spontaneous, fast-action laughs in an intimate setting—a hair salon. We sat close to the action on chairs at tables and with an open bar so we could buy drinks to enjoy during the performance. It may be the first play I can recall seeing where there's a lead gay character, the hairdresser of course. The audience voting on "who done it" determined the play's ending, which could be one of three different alternatives that the actors play out to the finish. We made a smart move by selecting this uniquely audience-involving production that is showing only in Boston.

Fortunately, the theater wasn't too far from our parked car because we were exhausted, but we made it back to our little gypsy camper in dry, clear and comfortably warm weather.

Bea was focused on reaching Gloucester where so many of the sea stories she's read have honored "They that go down to the sea in ships." This was etched in the town's Fishermen's Memorial monument, including the names of 10,000 Gloucester fishermen etched in the town hall wall. These men were lost at sea over the three hundred years since the founding of the seaport.

I took her picture, as is our custom with her at many ships' wheels, but this time she stood outside beside the ship's captain in rain gear wresting his ship's wheel steering his boat through the storms to bring home the crew and their catch for all to enjoy since the 1630s.

And did we ever enjoy the savory and tender fried clams at the harbor's dockside after we meandered through the docks where fishermen pulled their catches off the boats. We rested on the porch of a sailmaker's store absorbing the salty fishing smells from the ocean while watching a young woman sitting cross-legged on the lawn surrounded by yards of canvas as she stitched custom sail rigging by hand.

We drove a bit farther and ate supper dockside in Rockport, the famous artists' colony, on Cape Ann but we both decided that Wisconsin's Door County was as engaging and significant except for one major difference; here we ate our supper of seafood gumbo from the Atlantic Ocean rather than a fish boil dinner from Lake Michigan.

While Bea started driving west toward home, I spotted small red letters on the map while I negotiated our way to find the nearest Interstate heading for Niagara Falls. The tiniest print read "America's Stonehenge' and when I said it out loud, Bea pulled over and we decided to change our course a few miles into New Hampshire. How could we not go out of our way to discover a prehistoric site in our own country, one with the same name as that of our premier pagan pilgrimage of spiritual significance for us—Stonehenge.

If it had kept its name of Mystery Hill Caves until this year, we may have ignored the site all together. There are mystery places around in many states, but this seemed to be a prehistoric archaeological site that created questions in our imagination. We explored cave-like structures on thirty acres of land and were able to crawl around inside of many of them. Sacrificial altars with ridges carved in the tops to catch the blood sparked another conjecture from Bea who's read so many books on Celtic and Mayan formations similar to this and she put down the concept of human sacrifice because the culture was matriarchal and mothers would not have fostered human bloodletting.

Bea informed me of her theories of the Vikings coming here decades before Columbus in the Caribbean, John Smith in Virginia and the Pilgrims in Provincetown and Plymouth. Maybe descendants of the original Stonehenge builders came to America? What part could the American Indians have played in this site? But why had they come so far west from the ocean? We sought out the caves and stone forms more primitive than Stonehenge, but they too were astronomically aligned rock formations that captured the winter solstice. To prove this at home, we bought slides of the stone marking the winter solstice at the park's gift shop. We even watched archeologists dusting and sifting for more evidence to find answers of the history of the site.

I was mesmerized by the strange series of stones and cave dwellings. I could get into the concept of past lives as we freed our imaginations to absorb how these people lived. I saw ashes from a campfire in the distance and felt in my soul that I had been a woman potter in a previous life, an artist who created valuable bowls to serve and nourish my tribe. We were thrilled at finding this and being astute enough to enjoy it thoroughly.

We branched our way across Massachusetts through tollways and turnpikes, passing beautiful vistas and historic names, but we had to drive on while promising ourselves we'd return someday to explore this area. I would read from our guidebook the stories about what we were passing as that and the Interstate 90 helped make the miles fly by through New York towards Rochester and Niagara Falls. We decided to camp before Syracuse but not before I found a note in our

AAA Triptych that described a boat ride on the Erie Canal. We turned into our campsite and asked the manager about the ride.

"If you hurry up this road about ten miles, you can make the last ride at the little Erie Canal village that they're building as a museum."

We secured our camping space and jumped back in the car with dust flying to reach the little dock just before it was ready to head back east again for the last ride of the day. Another boating adventure found us on a completely different ride: being towed along the original Erie Canal by a mule tied to a rope. "I've gotta gal and her name is Sal/Fifteen miles on the Erie Canal."

The magic of the ride was envisioning how important this unique transportation was to the people of its era. It connected the Great Lakes to the Hudson River at Albany and then to the Atlantic Ocean. And it was dug out with immigrant labor through the entire state of New York. What an accomplishment. The tour guides were in costumes and told us stories as we slowly mule-powered our way through the narrow canal and back to the few homes and stores newly built to recapture those days.

Now, the St. Lawrence Seaway and the massive highway systems have not only made the Erie Canal archaic, but they're making railways almost obsolete as well.

"Failure is impossible," said Susan B. Anthony years ago and we follow in her footsteps in Rochester, New York as well as in our lives. We found her home, now a museum, at 17 Madison Street. I was disappointed that it was closed when we found it, but I posed for Bea to take my photo sitting on her freshly painted green front porch of her house, a rich contrast that was perfect for the auburn-colored tree-lined street.

And then we search for *The Feminist Review* and *The New Women's Times* that comes to our store for distribution. *The Review* comes to our store for free distribution and "provides an outlet for women to review women's work in an atmosphere of intelligence and respect," as quoted from the supplement to *The New Women's Times*, a bi-weekly from Susan B's hometown. *The Review* is published in cooperation with the New York City chapter of The Feminist Writers Guild, which we have attended in Milwaukee.

Though they send free samples to Mother Courage, they hope women subscribe for "only $10 a year" and they define feminism "based on a person's self-definition. They aren't going to presume to define it for you."

But when we arrived at the cluttered office, most of the feminist writers in the room looked like strong lesbians. We were greeted by a woman who showed us around the offices. Tables piled high with back issues. We didn't stay long because everyone looked as if they were meeting deadlines, but I was proud to have Mother Courage connect with these dedicated women.

I'm sure they don't make any money on their feminist endeavors either.

On the way to Niagara Falls, Bea entertained me with stories about someone I knew nothing about—Nikola Tesla, and she surely knew a lot about him. Her family had made a Tesla coil and she told me how it worked. Once when their bored family was all dressed up to go somewhere and they had to wait for her husband to get home from work, she involved them in experimenting with the Tesla coil that they had made. She asked her four children what would happen if they all held hands in a circle and each one next to the Tesla coil would touch it at the same time and complete the circle. Of course they did it, following their mother's scientific bent and curiosity. Standing in the circle, holding their breaths, those two closest to the coil finally put their finger on its power source. "Zap! Surprise! Good thing the device was weak or Jack would have finally come home to find his wife and children electrocuted."

Tesla came from Eastern Europe and was hired by Edison to do simple electrical engineering jobs and ended up redesigning Edison's inefficient equipment and wanted the company to change to direct current generators.

Edison and Westinghouse were into what we have today, alternating currents. That's where "AC/DC" comes from. He gave the Edison company profitable patents in the process. He even dug ditches for the Edison Company for a while and died penniless as a result.

Edison never wanted to hear about Tesla's AC designs. He was convinced that DC electricity was the future.

Tesla continued inventing devices for power and for electrotherapy, light systems, radio and using magnetic fields. His work would have benefited the world, but he lost out to the corporations who invested in Edison and his methods.

So it goes.

Before we knew it, we were at the edge of Niagara Falls, ready to park the car and make believe we could act as if we were honeymooners. But this wasn't Provincetown.

We had time only for an attraction or two, and we decided to take the Cave of the Winds trip below the Bridal Veil Falls, about as close as we could be to the water and to anything resembling a honeymoon.

We rode an elevator one hundred and seventy-five feet deep into the Niagara Gorge and donned bright yellow ponchos and special boots so we wouldn't slip and fall. Rock falls have altered the history of this passageway, but only fate would make that happen to us as we crossed over and climbed a series of wooden walkways to the Hurricane Deck.

Bea and I stood at the railing of the Hurricane Deck with the other tourists. We were about twenty feet from the torrents of Bridal Veil Falls and were doused with spray lashed by winds, but I didn't want to leave. Bea retreated to take some photos, but I was the last to let go of railings at the corner of the Hurricane deck because I experienced being in the center of a 360-degree rainbow. The sun blessed me at just the perfect time of day by giving me this gift and I didn't want it to stop. I heard Bea over the deafening roar hollering to me that the tour guide wanted me to come down. The rushing waters came down from above me, smashing on the rocks just below me, and I was surrounded by a perfect, complete rainbow! How can I not stay as long as possible.

I was high on something when I reluctantly turned to join the rest and take the elevator to the surface. My insides glowed in spirit as much as my red face. I tumbled out of the crowd with Bea following me, laughing together. I felt like a youngster with a natural high.

"Your hair is red," exclaimed Bea. "I have to take your picture!"

"That's how I feel all over, happy and full of energy." I gave her a huge hug and danced around her. Then I realized that we were standing directly in front of Nikola Tesla's statue. He was sitting with a folio of plans across his knees, but he was staring at me.

"Bea. Look who's here? How come you know so much about him and then tell me all those stories just as we become involved in this atmosphere? In this electrically charged atmosphere? Bea, you are magical."

"But Jan, it's you that is electrifying—and I love you."

"Thank the Goddess!" I cried. Yes, I actually cried—for the sheer joy of experiencing euphoria.

Cutting through Ontario north of Lake Erie, we made our way to the Detroit area as fast as we could go, then through Michigan. We decided to stop at a motel so we could spend a few hours seeing the Indiana Dune's lakeshore. That way we could get an early start to get through Chicago and make the last lap to our home after so many adventures.

The dunes were better than we had thought because we enjoyed not only the vast shoreline of smooth sand and sloping hills, but we watched so many hang-gliders take off from the thatch-topped dune and catch the wind moving a different sort of sail. It would take a lot of faith on my part to step into the air with only canvas to keep me from falling, but what a thrill it would be to know how to be so free.

This vast beach and lake, unlike those on the Atlantic coast, had no ebb and flow of tides to consider. No mussels, crabs, lobsters. I had never considered the effects of the tides before—and the pull of the moon—except for its pull on me and my spirit, our spirituality, our natural connections to the water, earth, air and fire.

If I am like the air and water, what is Bea? Earth and fire? We differ in the way we view our experiences. That's especially obvious after traveling together, the two of us for these two weeks. She must be fire for she sparks our lives with her intellect, her awesome ability to recall facts and teach them to me. She is also earth in her passion and her humor and, to me she is the air that I breathe, for without it I feel that I would expire. Ah yes, we are both and all to each other.

We've returned to live on our country's Middle Coast without the ocean's physical tides, yet we have forces that pull and push us in our moods, our energies, our priorities, and our emotions. Hopefully, even prayerfully, we'll flow with the motion of calm waters, yet we need the earth to ground us, the air to breathe new life and keep us alert and happy, and fire to warm us with our continued courage to love.

Chapter 14

Jan on October 4, 1982

Bea gained a granddaughter today, her second grandchild from her second offspring. We hope and even pray that they make good parents for her grandchildren.

And thinking of close relatives and friends, or ex-relatives and friends, Alex has been out of work for a while. He left his draining but successful career with relief, and I'm sure a handsome settlement, after incredibly long hours launching the computer and merging it into the company's system, traveling back and forth to Detroit and trouble-shooting computer problems for the company around the country. Still he found energy to take Marge and himself to Australia during the summer, supposedly to look for a job there. That would give him a tax-break on the expenses, and if he found a job there, he'd surely live far enough away from me to please him. Now I hear he'll be working for the State of Nevada—not as far away as the southern hemisphere but I guess he's far away enough to start a new life without having to live in his shadow of me and my lover's visibility.

He'll probably sell our house overlooking Lake Michigan, and Jenny will have to find another place to live. I wonder what he'll do with our Door County property? I haven't had time to bother him about going up there this year. Maybe he'll cool off about the visitation restrictions he put on me. Maybe I can help take care of the property. Meanwhile Jenny must make a lot of decisions about her future. I hope she and Matt don't plan to move out west with him.

Jan on November 1, 1982

Chuck McCarthy, Randy's clone, is now in charge of implementing a hospital-wide Quality Circles program, the latest employee motivational trend started in Japan. I wonder how that will work when our employees operate in quality circles now—without a campaign.

I met with Randy and Chuck to present the results of my survey that was brewing among the other administrators while I was gone. They sat questioning almost every detail. Don't they have anything else to do? How can I accomplish what is needed when I must defend myself, even when their peers' responses are affirming what our department is doing for them all.

One of my administrative confidants and I consoled each other when she handed me her response to my PR survey. She too is being demeaned in front of the other administrators at their weekly meetings. "They want me to get rid of staff and hire new, cheaper people when the science of hospital care needs more experience and skills than ever before. I never thought," she confided, "that I would see such hostility in our meetings. Administrators are fighting harder to defend themselves than they are in solving the problems we have. And it's so humbling to watch adult professional men and women belittled, especially when they all have given so much of themselves for this hospital. Jan, this place lost its humanity. We used to have compassion for one another. And now they expect us to do these damn Quality Circles when in fact we've had them all along."

And we talked each other down from our mutual frustrations, hoping we'd stay healthy and strong so our co-workers and teammates wouldn't have to suffer along with us.

They've fired some staff, yet I'm still there and can help others get through this, or at least set a pattern to survive. I'm not responsible for decisions made around me and now I'm making enough money so I should stop hurting myself by being angry that I'm not making more, and when I consider all of the wonderful, supportive people there, that's an invaluable treasure.

On Monday I worked on a story on hospital costs relating to Lakeshore Med. Randy and Chuck completely rewrote the media release after everyone in fiscal administration had approved it. Now Randy approves everything I send out so I took it to him, who read it with Chuck standing over his shoulder. I looked at them and thought, "Randy is trying to show Chuck how to be an asshole." This time I didn't take their nit-picking personally. It's their problem.

I endured the put-down of their rewriting the entire article and went back in my busy, noisy office, rewrote the article according to Randy and Chuck, then checked it out with our finance administrator.

"Why hasn't this been sent? How come it's taken so long?" he asked.

"It was waiting for Randy's approval."

He snickered a bit—and he's not a laughing person. He looks like Gonzo on *Sesame Street* and shows no sense of humor, but I felt his subtle acknowledgment.

"I won't put my name on it if this goes through," he said, so we rewrote what was changed.

"Well, I don't blame you for wanting your version back," I told him, "but would you please phone Randy and tell him that *you* want to return the release to our original version?"

Jan on November 3, 1982

It's fortunate that I was able to go to the 8th annual Woman to Woman conference at MECCA in Milwaukee. MECCA was jammed with several thousand women. In my evaluation, I wrote that there should be workshops for and/or about lesbians and their issues if it's to be a true Woman to Woman conference. I wonder what they'll do about that for next year.

Because of the inspiration I gained from motivational speakers like Patricia Durovy and those at various workshops, I've set some new goals: I'm caring for people—and myself; feeling responsibility toward them but not rescuing them.

But Randy King must not destroy me. I'm not being responsible for solving all problems. And Randy King cannot be changed.

Because of Woman to Woman, I took out my Ira Progoff Intensive Journaling workshop ring binder and books. I haven't gone there since the end of 1977 and I have some energy to revisit it now.

Dialogue Dimension: Special Personal Sections—Dialogue with Society: How am I really feeling?

The first pen I grasp for after so long is my Mother Courage pen. It is dry.

> I want to write how I'm feeling. Time wasted. Time at rest. Time grating against me as it passes by.
> Reaching for a second ordinary pen and scratching blank cracks on the brittle paper, I find that one empty too.
> I didn't throw the Mother Courage pen away. I have hope for it. The Bic hit the wastebasket. Who cares about it, poor ordinary thing.
> How am I really feeling?
> Frustrated. Tired. Wasted. Burnt out. But I'm not helpless about my own resources, not wasted in the long view of the seasons.
> I have dreams. But the dreams that I have are thorns and nettles to the person that I want to share them with.
> I have energy, and the energy that I have to offer is wasted in waiting, in watching for the 'right time,' in being considerate, in being 'practical.'
> Isn't it like a woman to write about feelings when the power around her measures in dollars, census, and surveys.
> Do feelings count?

Only by the light of the moon, full moon, when defenses are down and primal pulling of my senses breaks apart the pragmatic values of numbered results.

Do my feelings count?

Every day is quite a struggle—and those days that are less than "quite" are apparently free. I have an income. I eat, drink and live quite sensuously. My Bea, who has the wealth of all creative intelligence, cooks and shops for me; minds our checkbooks; pays our bills and works hard to be the a "Total Woman" for me—as much as food and drink is vital to my life.

She is frustrated. Feeling negative. She's rejected again in her dream of owning a successful bookstore. And when I share my frustrations of her life and mine, she assumes that my feelings are a rejection of her.

Better to say nothing?

I'm as much a part of our fear of failure, of rejection, of endless work, of the future.

I work hard but the end results of that work are discounted or criticized by my employer and by my partner.

I often feel lonely because my work is not acknowledged nor shared at home, and what I cherish, my life, my love, is not truly shared at work.

I feel vulnerable because it seems that whatever I do is either not good enough at work or is the object of competition and/or jealousy at home.

I feel tired now again. It's been a rough and intense day. I've had vibrating conflict and wasted energy at work. More problems than solutions.

I cleaned soot and shit, other people's shit and soot, out of a basement at our property. I helped my maintenance friend clean up a garbage-filled kitchen drain. I unstopped a toilet. I aired up a tire on my rusty Toyota that is symbolic of my diminishing resources.

I reached some resolution with my daughter after an emotion-filled conversation after her father left this place—his roots—her roots, our home that used to be—to live in Nevada.

The two of us seldom exchange our true feelings, but Bea forced us to confront our past and present anxieties in our mother-daughter lives. I hated to see Jenny cry and I hated to give in to my own tears while Bea scolded Jenny for her supposed indifference and neglect of her mother. Bea brought up some truths, but I never would have confronted her kids for their lack of supporting her. And I didn't want to argue with either of them, especially argue in front of each other. Bea may have been projecting some her own motherly feelings onto us, but I didn't argue with either of them.

All will be better with time. Jenny will understand as I now understand my father's life—after he has died.

And Bea confronts me with her hopelessness of her wasted genius—so afraid of rejection and compromise—and yet she challenges me to create again and to write again despite the obstacles that confront me. Her challenge seems hollow, an excuse for her wasting her creative time. What if I write my story and it is successful? It could destroy our life together.

I hope I have the strength to fulfill my goals, and I hope our lives have the strength to survive together if I should achieve any goals of my own—without her? —in spite of her? —hopefully with her and —with her, balanced and sensible.

Jan on November 5, 1982
Dialogue Dimension: Special Personal Sections—
Dialogue with Society

At first I thought tonight, "Society can go fuck itself!" And then I put myself in league with those criminals and politicians who say that same thing. And that's not where I want to be.

Society as it exists now—until this present day and somewhere in the future—will grow beyond its restraints if persons who have the courage to be different because of selflessness or because of love take the chance and challenge it.

I didn't want to challenge "society." I only wanted what I needed. And that need was to love someone who would return that love to me in the same context, in the same understanding, in the same freedom and acceptance of true love.

I'm so tired now. Living always on the edge, surviving the life's ambiguities, waiting to be cut down and chopped up by reality, by power abused and misused. I am so tired.

I thank the Goddess for leading me to journaling again. It's a safer way of blowing off emotions rather than confronting them with those that cause the hurt.

Stop whining, Jan, and get to back to work—or preferably get back to play.

Bea on December 15, 1982

Jan's took some time off early this month to rest up from all the constant stress at work plus the pressure from administrators for cost cuts goals and something she calls the TEFRA regulation that will eliminate $1.3 million from this year's hospital's budget. Of course, Jan or Carolyn have not been given their cost-of-living pay raises this year—and who knows when in the future.

She's been organizing photos and papers from her past and present—evidence for the future, spending hours filing and sorting. I wonder what she'll end up doing with it all? Perhaps she's preparing to sue Lakeshore Medical Center's administration for job discrimination, but she went to the Federal office of equal opportunity or something like that, and 9-to-5, a working women's help network, they told her she's in such a unique job without a union and few other examples to defend her case in court.

The famous feminist attorney Mandy Stellman told her to call her again when she has all her evidence together, but she didn't give her any hope for justice. Jan's got enough to write a book. That's a problem. There's too much.

She is going to two interviews in Milwaukee next week—on speculation. She decided after cleaning out her closets and trying on skirts, she'd have to wear her one of her pants suits to her interviews because, she said, she looks and feels terrible in a skirt. She heard that her HPRW friend at Children's Hospital is leaving and a Children's vice president and a former TV executive recommended Jan to for an interview. They'll have some other VPs meet with her next week.

She's been doing a lot of homework, trying to enter a field other than healthcare and will actually interview with the director of the Milwaukee Repertory Theatre because the same PR friend recommended Jan to her. And then she'll be interviewing for a prestigious PR agency, Bankman, Sherman and somebody. I know she's under a lot of stress about this, and she'll prove to them that she can shift into other PR areas.

Jan on December 23, 1982

After responding to invitations for job interviews in Milwaukee, I arranged to meet the administrator from St. Catherine's Hospital next to breweries, expressways and in the concrete inner city with a line of homeless people waiting to be given care, food or shelter. A humanistic guy, he appealed to the missionary fervor in my soul. Those jobs may pay more and they intrigue me, but I'll be careful if the positions are offered to me and will evaluate their plusses and minuses, which may be significant.

My retired Lakeshore Med's administrator, Clark Young, said he would be "honored" to be a reference person for me and he gave me good counsel on the problems of these two Milwaukee hospitals. Children's is politically motivated to move west to the Midwest Regional Medical Center on Milwaukee County grounds (wherever that is) and close to the Midwest Medical College. Mr. Young warned me that St. Catherine may not survive much longer. It's hard to attract regular patients when it serves so many poor people without insurance coverage, especially now with discounted hospital reimbursement costs for Medicare and Medicaid patients.

If nothing happens, at least I will have given my career potential a shot in the arm, and reviewing what other hospitals are about will help me judge the merit of my Lakeshore Med's environment.

Wouldn't it be great if I could meet with Randy and Nick and tell them that I have two job offers waiting for me and I will earn considerably more money and finally gain career and salary equity with my PR peers.

"Profiles-Winning Strategy" Speaking of careers, Anne Gregor, a UW business major, interviewed me for their *Women in Business* newsletter.

Jan Anthony is one of those lucky people who, when asked what she considers her greatest accomplishment, answers, "Just being here, doing a job I love." Jan is Director of Communications at Lakeshore Medical Center in Lakeshore Bay She is responsible for the hospital's internal and external communication but considers 'setting up a positive environment within the hospital and creating a positive image of the hospital are her major goals.

How are these goals achieved? "Synergy is the use of two or more elements working together to create a better product or result than any one of the elements separately, is the buzzword in her office." This feeling is reinforced by the title in their self-produced hospital publication, *synergy*.

Jan feels it's important to seek different perspectives. "Do not always look for similarity or agreement, look for stimulation."

When asked what advice she has for perspective women in business, Jan responded:

- Create your own network. Make contacts now.
- Don't be self-contained. Synergize.
- Ask for help when needed. Respond with appreciation.
- Become active in professional organizations.

204

- Whatever you do is reflected upon you and leaves a lasting impression on other people. You must be positive in your outlook and in your communication with other people.

If asked what my lasting impression is of Jan Anthony, I would say that here is a woman who is extremely talented, loves her job and the responsibilities that go with it, and has made a commitment to doing it well.

Therein lies the winning strategy.

Bea on December 23, 1982

Jan invited her mother's oldest sister, Aunt Ora, and her husband, Herman, over for supper. We had bumped into the eighty-plus seniors while we were out for a meal that happened to be at Ora and Herman's favorite supper club hangout. They hold court there and supposedly entertain people who think they're cute and buy them drinks. Sometimes people have to help walk them the few blocks to their little home.

Except for our kids, spouses and children, my ex- and Jan's father, none of our older relatives have been in our home. Jan hasn't connected with any relatives unless they were admitted to her hospital. Then they tell nurses to find her, as if they'd be cared for any better by being a member of Jan's family.

It was intense for Jan having them for drinks, of course, and supper, but Jan felt she needed to touch base. I was simply bored. That was after supper and a few more brandies when old Herman barked, "Isn't there a man living in this house?" That's when the indignant elders decided to leave and Jan had to drive them home.

That took her mind off the fact that she didn't land the Children's Hospital PR job. They hired a man. And the other job fell through too. The big bucks will be missed, but the extra stress and mileage will not be. Both administrators said she could have done the job, but they found someone in the area with more contacts. That was the only difference.

Jan on December 23, 1982

After a leisurely Sunday morning which included a lazy interlude after a shower together, then sheer decadence and delight, we indulged in being together in bed for hours. With my long days at work, it's been awhile since we've enjoyed each other so much.

During the quiet Solstice-darkening afternoon cocktail time arranging my table full of photos and stories, I looked up to see Bea looking at me. I searched through my stack of poems, and found this one from April 9, 1974, and read it to her.

> Mother Earth's eyes enfold me
> in their natural, nurturing beauty.
> And I, as Nature's own,
> creep along the stamen
> to sample the sweet goodness
> of the lush flower
> to unearth the secrets
> of its great power.

Chapter 15

Bea on December 26, 1982

Sharon and Marian have acquired a new family member after the last of their three golden retrievers, all named Bear, died. The first two dogs died of cancer, the last of eating pantyhose that twisted around in his digestive tract. Each of those deaths brought grief, but before that those big dogs brought lots of affection and fun, including the one Bear who had a special thing for me. When I'd sit on their sofa, he'd creep up on the back of the sofa behind me and wrap himself around my shoulders. I felt like a fur-clad dowager from my mother's fashionable days when she wore fox stoles that had its wearer fasten the dead critter's mouth to its tail.

After they bought a smaller dog, a Westie named Maxwell, they decided to get a parakeet. Sharon, as usual, went all out to train the little bird. Sharon would warble her voice up into the shrill nasal tones and repeat sweet words over and over until Merlin caught on to repeat one or two words back to her. Sharon whistled, made puckering noises and taught Merlin tricks that entertained us, even though Jan's a bit phobic about birds flying free in the house. They were told that the bird was a male when they bought it, the cage, all the fixings and toys.
Then Merlin laid an egg and became a female.
Their cat didn't bother Merlin because Sharon and Marian put the cage in a closed room when they left home and were watchful when Merlin was on the floor playing on her teeter-totter and many other little iddy-bitty toys.

Of course, Jan would sneeze from cat dander, but then she'd take an allergy pill and another glass of wine. No wonder her eyes were glazed and her nose looked red when they took pictures of us at one of the many times they fed and entertained us. This year they took our picture next to the Christmas tree that Sharon decorated with her passionate artistry and attention to aesthetically placing every light, garland and ornament.

Jan likes to make little crafty Christmas gifts to give to friends and family, and even some pets, and she went to Nelson's Variety Store to buy her supplies for Sharon and Marian's Merlin. She gathered the fixings to decorate a tiny Christmas tree for Merlin's birdcage. (Marian also makes creative and rainbow-colorful whimsical jewelry, boxes, picture frames and more, but she's a true artist.)

We exchanged our gifts before we ate another delicious gourmet and well-presented dinner in their home, and they treasured Merlin's Christmas tree that Jan had decorated and wrapped so extravagantly. Sharon carefully approached Merlin's cage and in baby-like, cooing words, she told Merlin not to be afraid of this trimmed little Christmas tree. She opened the cage to move the other bird toys around the bottom of the cage and placed the festive mini-tree in a safe cage corner so Merlin had plenty of space to move away from it in case the bird became fearful of this new object. We women went to share our holiday meal with our closest adopted-sister friends.

We lit candles and celebrated together. A Milwaukee friend had sent us a Yule winter solstice card and Jan read the card for our feast celebration.

> Help me coax the sun's return
> Light our candles all to burn
> As the days are growing longer
> Women's lives are growing stronger.

We raised our joined hands over our heads shouting together, "All Right!" What a feast we ate and what a pleasant conversation we had, but when we returned to the living room, I glanced into Merlin's cage and called the others to come and look! We were shocked to see that Merlin had arranged all her toys to fit under the Christmas tree. I wouldn't have been more surprised if Merlin had mimicked Sharon singing "Jingle Bells," and we all joined in.

Bea on December 26, 1982

In looking back for this year's artistic accomplishments, I haven't painted many canvasses but I built Jan the bed board cabinets that she wanted with a slanting back panel to hold us and our pillows that opens to store travel books, magazines and flyers. The long top board also covers the two sided cabinets for our reading lamps, beverage glasses, clocks, a radio and more books. The items stored below in the cabinets also hold books on the shelves, but primarily they served to keep our various bedtime toys behind the closed cabinet doors. We painted it white to blend with the walls, and I built it to fit under our double southern windows on our top floor. The windows can be open all summer long to mix with cross breezes from the open windows on the east—breezes that drift across our bare bodies.

I also created an Irish harp, which subsequently came unglued. So far our bed has held together and has not come unglued or unscrewed despite many nights of vigorous coupling.

I've also written "I Am Trying to Say That I Love You" song to use with my idea to compose a musical play about warehousing the aged. I roughed out the plot for *Senior Citizen* and completed four songs with more ideas coming all the time, many of them comical.

All my children are married, but one is getting divorced already. I have two grandchildren to add to my family worries that I try to suppress.

And it's snowing like hell again!

Our moon group is well organized and it has been spiritually rewarding—and fun too. Jan claims it's successful because I'm taking time to plan the rituals. But it's trust that makes our circle sacred. It's the awareness that our bodies are sacred, more so in our circle than in traditional religious church sacraments that males stole from us women centuries ago. We had historic and internal power and now we're taking it back. Our bonding with our women in family and as friends is positive. Our outer selves look inward to appreciate our value; the supernatural becomes natural and awesome again.

It's a good thing I've been studying and writing for years about Stonehenge and parapsychology and the esoteric subjects that have always appealed to me. The subject of Stonehenge brought Jan and me together years ago when we were UU Sunday school teachers who became friends then—and lovers now.

I always invite our circle women to take turns leading the group, but the circle always seems to end up with me organizing the gatherings. Because of our bookstore, we have easy access to the growing list of revolutionary books that called for change in the source of man's power over women—the omnipotent power of the male images of God. Many of these books help us with our rituals, but our favorites so far are Z Budapest's books. She is credited with bringing the Goddess religion to feminism by combining feminism theory, feminist activism and Goddess spirituality together into what she coined "feminist spirituality." The Dianic Practice of Witchcraft (though we only used the "witch" word among ourselves) celebrates feminist values and women's mysteries—the physical, emotional and psychic roots inborn into the female body.

I thank the Goddess for our moon celebrations. I appreciate our friendships and our gatherings so much, I wrote a song for us to sing together when we meet each full moon.

> Blessed be, blessed be. Worshiping the Goddess
> On the night of full moon. Helping probe the mystery
> And here are we—we have come to see,
> And to find the key to be free.

Blessed be, blessed be. Reverently assemble.
Draw the circle round us. West and North, we call power forth,
And South and East, Sky and earth not least.
After circle's ceased, then we'll feast.

Blessed be, blessed be. Keepers of the secret
Ways of all the women. Circle now. It is here we dare
Our ways to share, trying ritual rare
Our desires bare show we care.

Blessed be, blessed be. Find the power of women
Ancient as the old ones. There are those who have thought us meek
And our powers weak, but it's love we seek
Life without is bleak, so we speak.

Blessed be, blessed be. Honor all the holy
Women of our past times. Full moon rise at the setting sun
And we as one see our spell is spun.
It's a job well done—and we've won.

Jan on February 18, 1983

Dear Matt,

I hope you received my Valentine on time. I sent it at the last minute because my mind's been so crowded with events that I lose track of the days. I'm always planning far ahead, meeting an instant deadline, or thinking about something that happened in the past. But mailing you and Jenny a Valentine is certainly my top priority.

And as I've said before, your Indonesian slides and your master's thesis materials that you showed me are terrific.

I'm having new adventures taking eight scuba lessons at the YMCA pool. Bea came to my first class to watch me, and our instructor remembered her and her three sons in his class in 1971 and invited her to join the class as a guest. She is now able to help me with all the skills and equipment: the mask, fins, snorkel, tanks, regulators, weight belts and the BC—the buoyancy compensator. I hope I can pass the written test and then pass my open-water outdoors test in a gentle little lake somewhere.

I hope that you're feeling as good as I am and finding positive solutions to advance your goals.

Much love,
Mom

Jan on March 29, 1983

Happy Springtime, Matt!
I'm happy that you'll stick it out there until you're finished with school. I'm sure your dad is happy to have you near him.

It's exciting to hear that your Indonesian research is considered relevant and significant. We saw *The Year of Living Dangerously*, an excellent movie about Indonesia in the late 1960s that gave us a chance to see country and urban life—and the scary politics. We certainly felt closer to your experience of living there two years ago.

I'm working diligently with a grand open house planned for April 17, the Blue & Gold Lakeshore Med run on May 14 and St. Agnes Health Fair on June 4. Then who knows what?

I enjoyed two sessions of teaching journal writing at "Accent on Women" to classes of about twenty-five women. They wrote excellent evaluations and even applauded after the classes. It made me miss the classroom again, but teaching to hungry-for-stimuli women is easier that motivating many high school students struggling with all their issues.

Between the open house and the run, I'm taking a two-week camping trip to Florida for some scuba diving and relaxation. We want to go to Disney's Epcot too. We'll pull our little camper with Bea's Cutlass that she inherited from her father's estate, and we'll spend our money for air for our scuba dives rather than on airfare and hotels. Bea will retrieve her scuba gear back from her kids, including a set for me.

Your mother is reaching new depths! I spent an hour under water at the YMCA pool last night. There wasn't much room to move around and stay warm, and I turned into a prune. My mouth was worn out from biting on to the regulator and I'm a wreck today. But I did it and I'll pass the written test with great determination. I'll be taking open water tests in Florida.

We saw Judy Collins this week. Her show was quite sublime compared to some folk presentations of the past, more low key and high fashion, excellent and powerful. Do you remember when I took you and Anna and Adam Spence to see her at Ravinia years ago? Her songs have always been important in my life...especially her singing the Beatles' song, "In My Life."

The bookstore business is poor but our *Something Happened* sales are increasing. We sent forty-eight books to the State of Hawaii last week.

I'm off to a retirement party for a Lakeshore Med nurse with over forty years invested in this hospital. It's people like that who make my job worthwhile.

Bea on April 21, 1983

I did the wash and ran errands, cleaned the car and worked hard all day Saturday. After supper, I played with the VIC computer and wrote my first long program that I saved on the cassette, a long and complicated process but fun. Jan didn't come home from work until after 2 a.m.

Jan's open house was Sunday. I made my rounds to see my kids, picked up the scuba gear, took the tanks in to be hydrostated, bought an awl and sewed up the hole in the canvas top of the trailer and was bored, bored, bored. Jan didn't make it home until after 7 p.m. By this time I was in a rage.

I heard a noise in my car while I was driving around so I asked Jan to please take the car for a ride so if anything seems wrong, we can fix it before our trip. She was gone for hours—with my car. Well, that was it. I drove her rusty Toyota around to look for her—

even went to her office. I was boiling mad. When we finally connected at home, she told me she went to the cemetery! Whatever the hell that means.

Things quieted down with Jan on Wednesday after I held therapy sessions at the bookstore for three people in the space of an hour and a half. One session was with a mother of a lesbian; one was with a lesbian and then another with a regular woman.

While we were packing the car and trailer for our trip, Jan apologized and promised to help me more.

Chapter 16

Jan on April 22 to May 8, 1983

Marian and Sharon plus my Jenny and her guy all came over last night to wish us a good trip. Last year we'd met with Marian and Sharon to show them our little pop-up, canvass-top trailer that we were to pull to Florida. But Bea's daughter called us from our bookstore with urgent concerns about my father not showing up for his appointment. Sharon's a nurse so she and Marian went with us and we found my dad at home—collapsed, unconscious and tangled in his telephone cord. He never regained consciousness and died five days later.

This year the four of them could barely step through piles of scuba and camping gear. When they left, we packed it all in the trailer and car early in the morning and kept driving for an exhausting eleven hours

We discovered Cumberland Falls on the map and headed for it. Bea was pleased because when she was a teenager she'd traveled there with her dad and mom and her mom's four cocker spaniels. This time it was twilight and we were starving, but we rushed to set up our camper in a wooded area at the top of a hill and made it to the historic lodge in time to enjoy an elegant supper.

It was dark when we returned and moved about in the camper getting ready for bed. After snuggling together on one of the two beds that folded out to each side, we were ready for a well-deserved rest with a light rain dancing on our canvass top. Soon we felt a slight but unsettling shudder. We quickly found our flashlights, unzipped and jumped through our tent opening, ran to the back of the trailer and almost fell down a wooded ravine. We realized that the trailer's back corner jack supports were leaning toward the ravine like the Tower of Pisa. They were ready to give way and send the trailer down through the brush and trees. After hitching up the car and moving our trailer forward from the edge, we realized that we could have been asleep while the earth eroded under us, toppling us on a wild ride hurling us through the trees and into the Cumberland River valley below.

After a hardy, warm breakfast in the lodge, we climbed about the falls, wearing ponchos to keep off the misty rain that followed us and grew to pouring rain as we maneuvered for nine tense hours on mountain roads.

When it was my turn to drive, Bea kept me stress free with stories including one she recently read about a recent discovery in China of several thousand individually sculpted clay soldiers and hundreds of horses, even chariots. Some Chinese farmers were digging for a well and found a few soldier statues of an ancient emperor's army, and archeologists started digging to uncover this incredible discovery. That would be something to see, but visiting China was low on our priority list and too expensive for our resources.

Tornado warnings greeted us as we checked into a motel in a little North Carolina town. We considered ourselves lucky to have found a room rather than being under canvass as we listened all night to windstorm debris crumpling along the roadway.

We didn't get much sleep so we left the motel early and drove all the way to Orlando to set up our camper at 4:30 p.m. We grabbed something to eat and drink from our cooler and decided to spend an impromptu evening at Disney World. We went to the camp office to ask how late Disney World stayed open. Jan remembered it was at least until 11 p.m. when she was there with her husband and kids in 1977. We were reassured that it would still be open so we headed for the Magic Kingdom and arrived just as they were closing the ticket booths an hour earlier that what showed on our watches.

Undaunted, we went to the attendant standing at the end of a secure, chain-link, chest-high fence to tell him we wanted to get in. I wasn't so sure because it was expensive for such a short while, but Bea wanted to and I didn't want to look like a cheapskate again. When the attendant walked away to see about two tickets, a formidable man dressed in civilian clothes reached over the gate with his fingers to release the inside catch on the lock.

It all happened so fast. Bea and I looked at each other and without saying one word, we followed closely behind him until we moved faster to board the monorail pulling away from its station. We giggled our way to the Magic Kingdom entrance until we discovered another intimidating chain link fence where paying patrons showed their stamped hands to an official at a gate. Without missing a step, we headed to the unguarded gate at the deserted end of the fence with a brightly decorated tunnel on the other side. I reached over as I'd seen the formidable man do before, found the same pressure point under the latch and again we were through the gate and into the tunnel with Bea saying, "Where are those kids. I thought we said we'd meet them right here."

Then we realized it wasn't "kids we'd lost" but the hour when we crossed the time zone.

Sneaking into the park beat other thrills on my list of peak Disney World experiences.

We hopped on the frontier-style train to get off close to Space Mountain and on that ride before the park closed. It was a job convincing Bea to try it. Who needs teacup rides when you can soar into space on a rocket. The line was short so Bea didn't have much time to protest, and before she knew it, we were straddling the rocket behind a dad and his son. And off we went.

I held on to her hard with my arms wrapped around her chest. I was screaming in her ear while she was screaming in the dad's ear, "Jan! Let go of my boobs! You're squishing me to death." Of course I couldn't hear her and kept on squishing and screaming. When we tumbled out of the rocket, the dad gave us a weird glance but I was oblivious of what his look meant until Bea regaled me with the tumultuous, squeezeous, screamiest, uproarious few minutes of our lives together.

"I'll never go on a roller coaster again!" But she smiled as I almost toppled over laughing.

We hopped on another ride next to Space Mountain and entered the Michael Jackson Experience with his moonwalk dancing and with the kids around us cheering at his moves. By then, the street sweepers started their routine as we walked through the stores along Main Street. After buying so many shirts and souvenirs, we were certain that Walt himself would overlook our questionable entrance and celebrate our exciting exploits.

Epcot was ready when we got there at 9 a.m. the next morning. We passed the crowds lining up at Spaceship Earth and headed in the opposite direction to the huge dinosaur energy building. As we continued to the left to see more world exhibits, I couldn't believe it when we walked into the enormous Chinese exhibition entrance to be greeted by what Bea described to me yesterday: three of the terracotta soldiers and one horse in a sealed display case beyond the vast red and gold entrance doors.

We took in everything including the breathtaking fireworks at Epcot's center lagoon at sunset and then, before the park closed at 10 p.m., ran to make a return visit to experience the dinosaur era again.

We consumed Mexican beer with our enchiladas lunch, Japanese beer with chicken grilled on a stick, and a lime and lager and a bit of pot pie in England before we made our way back to collapse in our trailer at midnight.

<<<>>>

We headed for Cape Canaveral and landed at the Space Center Campground, a tropical paradise on the Indian River. At about 7 p.m. we drove north to find a restaurant, but on the way we walked out on a long pier and watched the sun setting in the west with the full moon rising on the Atlantic Ocean. We were alone so we could hug and dance at the horizontal clouds glowing red from the setting sun and howl at the orange globe radiating a rippling path directly from the rising moon that touched the two of us praising Mother Earth.

The Space Center was especially exciting for Bea who reads about astronauts and space science. New exhibits were added since I was here in 1977, but the huge launching stations are now off limits to tourists.

It took us five hours on Thursday to drive to Key Largo where we settled into our campground and checked out the Tropic Isle Dive Shop, but it was closed. So we went for another tasty seafood supper along the Atlantic coast—and lots of exotic drinks from Tiki-type bars.

Bea entertained me with stories of her family's Florida trip as we watched the glorious moon rising each evening sitting around our campfire with our drinks. She had me rolling off my chair with the tale of her trying to turn Husband Jake on with her minus 56-pound slim new body, but she thought she'd plus that on their trip one evening by wearing blue glasses and a blonde wig—and when she appeared in her outfit, no one in her family said a word.

While Jake and the older boys went charter fishing, she took Joel and Jill to find shells and, in addition, they found batches of orange sponges. The teacher-naturalist in Bea encouraged each of them to squeeze the sea critters. "See," she said, holding one out to her son and daughter, "they won't hurt you." And nothing hurt them until two weeks later when their hands broke out in an itchy, painful rash, and they couldn't do a thing about it except walk about in pain holding their hands in the air for days until the sponge toxins dissipated.

Of course, she always tells me the ludicrous tale about how she and Jake eloped and were married in Naples by Judge Jolly. Her mother offered to pay her to stay home and have a big wedding, but Bea had her mind made up and "went off to get hitched and start a family."

The winds on the next day were too strong and the waves too choppy to try for my scuba certification with my diving instructor from Key Largo's Tropic Isle Dive Shop, so Bea directed us into Pennycamp Park Beach where she helped me pull on the wetsuit, fins and snorkel mask that we borrowed from her skinny sons. Though I'd passed scuba lessons at our YMCA pool, this was the first time I wore a full diving outfit like this, but Bea assured me, saying I'd experience the feel of the suit before the weather finally settles and the dive boat can go to sea. I was lucky I could zip it up and still breathe.

Obediently I followed her into the water where we had great fun snorkeling, sighting fish, an anchor and cannon that had been planted by the park service. But what hadn't been planted floated before us, a glob of what looked like a giant transparent tapioca pudding made up of little slimy orbs with white spots at each center. I don't know why, but we decided to swim through them, and we couldn't tell when we began snorkeling how massive the cluster was. I remembered Bea's sponge story while I was in the midst of the goop, but all I could do was take one stroke at a time to swim through it.

Fortunately, we kept our cool, or claustrophobia a half mile off the beach could have been my undoing; yet we escaped again to live for another day.

Still too windy for my snorkeling test on Saturday, we rambled through tourist spots, including the Theater of the Sea, a water zoo with a bleacher covered by a rickety corrugated roof to watch porpoises doing tricks. The trainer explained that the hardest worker of all the porpoises was—TaDa!—Jean, the star of the show and the oldest who's been performing for fifteen years. Jean certainly proved her stuff by leading the porpoise pack and doing her tricks over and over, whistling and clicking on command. She could speak too, he claimed, and she chortled into his microphone, "I want one more!" each time she caught her sardine-sized reward.

I found my animal anima, my animal soul spirit guide who lives and works so hard to please one and all, and Bea agreed positively about my always wanting one more. Jean was the first porpoise to glide onto the wooden pier platform for the children to feed her and feel her snout, but Bea and I almost pushed the kids out of the way to be first in line to reward and pet Jean close to the wobbly pier's edge.

Bea, in turn, was invited by another trainer to get a hug from the sea lion propped up out of the water with his flippers on a perch. Not one to miss an opportunity like this, Bea cheerfully exchanged a full embrace that included the sea lion branching out her whiskers to surround Bea's face. Surprised at this level of intimacy, Bea backed off after the sea lion barked a belch into her face. "Bad breath. Really bad breath," Bea told me. "It reminds me of the times Marge conned me to go to those singles events and dance with the guys."

Finally the weather looked perfect on Sunday and we arrived at the dive shop early, excited to have the chance to pass my underwater test and be an authentic scuba diver like Bea. She helped me with the certification papers and arranged for John, the lead instructor, to test me. John introduced us to Guy, his intern who's learning to be an instructor. Guy was assigned to be Bea's buddy in the water.

We hauled our heavy gear and camping cooler full of food, orange drinks and beer on to the boat and waited for the rest of the divers.

Soon vans, busses and cars flowed into the parking lot and unloaded at least forty eager divers onto the boat. Many in that crowd had their own team leaders on tours from their hometowns. Good thing we were early because we had seats. The motors revved and the wave action grew choppier the farther we motored from shore. When we reached our destination, we waited for the others to disembark and I climbed down the wobbly rope ladder to pass a test run with only my snorkel. I couldn't believe my eyes when I looked into the water. I was going all the way down into thirty-five feet of the Atlantic Ocean? It certainly wasn't the ceramic floor of the YMCA pool!

After I passed that test, I climbed up into the boat again to put on fins and heavy gear, including weights, and descend into the water for my first dive. Naive me. I told myself I could do this if I did exactly what the instructor signaled me to do. I didn't worry about Bea who had Guy to follow us around. And she's done this before. She's adamant about taking photos too.

The waves billowed high, but the waters seemed calmer as we submerged and descending to land on the ocean floor and test my skill at exchanging breathing apparatus with John. I thought that would be hard to do, but I'd seen enough underwater movies and practiced in the pool, so it went well. Then he led me through a hole in a reef. I butted my tanks against it and plunged lower to swim through.

The time passed swiftly because there was so much to see and do, and soon it was time to reboard and move the boat to our second dive location. When I surfaced, Bea was nearby. When we were close to the boat, we grabbed the ladder quickly or we'd end up in a dip of the wave while the boat loomed above us on a crest with over ten-feet between us and the boat, and those distances changed all the time. We struggled to take off our fins and board the boat, but if we didn't grab the boat ladder just at the right time, we'd move away from it with fins in hand and couldn't make much headway returning to the boat again. But we made it with help from John below and the boat crew above.

After we staggered to our seats and removed our almost empty tanks from our backs, we could eat the food we brought while Bea told me Guy disappeared when her buoyancy jacket and weight belts wouldn't work together to take her down. She took one photo and said to hell with that, returned to the boat and hollered several times to the crew. Someone finally came and took her camera from her. Then she braved going down alone, saying the cardinal diver's rule to herself all the time, "Never dive without a buddy." And yet she went and found us and followed us.

I was somewhat comatose myself and out of it enough to concentrate on being brave enough to do my second dive in the new location. Meanwhile all the others seemed to be having a grand time with their comrades and leaders.

John chewed out Guy because he lost Bea, but Guy said he wanted to learn what John was doing and lost her. With a promise to do better next time, Guy was told to do his job and watch John and Bea at the same time. That was OK with Bea.

Just when I started to feel comfortable being tested in the ocean for the second time, I saw Bea holding up the middle finger of one hand with tendrils of blood rising to the surface. John grabbed each of us by the hand, headed for the surface and spotted the boat a distance away. Like a catamaran, we three paddled our fins to reach the boat with swells making the boarding ramp even higher—and more threatening should it come down and land on us.

When I took off my fins before boarding, I floated farther away and John had to leave Bea and come and help me. The crew finally pulled me on to the boat while my heart pounded and mind wished for a large crane hook reaching down, grabbing me by the tank pack and hauling me up on board. Somehow I made it.

I was ready to fall on the slippery, heaving deck and it seemed as if I staggered for a mile before I reached my seat. Bea helped me with my gear while a crewmember searched for his first aid kit. The second diver's rule is never touch the coral, and John chewed her out about that. Undaunted again, she defended herself. "I struggled to stay down and keep up with you and felt myself hyperventilating! I had to stop and rest so I grabbed a coral tube for a second until I got my heartbeat and breath under control. Then I looked and saw blood coming from my hand and swam toward you."

We both sat in a state of shock.

"Jan. You're shivering—and your nose is blue too."

One of the crew asked if we had any fluids to drink and I stammered, "There's orange juice in that red cooler over there, but if I get it myself, I'll fall flat on my face."

He retrieved a juice can for each of us and opened it for Bea still holding her cut middle finger in the air and for me with no strength left in my frozen body and my brain in shock. I clutched the quivering can and willed my hand to reach my mouth while my eyes watched my trembling arm shake its drunken way to my purple lips. What would we have done without that Vitamin C to revive us? And then we gnawed on our food while the other divers, younger and fit, returned, revved up from their adventures under the sea.

Back at the dive shop, John signed my certificate. Bea praised me saying that I'd earned my diver's flag, but John advised us both to work out to build up our strength before we dive again.

Somehow we drove back to the camp, found our trailer and fortified ourselves with alcohol with Bea finishing the last dregs in the bottle. I waited for several hours after to listen to Bea download her harrowing experiences over and over, thanking the powers that be that we survived. We pledged never again to go on a cattle boat like that one. We'd hire dive gigolos for each of us. Finally, she settled down and we took a long nap before we found a nearby restaurant and devoured stuffed crab and fried clams.

"I'm pooped," Bea declared when we returned to our little bed in the camper.

That's putting it mildly.

The next morning and still tired, we drove the long concrete ribbon across bridges over the rough blue ocean and between islands to Key West. Bea told me diving-for-treasure stories, including those of the Mel Fisher expeditions where he and his family spent years searching for Spanish gold, even after one of his sons and his daughter-in-law drowned during the search. Finally, Fisher found the Atocha's gold treasures off the sunken Spanish galleon hidden the sandy ocean bottom, and Fisher became famous and rich. She wondered what ever happened to him, and I guessed the moral of the story is "Never give up!"

When we entered Key West, I enticed Bea to skip past the mundane motels and campgrounds and head for Ellie's Nest, a lesbian-owned B&B that I'd seen advertised in *The Lesbian Connection* periodical that comes to our bookstore. Did they have a room, we asked. We were shown the Patience and Sarah room named after Isabel Miller's tender 19th century story of two bold women loving against the Puritanical prejudice that they overcame. It's one of my favorite books.

The owners welcomed us warmly and showed us the pool and hot tub in their intimate but tiny tropical garden. The room was a bit pricey but we decided to stay at least one night. Compared to yesterday's oceanic endurance feat, Bea and I felt free and full of joy swimming nude among the exotic plants surrounding their pool, tossing beach toys at each other and jumping high out of the water like porpoises and dolphins, diving between each other's legs, splashing and wrestling tenderly with the daylight shining brightly on our playful bodies. Other women guests who had been lounging in deck chairs joined in the fun, laughing with us.

Bea grabbed my hand and led me to our Patience and Sarah room to dry each other with white plush towels before we lie together on a brass bed with soothing ocean breezes caressing our bodies through one delicate lace-curtained window and out the other window with its white, intricately crocheted panels twisting together, wrapping and unwrapping in the softly flowing air.

The room was heady with lavender-scented potpourri, Victorian lampshades adorned with silk, oval-framed mirrors and historic pictures of American, English and Parisian women adorning the walls. We quickly completed the ambiance with our fresh supplies of wine and martini fixings that we served from the silver tray with etched glassware and ice bucket.

We had discovered this Tennessee Williams-type southern bedroom within an antique house for women only within a gay-friendly town reaching out to the ocean and the gulf, the vulnerable tip of the continent (like Provincetown) where the fear of loving each other, same sex or straight, has dwindled to nothing and where we can be completely relaxed and open to each other and to the world.

And open to each other we were—in compassionate joy and prolonged and leisurely totally loving release.

Before the natural light stopped shining through the shutters, we both felt that artistically posed nude pictures of each of us must be taken. We hadn't done that since Bea had her own apartment and I was still married, when we were new lovers heady on limerence and liquor. On this day, while Bea took aesthetically loving colored slides of satiated me in various poses, I watched her move her camera and her naked body about me to pose me to her choosing while I captured her image in my heart's album, and then it became my artistic time to capture her sensuous body on film.

We needed food. We were starving.

We dressed and found sake and ate sushi and tempura at a nearby restaurant before watching street entertainers and the Key West sunset near the Pier House where we consumed exquisite key lime pie for our dessert on its outdoor deck.

Walking about the wood frame buildings that showed evidence of surviving several hurricanes, we turned a corner and—we couldn't believe our eyes—Mel Fisher's Treasure Salvors Museum totally surprised us. Again she tells me a story and we quickly find the real thing. The museum would be open tomorrow and we'd be sure to spend precious time there. We climbed stairs to The Monster, one of several gay bars, for a drink but decided not to stay. We'd rather go back to our Ellie's Nest for a moonlight swim and celebrate again our own woman's gayness.

Awakening to a lovely morning and another visit to the pool and hot tub, we packed up and said goodbye to our hosts. We didn't ask for directions to a campground, thinking that would be a bit tacky. But quickly we found one near the shrimp boat docks. The permanent trailers and most of the newer bungalows were built on stilts and residents parked their cars under their houses. After we knew where we'd spend this night, we took a vacation from the car and walked to take a festive trolley tour around Key West, passing many of the places we had found the night before, except for Ernest Hemmingway's house with his famous cats that survive him. Bea doesn't like Hemmingway and I didn't care, but we did enjoy a drink at Sloppy Joe's, his favorite bar.

Our top priority was Mel Fisher's museum filled with gold bullion, jewelry, pirate mythology, exhibits of Fisher's escapades and documents about whether the state or the discoverer owns the found treasure. We actually held gold bullion by putting one hand through a hole in the display case to feel its weight. Wow!

And Wow again for Bea's intuitive storytelling that prepared me for our treasury of discoveries before we even knew about their place among our escapades.

We returned to the Pier House deck for a late afternoon lunch, and while we were luxuriating with our chewy conch salad served in huge shells, I was stunned at what unfolded before me. My eyes focused on a most exquisitely tall young woman wearing the tiniest bikini as she waded into the water touching the Pier House's beach below. When she swam to the raft, she emerged topless, step-by-step up the ladder and out of the water. A hundred or more pairs of eyes gazed on her as she gracefully reclined on her back on the raft carpet for some sunbathing. Bea told me she'd never seen me ogle so hard for so long.

We boarded the sailing schooner, the Western Union, for a sunset cruise with more than fifty other tourists of various ages. As usual, the two of us headed for the wheel deck to watch the captain's tactics; that is, Bea watches the captain's tactics and I enjoy.

After the handsome, tanned captain maneuvered the wooden sailing schooner away from land, I asked Bea, "What's that thing?" pointing to the wooden pillar covering the compass.

Bea answered, "It's a binnacle."

Oh. I thought it was a compass."

"The compass is in the binnacle," she said.

The captain then introduced himself as Scott Bottoms and invited Bea to take the wheel. Surprise and shock shown on her face. He explained, "I have to run down for my jacket," and left Bea at the ship's wheel for almost thirty minutes with all those people on board. Captain Bottoms stood beside her much of the time after he came up from below, but he didn't take over again until we changed our direction. The Key West sunset became secondary to Bea's standing at the wheel of the historic 120-foot wooden Western Union schooner breaking through the waves under full sail off Key West.

The next morning, we left our scuba gear in the camper to snorkel on the Coral Princess with Captain Jack and his mate John in the calm warm waters at two locations with coral reefs swarming with tropical fish. I was surprised that the coral colors were not what they looked like in the movies or in the *National Geographic* magazines, except for the dangerous fire coral. We were too close to civilization, I guess, because the coral had a grayish mossy look to it. The fish were beautiful and I dove down to pick up a small conch shell that was alive so we put it back. Bea was happy taking underwater pictures and we were satisfied when we left Key West to begin the long drive home.

It took two hard-driving days before we took time to rest at High Falls, Georgia, in a clean campground with marble bathrooms. After we took the camper off the car hitch, Bea decided that before we popped open the canvas, it would be wise to move it a bit forward off a little incline. OK. After Florida's flat terrain, we had returned to uneven country. Unfortunately, the camper's tongue was as stubby as our little camper, making it physically challenging to move.

"I'll do it," said macho me, and I straddled the short trailer hitch to lift it off the concrete block we toted as a leveler. Bea moved the block out of the way and went to the rear to push our little two-wheeler forward while I pulled the hitch from between my legs. We were straining together until my strength failed and I dropped the hitch that also supported our propane tank. The metal band that held the tank was joined at its front, its band folding out with sharp ends extended and connected by a nut and bolt. Those ends became a sharp edge that ran down my lower spine when I dropped the tongue. As with Bea's hanging on to coral and needing first aid, this time it was my body that was wounded.

Fortunately, it was a slight but bloody scratch that we could treat with items from our first aid kit. The bruise that bloomed along my backside was more dramatic. I'm grateful that the metal band didn't pierce the skin deeper down my spine and thankful to be on our way home after all these bizarre adventures.

We settled in our campsite and then realized we could walk a trail to a rushing river falls. That always makes me happy. Bea cooked a great supper and we enjoyed a campfire under a starry Georgia sky.

My purple and orange rainbow bruise on my back made my accident look worse than it felt, so the drive to Mammoth Cave and our 4 p.m. walk down into the cool inside of Mother Earth inspired us. Somehow we always seem to go to the tops of places and then into the lower extremes—and why not experience all that we can.

Yesterday we got up early and drove all the way home to see our dog, Luv, and our house sitter Bob Haban who told us everything went well except that he stepped with his bare foot in Luv's "accident" on the carpet. Before Bea's daughter Jill and her husband came over, we found six grape vines and three blueberry bushes waiting for us on our picnic table for Mother's Day gifts. Then on Mother's Day, Jan's Jenny and my Josh came by, and the stories of our adventures were beginning to be told.

Bea's Dive Log Book

April 29, 1983: Pennycamp Park, Florida, Atlantic Ocean. Windy, gusts up to 25 knots but visibility still 10 feet and up. Warm. Depth: 4 to 12 feet. Wet suit jackets and weight belts, snorkel. Time. 1 hour with Jan. Helping Jan get the feel of a wet suit jacket and then weights. We swam around sheltered area and found the cannon and anchor they have placed at the edge of a pretty good drop off. Fish a delight. All colors and sizes. Lots of fun. Jellyfish. Little, like globs of soap. Swam through clouds of them, like going through Jell-O. Atlantic Ocean. Key Largo. Pennycamp Park. Molasses reef and French Reef. 5 caves. Warm water. 30 to 50 visibility. Depth 30 plus feet. Cattle boat "Good time Charlie" gear: fully inflated BC jackets. Time: two dives. Buddy: Jan, John, and me, Guy. 4 to 5 foot waves. Comments. Like Wow. 1st I got into water with J. and John. Snorkel check out. Then we got tanks. He took her down and I had camera. I couldn't get down. Took one picture and brought camera back to boat. Back in water to find them. Lost Guy! Lots a Luck! Got down but alone. Then I found J. & J. Followed them. OK. Fine. Then I had 500 gauge. Had to go up. Breathing too hard. At top, dropped regulator and drank the Atlantic. OK and up. 2nd dive hustle. Had to catch up. Struggle to stay down. Pooped. Hyperventilating. Finally hung on coral and cut my finger. John took us up. WHEW?

May 1, 1983: Florida Keys: SCUBA dive. Taking our nude photos in lesbian-owned Ellie's Nest. THE MOST! Pool, hot tub.

May 4, 1983: Key West. Atlantic Ocean dive. Location. Dry Rocks, Sano Key. Visibility 20-30 ++ warm. 6 and 12 ft dives with snorkel. Jacket. 40 min. and 30 min. Buddy Jan on the "Coral Princes" Captain Jack. Comments: Lovely day. No clouds. Hot sun. Calm! First location reef shallowed up to 3 feet and down to 12-15 sand.

The reef kept trying to pull us into it so we had to swim off a lot. We went to take the camera back and I got up to rest. Second location. White sand. Beautiful. Coral. Islands everywhere surrounded by clouds of fish. Took pictures. Found lobster pot. J. got a conch. Live so tossed it back. Magnificent TIME!

Chapter 17

Jan on August 15 to 18, 1983

In this unique setting, this idyllic place, the Eighth Annual Michigan Womyn's Music Festival will host five thousand women this year—primarily lesbians living for a long weekend on six hundred and fifty acres of sisterhood and caring and friendliness where we could only hope that the freedom of being whole and liberated would be extended into the real world. "Real world" is incorrect. This land and these women are as real as our other world that we work and live in. It is all real except that this "real" is surreal.

Bea prepared everything and packed the camper and car so we could leave on Thursday night as soon as I came home from work. We missed most of Chicago's heavy traffic, camped near Warren Dunes in Indiana, and started early for Hart, Michigan, with a sketchy map and directions to find our outdoor women's festival in a secluded Michigan woodland.

Following the rural roads and finding the subdued signs eventually pointed us north, then right, then left passed a farmhouse and up a dirt road for three miles. It wasn't easy trusting those directions until we finally linked up behind a surprisingly long line of vehicles filled with women and their gear waiting to be admitted to the festival grounds. It had seemed to us, traveling on deserted Michigan roads, that we were the only two women looking for this remote site until suddenly, women played and sang while waiting in an hours-long line of pilgrims with backpacks marching and joking with women in campers, vans and cars with license plates from everywhere.

Gathering here is the largest women-only community in the world. Some women work year 'round to organize the event. Others come early for several weeks to pitch community camping and meeting tents, install cold water showers and water taps, set up various generators, musical equipment, two or more performance stages, organize and shop to fill several refrigerated semi rigs full of vegetarian food, clear the land for roads and walking paths, designate vendors and concert audience space, and make sure the "PortaJanes" are ready to use.

As we inched closer to the gate, we saw redneck white men standing behind barricades holding signs and spouting righteous rhetoric of their disdain and contempt. Those rednecks were the last males we were to see for our time on the land—except for the PortaJane cleaning men hired to come in the shadows late every night with women heralding their presenc= before their honey wagons approach each area, "Men on the land!" An occasional pilot in a low-flying plane would flit about over the concert audience to leer down on those naked, sunburned women who felt free to be that way. We also felt free to hold hands, hug, kiss and share our love of women and this women's culture.

Finally inside the gate, we registered and paid $63 each for our three-day stay with prepared vegetarian meals. We crowded through a brief orientation and then signed up for a four-hour work shift from hundreds of job options: staffing information booths, security, shuttle, garbage pick-up, traffic control, child care, medical aides for the women doctors in The Womb, assisting in support groups of every genre, helping handicapped women called "differently-abled"—whatever task it takes to make lesbians plus straight women's community function 'round the clock.

Not everyone is a volunteer. Kristie and Lisa Vogel produced the whole event working year 'round with some paid staff, others came early to create the infrastructure, the stage and sound set-up, healthcare, food service, and much more, including a vital service, garbage. What a sight to cheer when the team of waving and yelling husky dykes chucked our waste from blue containers into huge garbage trucks zipping along Lois Lane.

We decided to do kitchen duty on Sunday afternoon so we could chat with women while we worked.

The land is divided into special interest areas: general campers gather in Bush Gardens, Solaris Ferns, Nurd Knoll and Crone Heights. Bread & Roses is for chemical-free camping and Juniper Jump Off for the quiet ones. The loud and rowdy campers live on Lois Lane and Twilight Zone that's closest to the entrance and farthest from the others. Women with children are encouraged to camp near the Gaia Girls' Camp and Brother Sun Boys' Camp with daily activities for each, but the boys are not allowed onto the regular grounds. All these are linked along major shuttle stops on the main dirt roads.

We chose to position our little camper in an RV area that was close enough to the shuttle stop and PortaJanes yet far enough away to ignore the whopping slams of their plastic doors. We backed our car into a secluded circle of bushes and set up our camper, a little table, Coleman stove and cooler with some food and, of course, beverages.

All were advised to wear sunscreen and hats during the day, warm clothing after dark and drink lots of water to prevent dehydration, but we'd somehow always return to our campsite for our beer and cocktails.

With our program guide and map in hand, we walked for a long, long time on the woodsiest trail to the main activities areas, realizing how much of the land was natural and off-limits. Various paths and turns were marked with knee-high stakes tied with ribbons. One path crossed a four-foot deep gully, and women were posted to warn us and help us cross it.

We turned on an obviously major dirt road and passed shrubbery and tall grasses to cast our eyes on a most beautiful sight covering a gently sloping hillside. To our surprise we witnessed a playful performance of almost a hundred smooth and slippery women in a massage workshop—a rhapsody of relaxed, semi- and unclothed, gloriously happy women in various positions. Singles were welcome and easily matched. Assorted skin colors, shapes and sizes took part. WOW! What a workshop! What a vision to carry with me forever. And everyone was having a joyful time as the leaders stepped over women practicing massage techniques on each other. I could have jumped in right away, but Bea laughed and nudged me on to see the rest of our women's community.

She wanted to find the Day Stage location. She'd sent the organizers an audition tape of her singing her songs, but it was returned. "Rejected!" she exclaimed when it came in the mail. But she carried her guitar in case there'd be an open mike space where she could entertain and talk about her music.

We easily found the Night Stage area being set up for tonight's concert with Alix Dobkin, the Robin Flower Band, Something Special, Alive! and Margie Adam and Friends. When I saw the grand piano on the canvas-covered night stage, I appreciated how creative the woman was who designed the festival's logo—a grand piano with legs starting as tree trunks growing through the open piano top reaching to the sky and etched with the moon and stars.

We walked through the Mother Oak Differently-Abled (DART) camping in awe of the attention to detail for the many women who probably couldn't otherwise enjoy the rigors of this outdoor encampment. DART accommodates differently-abled campers with their variety of special needs, including visual guides. It was located close to the main activities using overturned carpeting paths for easier wheelchair mobility, super-sized PortaJanes for wheelchair accessibility, and they had the privilege of the only hot showers on the land.

Of course, all day and night stage concerts are interpreted for the hearing impaired, and interpreters are provided when requested for specific workshops. I'd seen that accommodation for the hearing impaired at my first women's concert in Milwaukee with Holly Near a couple years ago. I was overwhelmingly ecstatic during and after the concert when I won several arm wrestling challenges at a women's bar. I wonder if lesbians started that trend, the signing, not the arm wrestling.

We enjoyed watching about a dozen naked women shampooing their hair in the pipeline of icy showers close by and up a small hill to allow for drainage. The process is to jump in without fainting, hold your breath and get wet, then step out to breathe again, soap and lather your head and body parts. That forces you back into the cold showers to rinse off. A lot of whooping and screaming was going on and their beautiful bodies showed sunburn in butts and breasts that normally don't catch the sun. We took a photo, and I thought about that old joke that goes "Rump, titty, rump, titty, rump, rump, rump" to the "The William Tell Overture."

We walked through the rows of the Womyn's Bazaar merchandise "made by wimmin for wimmin," according to the sign. Amazons, nature and Goddess images abound: sculptures, pottery and jewelry of clay, metal, stone, glass, wood and bone; African, Goddess and tie-dye fabric clothing, T-shirts and batik; leather belts, bags and shoes made to order; paintings, photography, books, records, films and tapes; witchcraft, Tarot readers, altar objects and incense overwhelmed our senses, especially when vendors and customers shopped in various degrees of unadornment. We would return to shop many times.

At two sites, we came upon beribboned trees with bare branches reaching for the sky. Women had decorated the trees' aged limbs with beads, scarves, notes, poems and flowers. Some women meditated near them.

The food tent served salads, cheeses, and hot food like boiled eggs, grits, oatmeal, spaghetti with soy noodles, chili, corn on the cob, soups and more cooked in almost a third of dumpster-sized buckets set on metal grids over what seemed like a thirty-foot trough of open-fire burning wood and coals. It took four strong women to ease wooden shafts through metal rings on two sides of these huge black, cast-iron cubes to carry hot food to the servers. I saw one volunteer standing inside one of the cooled buckets, tipped on its side. She was scrubbing off oatmeal remains to clean it for the next meal. She wore an apron, a cap, boots and a happy face as she waved to women who cheered her.

Snacks were served all afternoon with breakfast from 8 to 11 a.m. and dinner from 4 to 6 p.m. Most every kind of fruit and bread was available. We each grabbed a banana. Potatoes, zucchini, collard greens and salads made in shiny galvanized metal livestock troughs were ready for servers when the women began to line up with their own utensils to pile the food on their dishes and find a place to eat on bales of hay, on the ground or at their campsites. We forgot to carry our utensils so when we reached the Triangle shuttle transfer point, we hopped on a tractor-pulled hay wagon and headed back up Lois Lane waving at the cheering throngs of campers set back from the road. Some cheerfully mooned us as the wagon of women applauded.

It was time for our drinks and our non-vegetarian supper that we cooked at our more intimate site where we could rest a bit before we hopped a shuttle for tonight's concert.

My excitement of watching five thousand women in various costumes and layers of clothing, hairstyles, in groups, as couples or alone, all looking for places to enjoy the women's music swirled around me like a rainbow kaleidoscope of liberated and laughing female images bonding under the twilight sky.

Elaborately adorned Black women drummed near the highest rim of the grassy amphitheater. Their drums vibrated exotic African rhythms, and their songs and the way they decorated their hair gave me a primordial memory rush and a wish that I too could make such rhythms. Their high spirits and Black chatter with those in the circles around them captivated me too.

I photographed a loving mother with her toddler ready to cuddle together in their blankets, lilac and lavender balloons and banners flying, and samples of every type of outfit—or none at all. One couple caused some ripples across the crowd as they paraded along the main path. Bare-assed leather dykes they were, with more black leather on their heads than on their exposed breasts, each with pierced nipples connected by hanging chains across their chests. Studded dog collars clutched their necks and wrists. I said perhaps their tattoos were faked for the occasion. Maybe not. Their motorcycle-black leather chaps on their legs surrounded and accented their exposed pubic hair and buttocks. They had their fun showing off and having their photos taken.

Finally, with lots of hugs exchanged all around, we found our friend Debbie and her gang and put down blankets and warm clothing to settle in with them. We'd brought wine and they'd brought pot and wine, which we all shared. My elation level was high enough without that, yet I joined in celebrating the freedom of my expanding cultural awareness.

Obviously, we were not seated in the roped-off, chemical-free area. Bea was uncomfortable as the sun started to set and the temperature dropped while we waited for the music to start. If an event is announced to start at eight, she eyeballed her watch and grumbled more as the lateness grew. Of course, we were enjoying a puff of our hosts' Mary Jane when it was passed to us. And the wine warmed us too.

The music started on Lesbian Time after what seemed like decades of announcements and program changes. By then a ceiling of Mother Nature's stars glowed above the hordes of high-spirited women. I wrapped a blanket around me and made sure that I kept cuddling Bea in her blanket to keep her warm.

As the acts progressed, energy rose from the waves of women—except for Bea who said she was so sleepy and she bundled up behind us to take a little nap. I continued to enjoy our friends' company but realized I'd had enough of our various treats.

The women yelled when pioneering lesbian musician Alix Dobkin sang "Leaping Lesbians." Everyone knew the words, sang along and wouldn't let her stop. I, of course, started crying when finally it was Margie Adam's turn to perform and she started out with her anthem, "Best Friend — The Unicorn" that we sang with her as we hugged our friends:

"When I was growing up, my best friend was a unicorn," she began, accompanied by the women's cheers, "Others smiled at me and called me crazy/But I was not upset by knowing I did not conform.../When I was seventeen, my best friend was the northern star.../I found my thoughts were very far/Away from daily hurts and fears and scheming/...Seeing is believing in the things you see/Loving is believing in the ones you love."

I reached around for Bea and she was gone. "Where's Bea?"

"Maybe she went to the PortaJane. I saw her walk away with her flashlight."

Margie Adam drew my attention away from Bea when she spoke to the crowd, describing her evolution as a women performer and an organizer. To the women in her audience, she said she found that the vulnerability of being open and exposed to be extremely powerful. "One person telling the truth empowers others to do the same."

And Margie Adam started with another number, shaking the living daylights out of that grand piano as we stood and cheered through the closing act.

With the music still pounding in my ears and the meaning of it in my heart, I was shocked and scared by worry and disappointment when I couldn't find Bea. No one had seen her return. And as we picked up our belongings and our litter so the field would be clean, I followed my friends as best as I could but lost them. I was carrying everything except a flashlight and Bea's blanket. I was exhausted and disoriented. "Think 'Right.' You don't want to fall in that trench that we crossed," I told myself. "And where's Bea? If she left, why didn't she tell me?" I slogged along in a line of women, down dusty trails like a chain gang member following those in front until the trail ran out.

"Hello in there," I said to a yellow tent still lit inside. A zipper opened and I asked the tousled head, "I'm looking for the RV section."

"Oh. You're in the Twilight Zone. The RVs are way down this road past the Triangle and on for a while. You'll find it if you keep to the right."

"Thank you." I had walked to the right but it brought me to this dead end and I still had to stumble along a path lit only by the night sky obscured by hundreds of trees. The shuttles packed with playful, singing festival women had long passed me.

I'm alone. I hope I'm on Lois Lane. Bea left me without warning and without a flashlight. How am I going to find our camper? I'm so tired and I have to carry this stuff. Maybe I should sleep in one of those community tents. If Bea doesn't find me back at the camper, what will she do? What will I do if I don't find her? Why didn't she tell me she was leaving? Why did she leave? The wine and whatever else I consumed didn't help me think. Where would I find help anyway? Just sit on the side of the road; something will go by, maybe a garbage truck.

Once in a while I'd hear laughing or a shout and hoped no one fell in that trench. My heart was pumping harder as each dusty step only led to the next. I'd been joyfully overwhelmed at the concert, and now I'm weary and broken.

Finally, I spied a familiar open space ahead and then the row of PortaJanes to the left across from our intimate camping circle. What will I do if Bea's not there? I zipped open the camper's canvass and found Bea sound asleep as if nothing in the world could bother her. My long, frightening journey and painful story is over. With my clothes on, I fell into the empty bed on the opposite side of the camper, covering myself with the blankets I'd carried.

I've never said a word about what I endured after I asked Bea why she left the concert. I didn't want to argue and ruin the rest of this vacation.

"I was tired," and she handed me the scrambled egg and sausage breakfast she'd cooked for us.

The festie rulebook says, "...you may pee in the woods if necessary—away from water resources and tents, though! And be sure to bring your toilet paper (and tampons) back in a little plastic bag to deposit in the garbage...With such a large group of womyn, do NOT shit in the woods. The ground can't handle it."

Fortunately, we didn't have to use anything other than the PortaJanes. I took my turn under the cold showers with other women. One of my sudsy comrades rinsing off in the shower was kind enough, and experienced, to remind me to breathe while I seemed in shock under the freezing water.

A smarter Bea heated water in our camp bucket and took a PTA bath at our site (PTA: pussy, titties and armpits) rather than submit to the festies' cold-water rite of passage shower. Of course, I photographed her more sensible bathing techniques accomplished with the sun shining on her, splashing about next to our car, tent, camp stove and bushes. I didn't have to remind her to breathe. She was as chipper as a robin in a birdbath on a summer afternoon.

We attended a Saturday workshop with Robin Tyler, Friday night's emcee and a stand-up feminist/lesbian comedian. We'd seen her a few years ago when we were newcomers to lesbian entertainment. We were surprised then when she filled a UW-Milwaukee campus auditorium. Within her wild story-telling jokes, her words empowered us. We often quote her when we talk about our hometown's homophobia, especially relating to our feminist bookstore. "A lesbian? P.S. Move to a big city."

We walked passed a rugby game, an open forum on non-chemical lovers' relationships with chemical lovers, recovery workshops from incest, from being in the military, from alcohol, from specific and general homophobia, drumming, fiddling, Frisbee, softball, football, a tattooed women's get-together, fat women's issues, peace meetings, legal workshops, a menstrual power ritual, a gathering of bearded women and those who love them, and many more.

In addition to performers' workshops, some of the hundreds of names printed in the program that I thought quite original were Wendy Sequoia, Rebecca Crystal, Feathermountaingrace, Newt, Sharon Fernleaf, Amber Moonborn, Sky Painter, Hawk Weed, Doodle, Bingo, Ace, and, of course, the producers Kristie and Lisa Vogel.

After carrying her guitar around, Bea never found a chance to perform. We found out later that the Jam Tent was in the Twilight Zone where women gathered after the Main Stage concert was over. That was too late for us, but it would have been fun to try it out and perhaps give Bea a chance to perform. And lesbian movies were shown after the Night Stage ended. I didn't know there were "lesbian movies."

We didn't realize that Kate Clinton was emceeing the Day Stage introducing Ginny Clements and the Women of the Calabash, the drummers from the night before. There's so much going on that can be disappointing when you miss something. Yet I'd think about what I'd enjoy next year.

We had our cocktails at our campsite, ate the supper Bea made and went to Saturday night's concert with Canadian singer/songwriter Heather Bishop, Jasmine and a group called Ibis. They usually end up with a wild band to please the younger women who dance wildly in front of the more subdued crowd until they move to the Twilight Zone and dance some more and play all night.

We stayed close to each other rather than join our group this evening, and we walked away together from the din of the concert activities to our more quiet camp to sit under the stars and drink our wine.

<<◇>>

Bea and I ate Sunday's breakfast at our site. So far all we've eaten of festival food have been a couple pieces of fruit, but we learned some details about how it's prepared when we turned up to do our four-hour shift in the food tent. We stood with six other women and pealed buckets of garlic and celery, chopping and chatting as we shared life stories with the other volunteers who had come from several states and even Australia. We decided wearing light clothing would be safe attire standing around high sturdy tables in the kitchen tent. It was disturbing to think of someone cutting off something.

We tried out a spirituality workshop but Bea said she was bored and we grabbed the shuttle and went home to wipe out. She made chicken soup for our supper and told me she did not have the energy to go to the concert and went to bed early. We opened all the zippered plastic window shields to let the evening breezes embrace us, but I sat outside under the calm August night sky. This wasn't how I thought our festival would end, but I knew I wouldn't enjoy going to the concert alone.

While sitting under the stars, I thought about so many issues that gnawed at me: relationships, children, salaries, bills, Mother Courage Bookstore's potential closing, car problems, work, lost land rights to my Door County vacation property because of my divorce, justice; yet I found peace on this women's land in Michigan.

Then I decided that this land in Michigan could be my land too—and I didn't have to worry about maintaining it. If I brought friends with me, I wouldn't even have to work to feed and entertain them. I have land—women's land— for all the lesbians who need this place to come to and feel free.

Fortunately, the weather has been perfect. It rained during the festive weekend last year; everything was wet, cold and muddy, but happy. The chance of bad weather didn't keep women coming back for more. The organizers hope to get ten thousand women here for the Tenth Anniversary in 1985. I plan to be among them. I wouldn't miss it.

I stumbled into bed with the concert music still reaching me across this hallowed land as I settled down for a heavenly sleep.

Bea on August 18, 1983

This weekend's festival workshops and music kept us involved, but finally I left my guitar in the car. I knew I wouldn't have a chance to sing and play my songs.

After breakfast and fooling around on Monday morning, we packed up and pulled our camper toward the exit. Women riding the shuttles to their cars parked in a vast area near the gate passed us all morning, cheering and singing on their way. Security women directed traffic with "See you next year" signs. When we pulled through the final chain-link gate on the dusty dirt road toward the county road, Jan started crying so hard and she couldn't stop.

"It means so much to me to be here," between her sighs and sobbing. "I loved being here and being ourselves, being myself. Being inspired. Being together with so many other lesbians. It felt so good."

"Except when it rained," I said, trying to get her to stop crying.

"It didn't rain! Well, maybe a sprinkle or two."

"And those damn mosquitoes."

"What mosquitoes?"

"That's so like you, Jan. No rain, no sunburn, no mosquitoes." And Jan started to laugh with me. With a deep breath, she shook off her sadness and we drove the long miles to our home.

From Mother Courage Press

All Books in
The Whistling Girls and Crowing Hens Series

Book 1—*Not to be Denied* captures humorous, sad and scary family life between 1900 and 1970: The Depression, war, life at home, schizophrenia; tomboy girls and teen girlfriends, sexual encounters, children, husbands, and individuals' choices that shape them. Passion explodes for two women in their early '40s. Liberal religion and Transactional Analysis weekends bring them together. Their paths meld when these naïve lovers test their magnetic attraction after Jan asks, "What could it hurt if we just let it happen?" (January 2024)

Book 2—*Gullibles' Travels.* Divorced Bea tries not to be a lesbian and her lover Jan strives to keep her children, husband and Bea happy. Bea and friends test the Sexual Revolution of the '60s and '70s. Jan recalls living in Cold War Germany in the '50s and touring Greece, Leningrad and Moscow with her husband in the '70s. Jan defuses a labor/management conflict and Bea and Jan escape to Europe for a rowdy and risqué three-week escapade in '76. (April 2024)

Book 3—In *Secret Transgressions*, Jan's hospital PR job expands with Bea as her assistant. Jan's marriage turns raw. Divorce. Bea is subject to sexual harassment in the workplace, is fired, and Jan is emotionally harassed on the job. Travel helps them heal and they create Mother Courage Bookstore and Press. (July 2024)

Book 4—*Being Mother Courage* embodies a dream come true: creating a feminist bookstore and experiencing historic events and adventures in the women's movement and the gay/lesbian world. They extended their first American Booksellers Association (ABA) trade show in Los Angeles starting with San Francisco's gay scene, on a night unlike any other, and ending by sailing with Seaworthy Women on a 31-foot wooden ketch launched from the 5000-boat Marina del Rey to Catalina Island. Women's spirituality circles and lesbian support groups in Bea and Jan's home inspire and support women. Jan confronts job harassment and Bea faces the bookstore's demise. Their Cancun vacation fun ignores sun-bathing on beaches to explore Mayan ruins. Jan enters the snorkeling world led by scuba-diver Bea. At home, their full moon circles begin with feminist and original rites and rituals. Tension turns to courageous laughter when conflicts are overcome. Bea uses her skills to pioneer Apple's Mac desktop publishing and was a guest speaker/teacher at the International Women's Booksellers Conference in Spain. (August 2024)

Book 5—In *Grit & Gratification*, Sailor Bea commands the boat and Jan, her bungling crew. Bea and Jan muster strength after Bea's homophobe father and Jan's supportive father die and they rehab their inherited rundown properties. Their new Mother Courage Press creates a significant, successful book for sexual abuse victims. When their retail bookstore closes, they are free to travel. As lusty lovers, they tow their camper to New York City, Provincetown, America's Stonehenge and Niagara Falls. Then they experience Michigan Woman's Music Festivals. Jan accepts that her lost Door County acres can be found on women's festival land. (January 2025)

Book 6—In *Moving On and Up*, Bea rejects joint therapy sessions with their friend. Jan goes alone to heal her stress asking to use her uniquely devised feminist therapy regimen that eventually benefits both women. Jan's boss eliminates her PR department and job, but her reputation earns her a better one at a major metropolitan hospital. Bea and Jan stay strong together. Mother Courage Press begins to thrive. Surviving scuba diving and wild camping trips, sneaking into Disney World, being inspired at women's music festivals and gatherings, traveling through the Great Northwest makes them feel on top of the world.

Book 7— In *Close to Fine* (1984 to 1995) Jan moves up to the 'Big Leagues' of hospital PR in an exciting but stressful job. Mother Courage Press is thriving and they dare to publish Entity Jeni's channeling via a friend's New Age psychic energy messages. Seaworthy Women sailor friends sail together across the Pacific in a small sailboat and send Mother Courage Press their manuscript so Bea and Jan fly to New Zealand and later to Australia. More fun starts with a trip to guitar heaven in northern California, and at home, Bea starts a woman's kitchen band to entertain audiences and themselves.

Book 8—In *Intimate Passages* (1984 to 2013) Bea challenges the intimate aspects of their long relationship but Jan persists as a new friend comforts Jan. Goddess searching journeys to England, Mexico, Malta, Egypt, Scotland and France sustain and inspire them

For additional information on the series, contact:
Publisher Jeanne Arnold
MotherCouragePress31@gmail.com
https://www.mothercouragepress.com

**Books are on Amazon, Google Books,
and available through Ingram for libraries and bookstores**

ABOUT JAN ANTHONY

Jan may brag about being a battled-tested warrior queen, but she's really an optimistic crone who blends truthful and imaginative words to recreate two women's audacious journey together. Their frustrated search for happiness as married women with teenage children fails. They fall in love, discover the depths of women-creative cultures and fight for successful careers while challenging socially acceptable norms. Jan's storytelling takes you into their intimate lives that enhance sensual and spiritual memories with their bodacious, risk-taking adventures.

Mother Courage Press
https://www.mothercouragepress.com
MotherCouragePress31@gmail.com

www.ingramcontent.com/pod-product-compliance
Lightning Source LLC
LaVergne TN
LVHW010158070526
838199LV00062B/4408